Easy Guide to the ♘ge2 King's Indian

Winning With the Hungarian Attack

Győző Forintos and Ervin Haag

D1374171

EVERYMAN CHESS

Published by Everyman Publishers, London

First published in 2000 by Everyman Publishers plc, formerly Cadogan Books plc, Gloucester Mansions, 140A Shaftesbury Avenue, London WC2H 8HD, in association with Gambit Publications Ltd, 69 Masbro Road, London W14 0LS.

British Library Cataloguing in Publication Data
A CIP catalogue record for this book is available from the British Library.

ISBN 1 85744 245 8

Distributed in North America by The Globe Pequot Press, 246 Goose Lane, P.O. Box 480, Guilford, CT 06437-0480
Telephone 1-800 243 0495 (toll free)

All other sales enquiries should be directed to Everyman Chess, Gloucester Mansions, 140A Shaftesbury Avenue, London WC2H 8HD.
tel: 020 7539 7600 fax: 020 7379 4060

EVERYMAN CHESS SERIES (formerly Cadogan Chess)
Chief Advisor: Garry Kasparov
Series Editor: Murray Chandler

Edited by Graham Burgess and typeset by Petra Nunn for Gambit Publications Ltd.

Printed in Great Britain by Redwood Books, Trowbridge, Wilts.

Contents

Symbols

+	check	Cht	team championship
++	double check	Wch	world championship
#	checkmate	Wcht	world team championship
x	capture	Ech	European championship
!!	brilliant move	Ct	candidates event
!	good move	IZ	interzonal event
!?	interesting move	Z	zonal event
?!	dubious move	OL	olympiad
?	bad move	ECC	European Clubs Cup
??	blunder	jr	junior event
+−	White is winning	wom	women's event
±	White is much better	mem	memorial event
±	White is slightly better	corr.	correspondence game
=	equal position	1-0	the game ends in a win for White
∓	Black is slightly better	½-½	the game ends in a draw
∓	Black is much better	0-1	the game ends in a win for Black
−+	Black is winning	(n)	nth match game
Ch	championship	(D)	see next diagram

Bibliography

Books

Encyclopaedia of Chess Openings vol. A (Šahovski Informator, second edition, 1996)

Encyclopaedia of Chess Openings vol. E (Šahovski Informator, second edition, 1991; third edition, 1998)

Encyclopaedia Modern Chess Openings vol. Closed Games (Wiener Verlag, 1998)

Königsindisch Sämisch-System bis Vierbauernvariante (Taimanow, Sportverlag Berlin, 1989)

The King's Indian Defence (Barden, Hartston and Keene, Batsford, 1973)

Beating the Anti-King's Indians (Gallagher, Batsford, 1996)

Periodicals

Informator Vol. 1-76
British Chess Magazine
Magyar Sakkelet
ChessBase Magazine
Scacco

Others

Notices from Heritage of Ferenc Jenei
Authors' games and analysis

Introduction

1 d4 ♘f6 2 c4 g6 3 ♘c3 ♝g7 4 e4 d6
(D)

Most of the main lines in the King's Indian, such as 5 ♘f3, have built up an enormous body of theory over the years. We may study them assiduously, and yet, when a game proceeds that way, we may find to our surprise that our opponent also knows it very well, sometimes even better than we do, because he has been studying it for decades!

We think that if you do not have your own repertoire worked out properly, or you are not satisfied with your old one, or even bored with it, then you will be interested in our book, which is the first summary of the topic.

We recommend another way to develop the g1-knight, which we have applied and developed for decades: the move **5 ♘ge2**, not in close connection with the move f2-f3, but instead

intending to meet **5...0-0** with **6 ♘g3** *(D)*.

One of the great advantages of the system with ♘ge2-g3 is that there is a great deal less to learn. Those who are in possession of this knowledge will enjoy a certain advantage against those who have not seen this move before or do not know the plans connected with it.

In this introduction we will examine typical strategic and tactical themes, and the starting points of some deep plans, taken from the two main branches of this opening (6...e5 and 6...c5), and from the smaller coverage of the 'miscellaneous' lines. These are, of course, examined in greater detail in the rest of the book, this material having been picked from nearly 1,300 games, among which many were played by outstanding grandmasters, but there are also several games by enthusiastic masters, and club-players who have been loyal followers of this system for a long time.

The knight's positioning on g3 may induce unusual turns, just through its unusual position. Let us start with one of the most interesting and typical topics.

The piece sacrifice on h5

Forintos – Baldauf
Berlin 1984

6...e5 7 d5 ♘bd7 8 h4 h5 9 ♗g5 a5 10 ♗e2 ♘c5 (D)

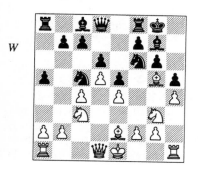

There now came the unexpected...
11 ♗xh5!
I found it difficult to make this piece sacrifice for two reasons. First: it seems reckless to sacrifice at such an early stage, and I usually prefer well-founded sacrifices. Second: I had never had exactly the same position before, so I was only partially able to count on my previous experience. After thinking over the possibilities, however, I decided it was worth the risk.
11...gxh5 12 ♘xh5 ♚h7

It will be pointed out in Chapter 1 that this sacrifice is correct even if Black defends more precisely. What is more, it ensures an advantage, which could hardly be achieved so quickly from the diagram position through other, positional, moves.

13 ♕f3 ♗g6 14 ♘xg7 ♚xg7 15 0-0-0 ♚g6 16 h5+! ♚g7 17 h6+ ♚g6 18 h7 ♘cd7 19 ♖h6+ ♚g7 20 ♕g3 ♚h8 21 ♕h4 ♖a6 22 ♖xf6 1-0

For a more detailed discussion of this type of sacrifice, see our summary and research in the relevant places in Chapters 1, 4 and 5.

The piece sacrifice on f5

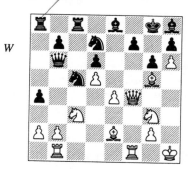

Jakab – Berkes
Paks 1998

20 ♘f5! ♗e5
20...gxf5 21 ♗e7! is very good for White, since 21...♗e5 loses to 22 ♕g5+ ♚h8 23 ♖xf5!.
21 ♘e7+ ♚f8
21...♚h8 22 ♘xc8.
22 ♕h4
Black is lost. The rest is instructive.
22...♗h8 23 ♘xg6+! hxg6 24 h7

Mate is threatened.

24...f6 25 ♗xf6 ♘xf6 26 ♕xf6+!
1-0

An unusual enhancement of a standard pin

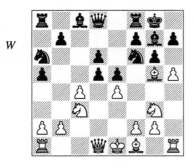

W

Serper – Watzka
Asiago 1994

Black may have overlooked that White has not yet played ♗e2 when he decided to try to transpose to the main line of the 7...a5 system by making the routine capture on d5 (10...cxd5). He doubtless expected the mechanical recapture 11 cxd5. However, his grandmaster opponent viewed the position in a rather more subtle way. It is worthwhile trying to guess what followed (only three moves have to be calculated).

11 h6!

A clever move, usually unexpected. Its aim is to stop Black playing ...h6, and thereby consolidate the position of the g5-bishop, and maintain the pin. Those who are interested in this and related motifs can see several examples in this book.

11...♗h8 12 ♕f3!

One of the advantages of the ♘g3 system is that the f3-square is free, and this is not usually taken into consideration by those who are accustomed to the main line with 5 ♘f3. Now a terrible pin has been created, and whilst it is possible to slip out of it, this also leads to a disadvantageous position.

12...♘b4! 13 ♘xd5! ♘bxd5! 14 cxd5 a4

Black has found the best defence, but nevertheless he cannot hope to equalize.

15 ♗e2 ♕a5+ 16 ♗d2 ♕b6 17 ♕a3 ♘e8 18 ♖c1 ♗f6 19 ♖c4 ♗d8 20 ♖b4 ♕a7 21 ♗e3

White has a clear advantage, and won quickly.

The strength of the f-pawn

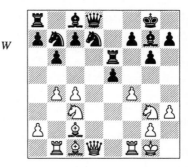

W

Novikov – A. Grigorian
Erevan 1996

17 f5!

One of the great advantages of the 5 ♘ge2 system, compared with 5 ♘f3, is that there is nothing to prevent White advancing his f-pawn. Several examples similar to this diagram, involving the breakthrough with e5 and f5 (generally with a sacrifice of the e5-pawn), can be seen in this book. One of the aims of this is that the diagonal of the g7-bishop will be closed. Another aim is to secure the pivotal e4-square for a white knight to augment the attacking forces. In the given example, Black cannot even provide any resistance against his opponent's ingenious and powerful play.

17...♖e8 18 ♘ce4 a5 19 c5!

The second pawn sacrifice serves to activate the light-squared bishop, and we will soon see how.

19...bxc5 20 fxg6 hxg6 21 ♗g5 f6 22 ♗b3+

The king is in a tight box, and the time has come for the queen to interfere.

22...♔h8 23 ♕g4 ♘f8 24 ♕h4+ ♘h7 25 ♖bd1 ♕e7 26 ♘xf6 1-0

Provoking light-squared weaknesses, and the good knight versus the bad bishop

Would you like to break up the bunker (pawns on f7, g6 and h7) that hides the black king so well? And would you like to occupy the key squares leading there? Then have a look at how Laszlo Szabo, three times a Candidate (who frequently used the 6 ♘g3 system), achieved this (*see following diagram*):

White launched a quick attack with h4-h5, thanks to the support of the g3-knight, but he understood that the opening of the h-file gives only a slight advantage. So, instead of this, by pinning the f6-knight with ♗g5, he

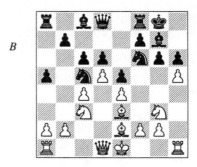

Szabo – Klundt
Bamberg 1968

tempted his opponent into releasing the pin with the weakening move ...h6. The diagram shows the position after ...h6 and ♗e3 have been played. The play now continues along positional lines:

12...cxd5 13 cxd5 g5 14 0-0 ♗d7

Now we can marvel at a real grandmaster-like recognition of how to take advantage of our positional pluses:

15 ♗xc5! dxc5 16 a4! ♘e8 17 ♗g4! *(D)*

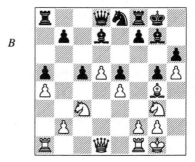

A key moment. The f5-square becomes even weaker after the exchange of light-squared bishops! Szabo has created two weak points (f5 and b5) with three excellent moves. The consequences of this can be seen from the game continuation.

17...♘d6 18 ♗xd7 ♕xd7 19 ♕e2 c4

19...f5 would provide a good example of the 'spreading of weaknesses': 20 exf5 ♘xf5 21 ♘xf5 ♖xf5 22 ♖ad1 and now, instead of the f5-square, White has obtained the e4-square, which is an ideal place for a knight.

20 ♖fc1 ♖fc8 21 ♘d1!

The knights are strong in closed positions, and Szabo went on to win the game confidently (see Line A113, Chapter 4).

A positional pawn sacrifice

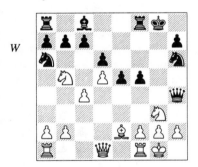

Van Gaalen – Van Laatum
Utrecht – Volmac 1991

When Black manages to play ...f5, then following exf5 gxf5, the move f4 should be forced through, even if it involves a pawn sacrifice. This fixes the f5-pawn so as to close in the c8-bishop.

14 f4! exf4

After 14...e4, instead, White will occupy the d4-square.

15 ♘h5 f3!? 16 ♗xf3! ♕xc4 17 ♕e1!

This is an improvement over the game Serper-Dannevig, Gausdal 1991.

17...♕xb5 18 ♕g3+ ♘g4 19 ♗xg4 ♕xb2 20 ♗xf5+ ♔h8 21 ♗e6 ♗xe6 22 dxe6 ♘c5 23 e7 ♖g8 24 ♖ae1! ♕d4+?! 25 ♔h1 ♘e4? 26 ♕h4 1-0

What shall the future of the g3-knight be, if the black h-pawn chases it away?

Again and again, the question must occur to Black: when and how is it possible to chase away the awkward g3-knight? Normally he will do so by ...h5 followed, if allowed, by ...h4. This can provoke two reactions from White, apart from cases when he sacrifices the bishop on h5:

1) White prevents it by playing h4;

2) He retreats the knight to a 'good' square. This is usually only h1, occasionally e2, but sometimes, and this is a remarkable plan, to f1. Why is it so remarkable? We will soon see, if we look at a recent game by Korchnoi (*see diagram overleaf*).

The famous grandmaster supposed, with good reason, that his opponent was planning the move ...h4. This was why he kept the f1-square free for a long time, contrary to normal practice, because he had far-sighted aims for it.

13...♖b8 14 ♗h6!

The goal of this move is not only the exchange of a strong piece, but also the weakening of the king's position as well. We shall see that the

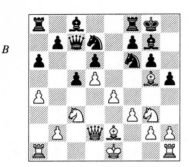

Korchnoi – Xie Jun
Arnhem 1999

removal of the g7-bishop gives rise to several combinational possibilities.

14...c4! 15 ♗xg7 ♔xg7 16 a5 h4 17 ♘f1 ♘c5!

17...b5 would be logical, but Black avoided it, because she did not want White's plan to come to fruition, for after 18 axb6 ♕xb6 19 ♖a2 ♕c5, the f1-knight goes to e3, 20 ♘e3, from where it can proceed to c4, thus justifying White's strategy.

18 ♗xc4 ♘cxe4 19 fxe4

This is fiercer, and perhaps even better, than 19 ♘xe4.

19...♕xc4 20 ♘e3 ♕c5 21 ♕f2

A cunning move. On the one hand it increases the threat on the f-file (after castling), and on the other hand it undermines the strong-looking queen position on c5. For example: 21...♗d7 22 e5 dxe5?? 23 ♘f5+. However, in Korchnoi's opinion, 21 0-0 is objectively best.

21...b5! 22 h3 ♘h5!? 23 0-0 ♘g3?

A natural move, but still a mistake. We could say that Black has now stepped on one of the mines laid by

Korchnoi. 23...f5 is far better, and gives approximately equal chances according to Sadler.

24 ♕f6+ ♔g8 25 ♖f3! ♗d7

25...b4 can be met by 26 ♘a4.

26 ♕xh4 b4 27 ♖xg3 bxc3 28 bxc3 ♕xc3 29 ♖f1 ♕e5 30 ♔h2?

30 ♘f5! wins, but is more complicated.

30...♖b4 31 ♖f4 ♖e8 32 ♖g5 ♕e7??

Black makes another blunder due to tiredness. 32...♕g7 (Korchnoi) would still have put up stout resistance.

33 ♕h6 ♖xe4 34 ♖xf7! 1-0

A nice final sacrifice. For further analysis see Line A2 in Chapter 8.

One of our 'intermediate innovations'

The theory of this unique opening has been developed at a rapid pace. We hope that with some novelties we have also contributed to this process. One of our improvements came from the following position:

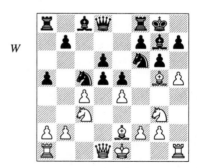

It is White's move. Players usually recapture with the c-pawn or sometimes with the knight. Our novelty is a *zwischenzug* (intermediate move):

12 hxg6!

An important and typical *zwischenzug* with the idea that 12...hxg6 is met by 13 cxd5!, and 12...fxg6 by 13 exd5!. It can be seen that it is not Black but White who determines what may happen in the position. Of course, Black may diverge with 12...d4, but, as we analyse in Chapter 4, 13 gxh7+ ♔h8 14 ♘d5 ♗e6 15 f3 ♗xd5 16 cxd5 ♕b6 17 ♘f5! can follow, with splendid tactical chances for White.

You can see an analogous idea in the game Forintos-Venegas Campo, Mexico 1999 in Line A12 of Chapter 4.

Rooks on the third rank
In the following example both rooks help in the attack on the 3rd rank in a spectacular way.

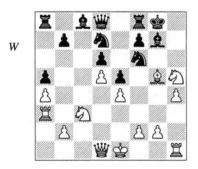

Mäki Uuro – Toikkanen
Espoo 1993

16 ♖h3
The king's rook also appears unexpectedly on the third rank.

16...♕b6 17 ♖g3 ♘xh5 18 ♕xh5 f6

18...♕xb2 is answered by 19 ♖a2.

19 ♗h6 ♖f7 20 ♗xg7 ♖xg7 21 ♖xg7+ ♔xg7 22 ♘b5!

This opens the way to the kingside for the second rook, which went to a3 with this intention, as well.

22...♔f8 23 ♖g3 1-0

But Black may also be OK
The examples so far have only shown White gaining the advantage. The balance of the opening is not so favourable, of course. Quite a few of the opening lines are close to equalizing if properly handled. This is no surprise, because often only a pair of pawns are exchanged, and all the pieces remain on the board for a long time. An advantage in space is White's most frequent accomplishment; the real fight starts later. However, although quick defeats for Black rarely occur in grandmaster games, this is a devastating opening to play against weaker players. As the above examples show, the slightest mistake by Black makes it possible for White to achieve a quick and decisive advantage.

However, if White struggles too hard, but is inaccurate, he may be outplayed, and then Black may retaliate. Here is a choice of the most interesting games on this theme (*see diagram overleaf*):

14...f5!
This pawn sacrifice is worthy of attention. It is often Black's last chance as at least it creates an unclear position. This was made possible because White played the manoeuvre ♘g3-f1-d2-b3 too early in this game.

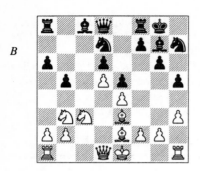

B

Szabo – Z. Bašagić
Sarajevo 1972

15 exf5 gxf5! 16 ♗xh5 b4 17 ♘a4?!

White underestimates Black's possibilities. Otherwise he would have retreated his knight to e2 instead of decentralizing it; then he would have had chances to exploit his extra pawn.

17...f4 18 ♗d2 e4! *(D)*

W

19 ♗xb4?

White judges that there is time to take the pawn on b4, and also that the bishop should not be in the way should Black play ...e3. However, this move is a mistake. 19 ♗g6 is necessary, with an unclear position.

19...♘e5 20 ♗e2 f3! 21 gxf3 ♘g5

21...exf3 (Burgess) is even better.

22 ♘d4?!

White should possibly have chosen 22 fxe4 followed by 0-0-0.

22...♘gxf3+ 23 ♗xf3 ♘d3+! 24 ♔e2 ♕h4 25 ♕g1 exf3+ 26 ♔d2 ♕f4+ 27 ♔d1 ♘xb4 0-1

When the advantage slips in the heat of the fight

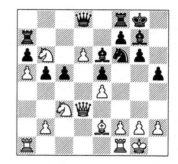

B

Ru. Rodriguez – Vogt
Thessaloniki OL 1988

20...♕b8!

White has made a mistake while working out a way to win: he advanced his d-pawn too early, which gave chances to his opponent. Black's 20th move is an important part of a plan to pile up pressure on the d6-pawn. The main threat is ...♘d7 and ...♖d8. White makes efforts to counter the dangers.

21 f4 exf4 22 e5 ♘d7!

The fate of the exposed pawns has been sealed. The only question is whether there remains any kind of counterplay.

23 ♘xd7 ♖xd7 24 ♕e4 ♗f5 25
♕c6 ♕c8! 26 ♕xc8 ♖xc8 27 ♘d5

The last flash of hope, which also
fades on the sacrifice of the exchange
by Black.

27...♗xe5! 28 ♘e7+ ♖xe7 29 dxe7
♗xb2

and Black won.

An experience of the author

I (GF) should possibly mention here
that, as one of the authors of the book,
I first become aware of the ♘g3 system when I was a schoolboy, and then
tried it out. Meanwhile, during the
Hungarian Championships, I also no-
ticed the excellent positions and several of the interesting and original
solutions of master Ferenc Jenei, a
player in the national team (our book
draws partly on his analysis). Later,
my club-mate Laszlo Szabo also employed this system. I tried this set-up
frequently in my games over the years,
and I managed to get to know many
subtleties of the system. A lot of my
own games appear in this book, in
their respective sections, but here I
evoke one of my games against the
famous ex-World Champion Mikhail
Tal.

I met the brilliant Tal personally
many times, at Olympiads, European
Championships and individual tourna-
ments. He may therefore have observed that I liked to play the ♘g3
system against his famous King's Indian Defence. I invited him into the
English Opening with my first move,
and only later did we transpose into a
type of King's Indian.

Forintos – Tal
Moscow Alekhine mem 1975

1 c4 e5 2 ♘c3 d6 3 d4 ♘d7 4 e4 ♘gf6
5 ♘ge2 g6 6 d5 c6 7 ♘g3 h5! *(D)*

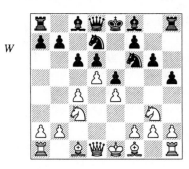

We put forward the view in this
book that this move is strongest when
Black has not yet castled (actually, it
was after the current game that I
formed this opinion about it). One can
say a great deal about the pros and
cons of delaying castling, but some
important knowledge may be gleaned
from this Tal game: for instance, that
Black may draw an advantage from
the fact that he has not put his bishop
on g7 yet, so he can instead play it to
h6 or e7.

8 h4 ♗e7!

White must now take care of his
h4-pawn.

9 ♗g5 ♘f8

Now ...♘8h7 is threatened, winning a pawn. Here I can mention my
overall game-plan that I formed during my morning preparation. I thought
that against Tal, who was famous for
his sacrifices, I would only be able to
obtain serious chances if I managed to

upset the material balance with the first sacrifice, and thus could gain some psychological advantage. This was the first occasion for a positional sacrifice, but it was not the h-pawn I sacrificed.

10 c5! *(D)*

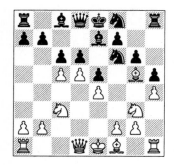

B

So, I managed to surprise him. He looked a little stunned and then started to analyse the position thoroughly. 'The proof of the pudding is in the eating', so he decided to accept the pawn.

10...dxc5 11 ♕b3 ♕b6

If 11...♘8h7, then 12 dxc6!.

12 ♕c2 ♘8h7 13 dxc6 0-0!

Typical Tal; he does not want to take the pawn by 13...bxc6, but after the text-move ...♕xc6 is threatened.

14 cxb7 ♗xb7 15 ♗xf6 ♘xf6 16 ♗e2 ♖ad8 17 ♘f1

Aiming towards c4, and yet at the same time a provocative move. It lures Black into a sacrifice, and Tal did not deny himself.

17...♘xe4!? *(D)*

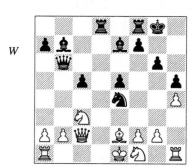

W

It is worth mentioning that both players were able to sacrifice, and this is not merely by chance, as on both sides a knight strayed onto the back rank, firstly to f8, now to f1.

18 ♘xe4 ♗xe4 19 ♕xe4 ♕a5+ 20 b4! cxb4 21 ♗c4!

White threatens to win at once by ♕xg6+.

21...b3+ 22 ♔e2 ♔g7

Now, in fact, after 23 ♗xb3 and following further mutual inaccuracies, I managed to win the game. However, I could have avoided a lot of unnecessary excitement with the accurate continuation 23 ♕b1! bxa2 24 ♕xa2, which would have led to a clear advantage for White.

One final point: statistically, White has scored 54.8% in the games of the 5 ♘ge2 theme taken from our database.

1 6...e5 7 d5 ♞bd7

1 d4 ♞f6 2 c4 g6 3 ♞c3 ♝g7 4 e4 d6 5 ♞ge2 0-0 6 ♞g3 e5 7 d5 ♞bd7 *(D)*

This line of defence was common in the golden age of the King's Indian Defence, i.e. the 1950s and 1960s, when development was mainly based on 7...♞bd7. However, this is less effective against the ♞ge2-g3 system than against the other systems with ♞f3, especially when Black follows up with ...a5 and ...♞c5. For this reason 7...a5 followed by 8...♞a6 is recommended, where either ...♞c5 or ...c6 can come next.

White has two promising ways to fight for the advantage:

A: 8 ♝e2 15
B: 8 h4 19

A)

8 ♝e2

A natural developing move. Black can reply:

A1: 8...♞e8 15
A2: 8...a6 17
A3: 8...a5 17

8...h6 prevents the pin by ♝g5, but White has the strong answer 9 h4!. The plan is 10 h5, and if Black replies ...g5 then the f5-square will be weak. After 9...h5 Black loses a tempo.

8...h5 provokes White into playing h4 himself: 9 ♝g5 a6 10 h4, transposing to Line B.

A1)

8...♞e8 *(D)*

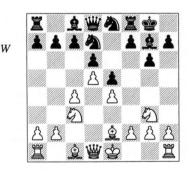

Black prepares ...f5 or ...♛h4 followed by ...♝h6.

9 h4!

Black can now choose from three possibilities:

A11: 9...c6 16
A12: 9...h5 16
A13: 9...f5 16

A11)

9...c6

The advantage of ...♘e8 is not the follow-up ...c6.

10 h5! cxd5

An instructive position! Now, instead of the routine 11 cxd5 (Long-Gullulu, Arnhem jr Ech 1988), we suggest:

11 hxg6!

This *zwischenzug* places Black on the horns of a dilemma. Namely after 11...fxg6, 12 exd5! can come, securing the e4-square for the knights, while after 11...hxg6 12 cxd5! White can generate play on the h-file.

A12)

9...h5 10 ♗g5

Now:

a) 10...♘df6 11 ♕d2 c5 (seeking counterplay) 12 0-0-0 ♕a5 13 ♗h6 ♘g4 14 ♗xg7 ♘xg7 15 ♖df1!. It is instructive how the advantage should be sought:

a1) 15...f5 is the move Black was planning, but it fails to 16 ♗xg4! hxg4 (16...fxg4 17 ♕h6 ♖f6 18 f4!) 17 ♕h6 f4 18 h5! +−.

a2) 15...a6 plans the pawn sacrifice ...b5, but it is convincingly countered: 16 f3 ♘f6 17 f4! (this had to be played now, lest a knight should go to e5) 17...♘g4 (17...exf4 18 ♕xf4!) 18 f5 (threatening fxg6 and ♕g5) 18...♕d8 19 ♗xg4 hxg4 20 f6 ♘e8 21 ♕g5 1-0 Szabo-Kern, Ludwigsburg 1969. There is no defence against h5.

a3) 15...b5 intends to accelerate the counterattack with a pawn sacrifice after 16 cxb5 a6. However, Szabo's

recipe, 17 f3 ♘f6 18 f4!, can still be used, e.g. 18...exf4 19 ♕xf4 ♘fe8 20 ♖f2 axb5 21 ♗xb5 ♖b8 22 ♗xe8 ♘xe8 23 e5, and White is clearly faster.

b) 10...♗f6 is a better plan. One idea for Black is ...f5 after ...♘g7 and ...♗e7. 11 ♕d2 and now:

b1) 11...a5 (Black does not have time for this) 12 0-0-0 ♗xg5 13 hxg5 f6 and now, instead of 14 gxf6 (De Wachter-Vingerhoets, Huy 1992), we suggest 14 ♗xh5 gxh5 15 g6!, when White's attack is decisive.

b2) 11...♘g7 12 0-0-0 ♘c5 13 ♖df1 ♗d7 14 f4 exf4 15 ♕xf4 ♗xg5 16 hxg5 ♗g4! 17 ♕f6! ♗xe2 18 ♘cxe2 ♘d3+ 19 ♔b1 ♘e5 20 b3 ♕xf6 (better is 20...♕e8 and ...b5, or the ...♘g4 and ...♕e5 plan) 21 gxf6 ♘e8 22 ♘d4 ♘g4 23 ♘xh5! gxh5 24 ♖xh5 ♘gxf6 25 ♖g5+ ♔h8 26 ♖h1+ ♘h7 27 ♖gh5 ♘f6 28 ♖h6 ♔g8 (Jakab-Leenhots, Rimavska Sobota jr 1996) 29 e5!? dxe5 30 ♘f5, followed by g4, gives Black some problems.

A13)

9...f5 *(D)*

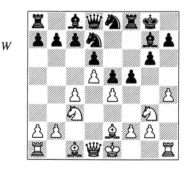

W

The only really logical continuation.

10 ♗g5

Not essential, but it is good to pin the knight and prevent ...f4. Now:

a) 10...♗f6 11 exf5 gxf5 12 ♕d2 a6 13 ♘h5 ♗xg5 14 hxg5! (instead of 14 ♕xg5+, Hoogendoorn-Van de Martel, Eindhoven 1991) is good enough for a slight advantage. One example of the threats: 14...♘g7? 15 ♘xg7 ♔xg7 16 g6! ±.

b) 10...♘df6 11 exf5 gxf5 and now:

b1) 12 ♘h5 ♕d7!? 13 ♘xg7 ♕xg7 14 ♕d2 f4! 15 ♗xf6 ♘xf6 16 0-0-0 ♗g4 17 ♖dg1 ♔h8 with equality, Gerstenhauer-Sonnenberger, German Cht 1993.

b2) 12 ♕d2 c6?! (12...f4!? is better; then 13 ♘h5 ♕d7 14 ♘xg7 ♕xg7 transposes to line 'b1') 13 h5! ♕c7 14 h6 ♗h8 15 0-0-0 c5? (again, 15...f4 is necessary; closing the position strengthens White's attack on the kingside, as demonstrated by the continuation) 16 ♗d3! e4 17 ♗c2 ♘g4 18 f3! (this counters the opponent's combination) 18...e3 (attempting to win an exchange or a piece; however, White has seen further) 19 ♗xe3! ♘xe3 20 ♕xe3 f4 21 ♕e1! ♗xc3 22 ♕xc3 fxg3 23 ♖h5! (the point: ♖g5+ cannot be countered) 23...♕e7?! (23...♕d8 24 ♖e1! ±) 24 ♖e1 ♕f6 25 ♖xe8! and White won in Vodep-Wittmann, corr. 1987. A well built-up attack.

A2)

8...a6 *(D)*

This prevents ♘b5 and helps to get rid of the pin by ...♕e8. Now:

a) 9 ♗e3 (after this move either Black can accomplish his plan, or

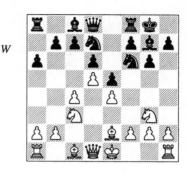

White loses a tempo; that is why it is instructive) 9...h5! (the plan is ...h4, ...♘h7 and ...f5) 10 ♗g5 (10 ♘f1!? would give sense to 9 ♗e3, e.g. 10...♘h7 11 b4) 10...♕e8 11 h4 ♘h7 12 ♗e3 ♔h8 (this invites a sacrifice on h5, but this is not relevant now, as there are too many black pieces there) 13 ♘f1 ♘df6 (Black has defended his king properly) 14 ♘h2 ♗d7 15 0-0 (15 c5!?) 15...♕e7 = Forintos-K.Maeder, Wijk aan Zee 1970.

b) 9 0-0 is also playable. Then 9...h5 10 ♗g5 ♕e8 11 ♕d2 ♘h7 12 ♗e3! h4 13 ♘h1 f5 14 exf5 gxf5 15 f4 ± is a typical position, of a type that often occurs.

c) 9 h4 is our suggestion, planning to answer 9...h5 with 10 ♗g5, transposing to Line B.

A3)

8...a5 *(D)*

9 h4!

Taking advantage of the knight's position on g3.

9...h5

For 9...♘c5, see Line A11 of Chapter 4.

10 ♗g5

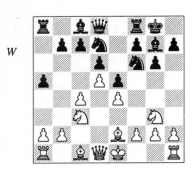

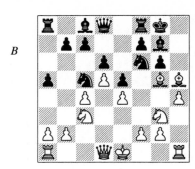

An uncomfortable pin, after which both players have to take the sacrifice on h5 into consideration.

10...♘c5

Another plan is 10...♖e8 aiming for ...♘f8-h7. Then:

a) 11 ♗xh5!? (a typical sacrifice) 11...gxh5 12 ♘xh5 ♘f8 13 ♕d2 ♘8h7 14 ♘xg7 ♔xg7 15 0-0-0 ♖g8 and now White let the king out after 16 f3 ♔f8 in Szekeres-Kock, Budapest 1992. Although he won the game, it was still more precise to play f3 and g4 following 16 ♗h6+!. How did Bronstein put it? Two pawns are worth a piece if they are united and there is also some activity. The opposite-coloured bishops just strengthen the attack.

b) 11 ♕d2 ♘f8 12 f3 (12 ♗xh5 gxh5 13 ♘xh5 transposes to line 'a') 12...♘8h7 13 ♗e3 gives White a slight advantage. After 0-0-0 and ♔b1 White can advance the g-pawn sooner or later.

11 ♗xh5!? *(D)*

Again a sacrifice! But always in slightly different circumstances! The pin and the two pawns promise a strong attack.

11...gxh5 12 ♘xh5 ♔h8

Comparatively best: Black prepares ...♗g4.

a) 12...♘cd7? 13 ♕f3 c6 14 ♖h3! and Black cannot prevent ♖g3, Hoogendoorn-Kocken, Breda rpd 1991.

b) 12...♔h7? (trying to defend the f6-knight with the king; we'll soon see the drawbacks of this) 13 ♕f3! ♔g6 14 ♘xg7 ♔xg7 15 0-0-0 ♔g6? (this leads to an abrupt finish; after the slightly better 15...♖h8 or 15...♘cd7, it would also be difficult to defend against the attack following h5 and ♖h4) 16 h5+! ♔g7 17 h6+ ♔g6 18 h7! ♘cd7 19 ♖h6+ (19 ♕g3! forces mate) 19...♔g7 20 ♕g3 ♔h8 21 ♕h4 ♖a6 22 ♖xf6 1-0 Forintos-Baldauf, Berlin 1984. It cannot be a coincidence that this attack with the piece sacrifice attracted many followers.

13 ♘xg7 *(D)*

This is simple and strong, but 13 ♕f3 is also playable. 13...♗g4 14 ♕xf6 (14 ♗xf6!? ♗xf3 15 ♗xg7+ ♔h7 16 gxf3 is riskier and unclear) 14...♗xh5 15 ♕xd8 ♖axd8 16 ♗xd8 ♖xd8 17 f3 occurred in Remlinger-Erlikhman, Las Vegas 1992. The united pawns and a little help from the opponent were sufficient for White to win the game.

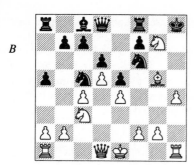

B

B

13...♔xg7 14 ♕f3

Although Black has won a tempo as compared to Forintos-Baldauf in note 'b' to Black's 12th move, this has little importance. Our analysis shows that White's attack is so strong that even here Black cannot get rid of the problematic pin in time. There are two examples from this position (although by transposition):

a) 14...♖h8 15 h5 ♗d7 16 0-0-0 ♕e7 (Chilingirova-Mastrovasilis, Komotini girls Ch 1992) and now 17 h6+! ♔g6 18 h7! ♗g4 19 ♖h6+ leads to mate or win of the queen.

b) 14...♘cd7 15 h5 ♖g8 (Chilingirova-Nestorova, Bulgarian wom Ch 1992) and now 16 g4!, followed by ♗h4 with a later 0-0-0, gives White a clear advantage.

B)

8 h4 *(D)*

White starts the advance immediately, delaying ♗e2.

8...h5

8...♘e8 transposes to note 'b' to White's 8th move in Line A of Chapter 3.

9 ♗g5

We now have a basic position.

9...a6

Black prepares 10...♕e8 by ruling out ♘b5 ideas. Other moves:

a) 9...♘b6?! 10 ♗e2 ♕e8 (Palsson-D.Olafsson, Reykjavik 1990) 11 ♘b5!, with a later a4, gives White the advantage.

b) 9...♖e8 10 ♗e2 ♘f8 11 ♕d2 ♖b8 12 f3 c6? (better is the immediate 12...c5, planning ...a6 and ...b5) 13 0-0-0 c5 14 ♖dg1 a6 15 ♘f1 ♕a5 16 g4 (an old saying from the past: he gets milled first who comes first to the mill) 16...b5 17 ♗xf6! ♗xf6 18 gxh5 b4 19 ♘b1 ♕xa2 20 hxg6 fxg6 21 h5 and White won in C.Flear-Duponchel, Le Touquet 1992.

c) 9...a5 10 ♗e2 ♕e8 and now 11 ♘b5! is most awkward, and causes problems for Black.

10 ♗e2 ♕e8 *(D)*

10...♘c5 11 ♗xh5! is the same as Line A3, except that there the pawn is on a5.

11 ♕c2!?

White can also develop by 11 ♕d2:

a) 11...♖b8 is best answered by 12 b4 or 12 ♗e3. Instead, 12 ♗h6 ♘h7 transposes to line 'b11'.

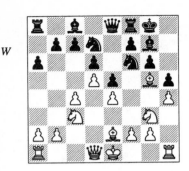

W

b) 11...♘h7 and now:

b1) 12 ♗h6 (the exchange of these bishops is effective only with an open file):

b11) 12...♖b8 13 0-0-0 ♘df6 14 ♗xg7 ♔xg7 15 ♔b1! b5 16 cxb5 axb5 17 ♖c1! (Black understands that he also has to keep an eye on the c-file) 17...♗d7 18 f3 ♖b7. In Vigh-Raeber, Biel 1995 White played ♘d1-e3, instead of strengthening the centre with ♘f1-e3, preparing g4 as well, with slightly better chances to White.

b12) 12...♗xh6 13 ♕xh6 ♘df6 14 ♕e3! ± Minev-Busquest, USA 1994.

b13) 12...♘df6! 13 ♗xg7 ♔xg7 14 0-0-0 (risky, because the black pawn is not yet on a5) 14...♗d7 15 ♖dg1 b5 16 f3 ♕b8! 17 ♘f1 ♕b6 18 ♘e3 ♖fb8 19 ♗d3 ♕c5 20 ♘cd1 c6 and now a draw was agreed in Udovčić-Gligorić, Titovo Užice 1966, which must have pleased White mostly.

b2) 12 ♘f1 ♘df6 (now ...♘xg5 and ...♘h7 is the threat) 13 ♗e3 ♗d7 14 f3 b5 15 ♘h2 and now instead of playing 15...b4, closing the queenside (U.Schmidt-Ahrens, Kassel 1995),

Black should keep the tension with 15...♕b8.

11...♘h7 12 ♗e3 ♕e7!

Now ...♗f6 is threatened, and this forces White to regroup his pieces, which is not advantageous for him.

13 ♘f1 (D)

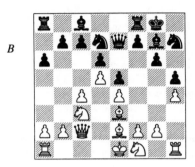

B

Now:

a) 13...c6 14 a4 ♘df6 15 f3 ♗d7 16 a5 ♘e8 17 ♕b3 ♗c8 18 c5! (a sudden change of direction, instead of the expected 18 g4) 18...♘hf6 (18...dxc5 can be answered by 19 dxc6 and ♕b6) 19 dxc6 bxc6 20 cxd6 ♕xd6 (better is 20...♘xd6 21 ♗c5 with just a slight advantage for White) 21 ♖d1 ♕e7 22 ♕b6 ♕e6 23 ♕b4! and Black is unable to counter the threats of ♗c5 and ♗c4, Forintos-Høi, Esbjerg 1978.

b) A more accurate continuation is 13...♘df6 14 f3 ♗d7 15 ♘d2 ♖fb8!? 16 a3 c5 (16...b5 17 cxb5 axb5 18 b4! gives White a minimal advantage) 17 b4 b6 18 ♗d3 ♘e8 19 ♖b1 ♘c7 Remlinger-Busquest, San Mateo 1994. Now 20 ♔e2 leads to a rich position with chances for both sides.

2 6...e5 7 d5 ♘g4

1 d4 ♘f6 2 c4 g6 3 ♘c3 ♗g7 4 e4 d6 5 ♘ge2 0-0 6 ♘g3 e5 7 d5 ♘g4 *(D)*

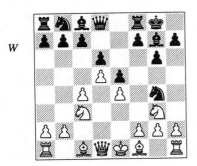

A provocative idea. The basic assumption is that in the case of White answering with 8 f3 or 8 h3, the reply 8...♘h6 helps Black's counterplay with ...f5, and if 8 ♗e2, then 8...♕h4 restricts White on the kingside. But this is only part of the truth. Now:

A: 8 f3   21
B: 8 h3   22
C: 8 ♗e2   22

A)
8 f3 ♘h6 9 ♗e2

9 ♗e3 (9 h4 f5 =) 9...f5 10 ♗f2 is an interesting plan from Soos: contrary to the usual method, he does not take on f5, but places his bishop on f2, ready to play on both sides. He allows ...f4, but at the same time he postpones castling until later, and will choose a location for his king according to

circumstances. After 10...f4 11 ♘ge2 g5 12 h3 c5 13 dxc6 ♘xc6 14 c5 White took the initiative on the queenside in Soos-Dzindzichashvili, Tbilisi 1965. We suggest the better 10...fxe4 11 ♘cxe4 ♘f5, with complications.

9...f5 10 exf5

10 0-0?! is less good. Seeing this position I recall a story from 1991, when I played for a German team in Stadthagen. Before the Sunday match, one of the club members approached me with the problem that he did not know what he should play in the King's Indian Defence against the ♘ge2-g3 Hungarian Attack. I thought for a while, then I recommended the continuation 7...♘g4, where White has to play really accurately because of the tactics, and if he does not know them properly he may easily go astray. In Ulrich Rohde's game it turned out quite well. Both he and our club won. Instead of castling it is better to take on f5, which is typical in positions after ...f5. However, it is worth following the game for a while because of its lessons: 10...f4! 11 ♘h1 ♔h8 (the flaw in White's position is that whereas after castling Black gets a free hand on the kingside, White lags behind with the typical advance on the other wing) 12 g4 ♘f7 13 ♗d2 h5! 14 ♘f2 hxg4 15 ♘xg4 ♗xg4! 16 fxg4 ♘d7 17 ♔g2 ♗f6 18 ♗f3 ♔g7 with advantage to

Black, Tyrtania-U.Rohde, Germany 1991.

10...♘xf5 11 0-0 ♗h6 12 ♘xf5 ♗xc1 13 ♖xc1 gxf5 14 f4!

It is important to block the f5-pawn, to impede the c8-bishop.

14...♘d7 15 ♕d2 exf4 16 ♖xf4 ♘e5 17 ♘b5 ♗d7 18 ♘d4 ♕f6

If 18...♕g5?? then 19 ♖g4 is an instructive trap.

19 ♖cf1

White has the advantage, Bönsch-Lesiège, Berlin 1992.

B)

8 h3 ♘h6 9 h4!

Preventing 9...♕h4.

9...f5 10 exf5

An important and typical move, making room for the g3-knight on e4 or on h5, depending on Black's answer.

10...gxf5

After 10...♘xf5 11 ♘ge4 the h4-pawn is taboo.

11 ♗g5 ♕e8 12 ♘h5 ♘g4!? 13 ♘xg7 ♔xg7 14 ♗e2 ♕g6

Our analysis shows that White has a slight advantage in this somewhat difficult position.

15 f3!?

Or 15 ♗xg4 fxg4 16 ♕d2 h6 17 ♗e3 ♗f5 18 h5 ♕f6 19 f3 ♔h7 20 0-0-0 ♘a6 Oei-Skripchenko, Bad Mondorf 1991. Now White should observe two instructive factors: 1) With opposite-coloured bishops the attack is stronger; 2) He has an extra pawn on the kingside. The right plan is therefore 21 fxg4! ♗xg4 22 ♘e4 ♕g7 (22...♕f5 23 ♘g3) 23 ♖dg1 with an initiative for White on the kingside.

15...♘f6 16 f4! *(D)*

An unusual but many-sided pawn sacrifice. If Black takes on f4 then on the one hand the position opens up, which favours the bishop-pair, and on the other hand ♕d4 and 0-0-0 may follow. What is more, the blockaded pawn on f5 obstructs the c8-bishop.

a) 16...♘e4?? 17 ♗h5.

b) 16...h6 17 h5 ♕f7 18 ♗h4 ♔h7 19 ♕c2 with the idea of castling long. Capturing the h5-pawn would only strengthen White's attack: 19...♘xh5 20 ♗g5!.

c) 16...♘g4 17 h5 ♕f7 18 h6+ ♔h8 19 ♕d2 with an advantage for White.

C)

8 ♗e2

The traditional reply.

8...♕h4 *(D)*

If 8...♘h6 9 h4! White has a tempo more than the variations starting with 8 h3 as the bishop is already on e2. 9...f5 10 ♗g5 ♕e8 11 exf5 gxf5 (11...♘xf5 12 ♘ge4) 12 ♘h5 ♘a6 13 ♕d2 ♘f7 (Spittle-R.Vann, corr. 1986) and now the awkward 14 ♘f6+ grants White an advantage.

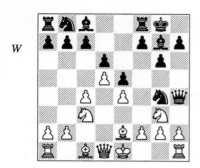

Bringing the queen to h4 is highly committal and has far-reaching consequences. Black both prevents White from advancing his h-pawn, and also sets two traps: 9 h3?? ♘xf2! 10 ♔xf2 f5 ∓ and 9 f3?? ♘xh2! 10 ♔f2 f5 11 ♕g1 f4! and Black wins.

Now White's main continuations are:

C1: 9 ♗xg4   23
C2: 9 ♘b5   23

C1)

9 ♗xg4 ♗xg4 10 f3
Now:

a) 10...♗d7 and then:

a1) 11 0-0!? may lead to rather difficult play, but is the natural continuation. 11...f5 12 exf5 gxf5 13 f4! ♘a6! (13...♗e8!? gives room for the knight on d7, Rauch-Kosztolanczi, Hungarian Cht 1995; now White should play ♗e3 and ♕d2) 14 ♗e3 ♖ae8 15 ♕d2 with only the usual minimal advantage for White in the opening.

a2) 11 ♗e3 ♗h6! 12 ♗f2 and now instead of 12...♕g5 (as in J.Johansson-Degerman, Stockholm 1992; h4 should not be provoked) the immediate 12...♕e7 leads to equal chances.

b) 10...♗c8 (the point of this retreat is that it leaves d7 open for the knight):

b1) 11 ♗e3 f5 12 ♗f2 ♕e7 13 exf5 gxf5 14 0-0 ♖f7 15 f4! (this is just a temporary pawn sacrifice) 15...♘d7 (15...exf4 is met by 16 ♘h5, and then 17 ♕f3) 16 ♘h5 ♗h8 and in the game Szollosi-Dely, Hungarian Cht 1961 White should have continued 17 ♖e1, ♕d2 and ♖ad1 with a queenside advance.

b2) 11 0-0 ♘d7 (if instead 11...f5, then 12 exf5 gxf5 13 f4 is the usual strategy for White) and now:

b21) The surprising 12 ♘b5 a6 13 ♘xc7 ♖b8 14 ♘e6 fxe6 15 dxe6 ♘f6 16 ♕xd6 ♖a8 17 e7 ♖e8 18 ♕xe5 h6 19 ♖d1 is quite good for White.

b22) 12 ♗e3 f5 (12...♗h6) 13 ♗f2 ♕d8 and now in Navarovsky-Stein, Kecskemet 1968, White did not insert the exchange on f5, so the important e4-square was not available for his knights. The proper line is 14 exf5! gxf5 15 ♕c2, with slightly better chances to White.

b23) 12 ♕c2! a6 (Szollosi-Ozsvath, Hungary 1962) and now the best line is 13 ♖b1 with a quick initiative on the queenside, making use of the fact that ...f5 cannot come for a while, e.g. 13...♗h6 14 b4 ♗f4 15 ♘ce2 and then c5.

C2)

9 ♘b5 *(D)*
This novelty from 1968 became popular after it was published in *Informator*. See the game Forintos-Dely, Kecskemet 1968, Line C221. The aim

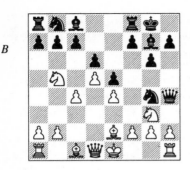

B

of the move is to press on the pawns on a7, c7 and d6, divert the b8-knight to a6, and tie down Black's queen's rook. It also stops ...a5.

9...♘a6

9...a6 is a risky pawn sacrifice that has not occurred in practice. 10 ♘xc7! ♖a7 11 ♕a4! (after this move the knight can come back via b5) 11...f5 12 ♗xg4 ♕xg4 13 ♘b5 ♗d7 (13...♖a8 14 ♘xd6 ♗d7 15 ♕d1) 14 h3 ♕h4 15 ♕a3! gives White an advantage.

Now:

C21: 10 ♖b1!   24
C22: 10 ♗d2   25

C21)

10 ♖b1!

The move we propose here is a novelty. The gist of the idea is that, after Black's natural moves, White will have a tempo more in comparison with the alternative continuation 10 ♗d2. After 10...♗h6, for example, the bishop takes on h6 in one move. The rook move aims at supporting the advance on the queenside later on, of course.

10...♗h6

After 10...♗d7 the bishop move 11 ♗d2 is possible here too (like 10

♗d2). The idea is also to play ♕c1 now. Then 11...f5 12 ♗xg4 fxg4 13 ♕c1 is similar to Line C221; after 11...♗h6 the simplest is 12 ♗xg4 ♗xg4 13 f3 – see Line C223.

11 ♗xh6

Those players who like complications should choose this variation, and those who prefer quieter positions should choose 11 ♗xg4, directing the play towards less troubled waters by exchanging two pieces. The play is similar to the note to White's 11th move in Line C223; the only difference here is that the rook is already on b1, which favours White. This difference is also important in the following continuation.

11...♘xh6 12 0-0 ♗d7

This move is more effective when the rook is still on a1; compare Line C223. After 12...f5 White can reply with the familiar idea 13 exf5 gxf5 14 f4 – compare Line C223.

13 b4

This is the logical continuation (not 13 ♘c3 ♖ae8!). If the a8-rook moves now, then the a-pawn can be captured because the knight can easily return.

13...f5 14 exf5 gxf5

14...♘xf5 15 ♘xf5! ±.

15 f4! exf4 16 ♘h5 f3! 17 ♗xf3

Compare this with the analogous position after White's 16th move in Line C223.

Now after 17...♕xc4, as the c5-square is now under control, 18 ♕d2! decides: 18...f4?? 19 ♘a3 wins the queen as the pawn is on b4; 18...♗xb5 19 ♕g5+ is decisive; 18...♖f7 19 ♘a3! ♕h4 (there is nothing else) 20 ♕xh6 with a piece more; 18...♘f7 loses to 19 ♘f6+ ♚h8 20 ♘a3 and ♘xd7.

C22)
10 ♗d2 *(D)*

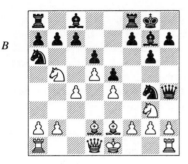

White plans ♕c1 while also preparing b4. Now Black can choose:

C221: 10...f5   25
C222: 10...c6   26
C223: 10...♗h6   28

C221)
10...f5 11 ♗xg4!

The e2-bishop is not so important. The opening of the f-file is not dangerous for White either.

11...fxg4 12 ♕c1

This threatens to win the black queen by 13 ♗g5.

After 12 0-0 instead, here is an instructive example, where both sides played rationally, and Black pushed her pawn as far as h3: 12...♗d7 13 ♕c1 h6 (now the position recommended by Florian has been created) 14 b4 ♚h7 15 ♖b1 ♖f7 16 ♖b3 and White's chances are better, Muresan-Lelchuk, Dresden wom 1990.

12...♕e7

Or:

a) 12...h6!? is Florian's idea, and should be compared with the note to White's 12th move.

b) 12...♗f6 (Black first regroups his bishop to e7 and only then retreats his queen) and now, rather then 13 b4 (Baigno-Mauro, 1994), first 13 0-0 is more accurate since then 13...c6 could be met by 14 ♘xd6!.

c) 12...♘c5 can be answered by 13 ♕c2!, e.g. 13...♖f7 14 b4 ♘a6 15 ♕c1 renewing the threat.

13 ♗g5

A little trick to lure the bishop into the rook's path.

13...♗f6 14 ♗e3 c5

This closing of the position rather favours the knights. An alternative is 14...c6, when 15 ♘c3 ♘c7 maintains the tension. It must be noted, however, that Black also has to reckon with 15 ♘xa7 ♗d7 16 ♕d2, e.g. 16...♘c5 17 b4 with complications.

15 ♕d2! ♘c7 16 ♘xc7 ♕xc7 17 0-0 b6 18 ♘e2

As Black may advance with ...h5 some time, the knight would only be a target on g3. Also, it could be more useful on the queenside.

18...♗a6?!

Hoping for 19 b3, slowing down White's advance on the queenside. However, 18...♗d7 or 18...h5 is better.

19 ♖fc1 ♗h4 20 ♖c2 ♕f7 21 ♖f1 ♗c8 22 ♖cc1

Both players manoeuvre for position.

22...h5 23 ♘c3

White does not commit himself to b4 yet, which is sometimes a good practical ploy in tournament games. His plan is to meet 23...♗d7 with 24 b4 cxb4 25 ♘b5, when the position opens. This is also a sign that White enjoys a slight advantage, as only he can decide when to break through.

23...♗a6

Manoeuvring again. Some more moves are of interest:

24 b3 ♕e7 25 ♘d1

Another regrouping, which hides a little trap at the same time. Black now decides it is the right time to take the initiative.

25...b5?!

Black intends to close the queenside to get a free hand on the kingside. However, 25...♖f7 is better.

26 ♕a5 ♕b7 *(D)*

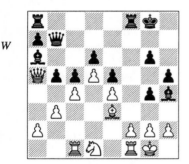

Now ...b4 is threatened, and it can even result in the win of the queen. But the white queen did not go to a5 to allow that.

27 b4!

This can be considered a leitmotif. Black can never open the files because of his draughty king position, so has to accept a weakening of his pawn-structure.

27...♖fc8

27...cxb4 is met by 28 c5!, and 27...♕b6 by 28 ♕a3! cxb4 29 ♕xb4 ♕d8 30 c5.

28 bxc5 dxc5

If White manages to force a pawn-structure like this (pawns on c5 and e5 without a d6-pawn), against the King's Indian Defence, then it usually means he can be happy. It is difficult for Black to defend the weakened pawns.

29 ♘b2! ♕b6 30 ♕c3 b4 31 ♕d2

Not, of course, 31 ♕xe5?? ♗f6!.

31...♗e7 32 ♘d3

This is the right place for the knight.

32...♗d6 33 ♗h6

White is ready to attack the weakened kingside with f3 or ♕g5. He went on to win in Forintos-Dely, Kecskemet 1968.

C222)
10...c6 *(D)*

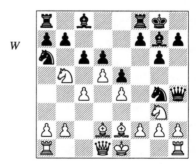

This tactical line took me by surprise when I first met it over the board. It is understandable that I did not dare to venture the unclear 11 ♘xd6 ♘xf2 12 ♔xf2 ♕f6+ 13 ♘df5 gxf5 14 ♘h5! ♕d6 because of the uncertain position of the white king. What is more, I feared it might be a prepared variation.

11 ♕c1!

There are other threats beside capturing the queen, as we can see later on.

11...♕d8

This time, had my opponent tried 11...h6, I would have seriously considered taking the d6-pawn, because I did not think that the position of my king was so dangerous after 12 ♘xd6 ♘xf2 13 0-0! ♘g4 14 ♗xg4 ♗xg4. I only calculated as far as this, and if it had occurred I would have made a plan here. I learned this method from Smyslov, as one day an amateur asked him, in my presence: "Master! For how many moves do you calculate?" "Mainly for one move" was the laconic answer. Then, when we were heading for our hotel, in private, he added: "I meant that I count for as few moves as absolutely necessary". To do this well, his good and quick assessment of the position was necessary. Now White should play 15 ♘xb7!. Taking the b7-pawn is a difficult decision, but still the best. Then:

a) In case of 15...f5 16 dxc6 f4 17 ♘h1 f3 there is 18 ♕e1! and Black's attack loses its wind on the kingside. Only White's advantage on the queenside remains.

b) 15...cxd5 16 exd5! brings about a difficult but instructive position. Play occurs all over the board, and the plans are already determined: Black attacks on the kingside, while White has to advance in the centre and on the queenside. Both players must attack where they are stronger! Then:

b1) 16...f5 17 c5! f4 18 ♘e4 f3 (or 18...♗e2 19 ♕e1 ±) 19 ♕e1! ±.

b2) 16...♖ab8 17 ♘a5 e4 (17...f5 18 ♘c6 ♖be8 19 ♗e1! ±; 17...♘c5 is met by 18 ♘c6) 18 ♘xe4! ♗xb2 19 ♕e1! (a recurring motif) 19...♗d4+ 20 ♔h1 +–.

12 ♘c3

As the g4-knight is under attack and has to move sooner or later, the tempo won here is enough for a little advantage.

12...♗d7 13 0-0 ♖c8 14 h3 ♘f6 15 ♗g5 cxd5 16 cxd5 ♘c5

16...b5? 17 ♕e3! wins a pawn for White.

17 ♕d2 ♕b6 18 ♖ab1 a5

A reasonable alternative for Black is 18...♕b4, followed by ...♕d4, trying to exchange queens.

19 ♖fc1 ♖c7?!

19...♘e8 is of course premature because of 20 ♗e7, while 19...♕b4 is still the lesser evil, with a slight advantage for White.

20 ♗e3! ♘e8 21 a3! a4

Here follows a typical sacrifice by which White aims for the better pawn-structure.

22 ♘xa4!! ♗xa4 23 b4 ♘xe4

After 23...♕a7 24 bxc5 dxc5 Black has the previously mentioned poor pawn-structure.

24 ♘xe4 ♖xc1+ 25 ♖xc1 ♕d8 26 b5

The main point: the a4-bishop is trapped. Although Black managed to rescue the bishop in Forintos-Sinkovics, Hungarian Cht 1986, he got into a disadvantageous ending, which he lost.

C223)

10...♗h6 *(D)*

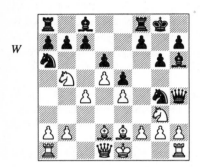

W

11 ♗xh6

This leads to complications. White has a major alternative in 11 ♗xg4. By exchanging the potentially dangerous knight, White follows a quieter path; there are fewer tactical chances here for either side. 11...♗xg4 12 f3 ♗d7 and now:

a) 13 0-0 f5 14 exf5 gxf5 15 ♗xh6 ♕xh6 16 f4 ♗xb5 (16...exf4 17 ♘h5) 17 cxb5 ♘c5 18 b4 ♘e4 19 ♘xe4 fxe4 20 fxe5 and White has the better ending.

b) 13 ♗xh6 ♕xh6 14 ♕d2 and then:

b1) 14...♕xd2+ 15 ♔xd2 f5 and Black equalized in Forintos-Balogh, Budapest 1991 with a later ...♖f6 and ...c6.

b2) 14...♕h4 15 0-0 f5 16 exf5 gxf5 17 f4! e4 (Markotik-d'Amore, Karpovac 1988) 18 b4 gives White a slight advantage, as his opponent has problems bringing the a6-knight into

play. Black also has to be careful because of his more open king-position.

11...♘xh6 12 0-0 f5

Or 12...♗d7 13 ♖c1 f5 14 exf5 gxf5 15 f4! exf4 16 ♘h5 f3 17 ♗xf3 f4 18 ♕d4! and White has the better chances because of the good coordination of his pieces.

13 exf5 gxf5 14 f4! exf4 15 ♘h5 f3!?

15...♘g4 16 ♗xg4 fxg4 17 ♘xf4 ± Knaak.

16 ♗xf3!

Not 16 ♖xf3? ♕xh5 17 ♖g3+ ♘g4 (Knaak).

16...♕xc4

An important position. Now:

a) 17 a4 ♗d7? (Knaak is right in saying that 17...♕h4 is best here, when White's advantage is questionable, though his compensation is not in doubt) 18 ♕d2! f4 19 ♖fc1 ♕b4 20 ♕xb4 ♘xb4 21 ♖xc7 favours White, Serper-Dannevig, Gausdal 1991.

b) 17 ♕e1! (this novelty of Van Gaalen's ensures an advantage for White) 17...♕xb5 (17...♖f7 18 ♕e8+ ♖f8 19 ♕e7 ♖f7 20 ♕d8+!) 18 ♕g3+ ♘g4 19 ♗xg4 ♕xb2 (19...fxg4 20 ♖xf8+ ♔xf8 21 ♕f4+ ♔g8 22 ♕f6) 20 ♗xf5+ ♔h8 21 ♗e6 (21 ♗xh7 is also strong) 21...♗xe6 22 dxe6 ♘c5 (everything loses here, e.g. 22...♕d4+ 23 ♔h1 ♖g8 24 ♕f3 ♖ae8 25 ♖ae1 ♖e7 26 ♕f7!) 23 e7 ♖g8 24 ♖ae1 ♕d4+ 25 ♔h1 ♘e4? 26 ♕h4 1-0 Van Gaalen-Van Laatum, Utrecht-Volmac 1991.

3 6...e5 7 d5 ♘e8

1 d4 ♘f6 2 c4 g6 3 ♘c3 ♗g7 4 e4 d6 5 ♘ge2 0-0 6 ♘g3 e5 7 d5 ♘e8 *(D)*

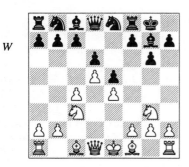

Black is planning to play ...f5, without any further preparation, but this way too many of his pieces are on the back rank. Now:

A: 8 h4 29
B: 8 ♗e2 34

A)

8 h4

This is the main line. White intends to play 9 h5. We now consider four main moves for Black:

A1: 8...f5 30
A2: 8...c5 32
A3: 8...♗f6 33
A4: 8...h5 34

There are also some lesser possibilities, the idea behind them being that the time White spends playing h4-h5 can be used to develop:

a) 8...a5 9 h5 (9 ♗g5 is also possible) 9...♘d7 (here 9...f5? is feeble since after 10 hxg6 hxg6 11 exf5 gxf5 Black's king position is quite uncertain – Taimanov) 10 hxg6 fxg6 11 ♗e2 ♘c5 12 ♗e3 ♕e7 13 ♕d2 ♕f7 (preventing f2-f4; slightly better is 13...♗d7 followed by ...a4) 14 0-0-0 ♘f6 15 ♖h4! (this move serves both to control the g4-square and to double the rooks; in reply it is not easy to find a good plan for Black) 15...♖e8 (making room for the knight on f8) 16 ♖dh1 ♘cd7 17 ♘f1 ♘f8 18 g4 and in Fyllingen-N.Hagesæther, Gausdal 1995 White soon won with the manoeuvre ♘h2-f3-g5.

b) 8...♘d7 and now:

b1) 9 ♗g5 is playable: 9...♗f6 10 ♕d2 ♘g7 11 0-0-0 a6 12 ♗e2 (now ♗xf6 followed by h5 has to be prevented) 12...h5 and now the prophylactic move 13 ♔b1 makes it difficult for Black to find a good plan other than 13...♕e7. He has to wait idly by for White to play either g4 or f4. The player who can make plans gains the upper hand.

b2) However, everybody plays the natural 9 h5. 9...♕e7 (9...a5 transposes to line 'a'; 9...♗f6 can be met by 10 ♗h6 ♘g7 11 ♕d2 preventing ...♗g5) and then:

b21) After 10 ♗e3, White must face the reply 10...f5.

b22) 10 ♗d3 ♘c5 11 ♗c2 a5 would only please Black.

b23) For the obvious 10 ♗e2 see Line B.

b24) 10 hxg6 fxg6 11 ♗e3 a6 12 ♗e2 ♘ef6 13 ♕d2 ♖f7 14 0-0-0 ♘f8 sees Black concentrating all his forces on the defence of the kingside, but White is better. He can make plans as he wishes, but it is important that he first plays the preparatory move 15 ♔b1.

A1)

8...f5

White now has two options:

A11: 9 exf5　　30
A12: 9 ♗g5　　31

9 h5 is feeble since it can be met by 9...f4 and a later ...g5, so Black will be active on the kingside.

A11)

9 exf5 gxf5 10 ♘h5 *(D)*

10 ♗g5 is also playable:

a) 10...♘f6 can be met by 11 ♗d3 – Taimanov.

b) 10...♕d7 11 ♗d3 ♘a6 12 ♗c2 ♘c5 13 ♘h5 a5 14 ♕e2 (Daskalov-Bobekov, Bulgarian Ch 1960) with advantage to White (Taimanov).

White will win an important tempo when the bishop moves; otherwise, the exchange on g7 would give White the advantage.

10...♗h8

Or:

a) 10...♕e7 11 ♗g5 ♕f7 12 ♘xg7 ♕xg7 13 ♗d2 (White preserves his bishop-pair) 13...♘f6 14 ♕c2 ♘a6 15

B

0-0-0 ♘g4?! (this is tempting because it secures the e5-square; nevertheless, it is more natural to play 15...♘c5 16 f3 a5) 16 ♗e1 e4 17 ♘b5! ♘e5 18 ♗c3 ♗d7 19 ♔b1 ♗xb5 20 cxb5 ♘c5 21 f4 exf3 22 gxf3 and White soon won on the g-file in Schurman-Jens, Soest 1995.

b) 10...♘d7 11 ♗g5 ♘df6 12 ♘xg7 (better than 12 ♗e2, Nikolić-Smailbegović, Yugoslavia 1957) 12...♘xg7 13 h5 with a slight advantage to White. Black is somewhat vulnerable on the dark squares.

11 ♗g5

A lot of things are a question of fashion in chess. At least, that is probably the reason why 11 ♗h6 is not currently favoured, although it is just as good. Anyway, we recommend playing the text-move.

11...♘f6

Now White has two promising lines:

a) 12 ♗d3 led quickly to a win for White in Remlinger-Schemm, Las Vegas 1995. The instructive continuation was 12...♕e8 13 ♘xf6+ ♗xf6 14 ♕d2 e4 15 ♗c2 ♕h5?! (it is understandable that Black wants to prevent White from castling queenside, and stops the h-pawn, but White unlocks the blockade amusingly; 15...♘d7 is only slightly better since it can be met by 16 ♘b5) 16 ♗xf6 ♖xf6 17 g4! ♕xg4 18 ♘e2 ♕f3 19 0-0-0 with an inevitable attack on the g-file.

b) 12 ♗e2 ♕e8 13 ♘xf6+ ♗xf6 14 ♗h5 ♕e7 15 ♕d2 a6 16 0-0-0 b5!? (this pawn sacrifice is the consistent continuation; 16...♘d7?! 17 g4! ♘c5 18 ♗xf6 ♕xf6 19 g5 gave White an advantage in Keiwe-Howe, Copenhagen 1993) 17 cxb5! (White has a 'chance' to go wrong with 17 g4?! b4! 18 ♘e2 f4) 17...axb5 18 ♘xb5 ♖xa2 19 ♔b1 ♖a8 20 ♗xf6 ♕xf6 21 ♘xc7 with a slight advantage for White.

A12)
9 ♗g5 *(D)*

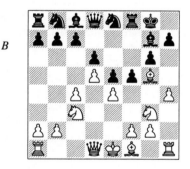

9...♕d7

Or 9...♗f6 10 exf5! gxf5, and now:

a) 11 ♗h6 ♖f7 (11...♘g7 12 ♘h5) 12 ♗e2 ♘g7 13 ♘h5 ♘d7 14 ♕d2 ♔h8 15 0-0-0 favours White, L.Johannessen-Lysedal, Norway 1992.

b) 11 ♗xf6 ♘xf6 12 ♗d3 e4 13 ♗c2 ♘g4 14 ♕d2 ♘a6 15 0-0-0 ♘e5

16 f3! exf3 17 gxf3 ♘xf3? (17...♘xc4 18 ♕d4 ♘e5 19 ♖hg1), Fitzko-Eliseev, Philadelphia 1990, and now 18 ♕g2! gives White an overwhelming advantage.

c) 11 ♕d2 ♘g7 12 0-0-0 a5 13 ♗d3 ♘a6 14 f3 ♘c5 15 ♗c2 ♗d7 16 ♔b1 (a good move in nearly all cases of queenside castling; the only important point to note is that, whilst it should be played quickly, it should only come after any other useful moves) 16...a4 and now instead of 17 a3 (J.Gonzalez-Nestler, Helsinki OL 1952) 17 ♖dg1 with a later ♘ge2 and g4 gives White slightly better chances, and 17...a3 can be met by 18 b3.

10 exf5 gxf5

Now:

a) 11 ♗d3 and then:

a11) 11...f4?! 12 ♕h5 and here:

a111) 12...♘f6 13 ♗xf6 ♗xf6 14 ♗f5 ♕g7 15 ♗xc8! ♖xc8 16 ♘ge4 with a decisive positional advantage to White.

a112) 12...h6 13 ♕g6! ♖f7 (not 13...hxg5? 14 hxg5 and ♖h8+) 14 ♗f5 ♖xf5 15 ♘xf5 hxg5 16 ♘h6+ ♔f8 17 hxg5 gives White a powerful attack.

a12) 11...e4 and then:

a121) 12 ♗c2 ♘a6 13 ♕d2 (first 13 a3 is better) 13...♘b4 14 0-0-0 ♘xc2 15 ♔xc2 a6 with chances for both sides, Dale-Wilkinson, corr. 1990.

a122) 12 ♗e2 ♘f6 13 ♕d2 ♕f7 14 0-0-0 (14 f3 is also good) 14...♘a6 15 f3 ♘c5 16 ♖hf1 with an initiative for White, Zwirner-Adair, German Cht 1994.

a13) 11...♘a6 12 ♕e2 ♘b4 (an instructive manoeuvre, forcing White to play a3) 13 ♗b1 a5 14 a3 ♘a6 15 ♗c2 ♘c5 16 0-0-0 ♕f7 (the bishop must leave g5 since ...f4 is now a serious threat) 17 ♗e3 b6 18 ♘h5 ♘f6 (Ker-Booth, Australian Masters 1989) and now White should play 19 ♘xg7 planning f3, ♖dg1 and g4, as in other similar cases.

b) 11 ♘h5 ♗h8 (Black has other moves – compare other variations throughout Line A1) 12 ♕d2 ♘f6 and now, rather than the dubious 13 ♘g3?! (Keri-Puri, Gausdal 1986), our recommendation is 13 ♗h6!:

b1) 13...♘xh5? 14 ♗xf8 ♔xf8 15 ♕h6+ ♘g7 16 ♕xh7 +–.

b2) 13...♖e8 14 ♕g5+ ♔f7 15 ♗e2! leads to a serious advantage for White.

A2)
8...c5 *(D)*

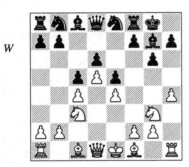

This sideline has not become popular since it does not help Black to generate play on the queenside. Now:

a) 9 ♗e2 f5 10 exf5 and now:

a1) 10...gxf5 is Black's usual reply. It can be answered by 11 ♘h5 as we can see in other lines, with the difference that ...c5 has been played.

a2) 10...♗xf5 11 h5 and then:

a21) In case of 11...g5? White can control the light squares, viz. 12 h6 ♗h8 13 ♘xf5 ♖xf5 14 ♘e4! and ♗g4 followed by ♗xg5 is inevitable.

a22) 11...♘d7 12 hxg6 ♗xg6 13 ♘ge4 (White is better since the position of the black king is not safe enough; the rest of the game is quite instructive) 13...♘df6 14 ♘g5 ♘c7 15 ♗e3 (the knight on g5 is very unpleasant – in addition it is not advisable to chase it away) 15...a6 (15...h6 can be met by 16 ♘e6!) 16 a4 (not only directed against ...b5, but also to prepare ♖a3-g3) 16...♖b8 17 ♕d2 ♕d7 (planning ...♘g4 in order to exchange one piece) 18 ♖h4 ♖fe8 19 ♔f1! (the king looks for a safe place) 19...b6 20 ♔g1 ♖e7 21 ♖a3! ♕e8 (...♘h5-f4 is the plan) 22 ♕d1 ♕f8 23 ♗c1 (opening the third rank) 23...e4 24 ♗f4 ♖ee8 25 ♕c1 ♕e7 (now the rook on h4 is in danger) 26 ♖h1 ♖f8 27 ♘d1 (better is 27 ♕e3 but it is almost impossible to play a whole game without mistakes) 27...♗h8 (the only chance was 27...b5) 28 ♕e3 b5? (too late!) 29 ♕g3! ♘ce8 30 axb5 axb5 31 ♘xh7! ♘xh7 32 ♕xg6+ ♕g7 33 ♕e6+ ♕f7 34 ♖g3+ and White won in the game Forintos-Karl, Zurich 1984.

b) 9 ♗d3 (one can generally take this move into account whenever ...c5 has already been played, as in this case) 9...h5 10 ♗g5 ♗f6 11 ♕d2 ♘d7 12 f3 ♗e7 13 ♘f1 ♘df6 14 g3 ♘g7 15 ♘e3 ♔h7 16 0-0-0 ♘g8 17 ♗xe7 ♕xe7 18 f4 f5 (Black could not allow the opponent's pawn to advance to f5; at the same time ...f5 is a leap in the dark since the position will be opened not far away from the black king) 19 exf5 gxf5 20 fxe5 dxe5 21 ♕c2 ♗d7 22 g4 (this is the proper continuation for those who have an attacking vein, but it is not without some risks; a quieter line is 22 ♖hf1 or 22 ♗e2; for example, 22...♘h6 23 d6 ♕e6 24 ♗f3 with an initiative for White) 22...hxg4 (22...e4?! 23 ♗xe4! fxe4 24 ♘xe4 ♔h8 25 ♖de1 with a later ♘g5 gives White a very strong attack against the opponent's king) 23 ♘xg4 ♕d6? (an instructive and important observation concerning this typical mistake: as Black avoided – rightly – the move 22...e4, he does not even consider it on the next move; however, now 23...e4! would give Black the better chances) 24 ♕h2!. One more pin, and Black lost on the e5-square in Van der Marel-Pel, Groningen 1997.

c) 9 h5 is our suggestion. It can hardly be answered by 9...f5 since the g- and h-files will be opened soon. 9...♗f6 can be met by 10 ♗h6 ♘g7 11 ♕d2.

A3)
8...♗f6 *(D)*

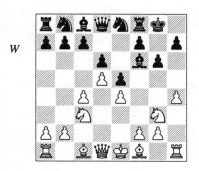

Black urges the h-pawn forward, so that later on he can check on the dark squares from g5. This looks like a good idea, but still does not solve everything.

9 h5 ♗g5 10 ♗d3!

White foresees that in the fight for the f4-square, he will need the e2-square. That is why 10 ♗e2 is weaker. Then Merlini-Soppe, Buenos Aires OL 1978 continued 10...♗f4! 11 hxg6 fxg6 12 ♗f3 ♕g5 13 ♗xf4 ♕xf4 14 ♕d2 ♘a6 15 0-0-0 ♗d7 and Black was OK.

10...c6

10...♘a6 11 ♗d2 ♗d7 12 ♕c1 ♗xd2+ 13 ♕xd2 ♕f6 14 0-0-0 ♕f4 brings about an instructive position. Black has secured the f4-square and managed to exchange the queens, but not all his problems are solved, as White has serious resources, and can obtain the f5-square: 15 ♕xf4! exf4 16 ♘ge2 g5 17 ♘d4 ♘f6 18 f3 h6 19 ♘ce2 c5 20 dxc6 bxc6 21 g3! (fighting for the f5-square) 21...c5 22 ♘c2 fxg3 23 ♘xg3 ♗e6 24 ♘e3, Farina-Agnello, Italy 1994. White has carried out his plan to occupy f5. From there a knight can keep two pawns permanently under fire.

11 ♗d2 ♘a6 12 ♕c1 ♗xd2+ 13 ♕xd2 ♕f6

We have been following the game Forintos-M.Schlosser, Münster 1992. After analysing the game I suggested an improvement: instead of 14 ♘ce2 to play 14 0-0-0, allowing 14...♕f4 as after 15 ♕xf4 exf4 16 ♘ge2 g5 17 dxc6 bxc6 18 ♘d4 White has the better chances in the middlegame. We saw the same clever idea in the note to Black's 10th move.

A4)
8...h5 *(D)*

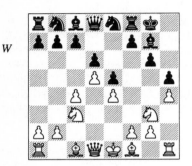

W

Whereas 8...f5 was all about counterattack, 8...h5 means 'blockade'. This move blockades the h4-pawn, but renders the move ...f5 no longer feasible. There are other plans for Black as well, depending on White's reply.

9 ♗g5

The alternative is 9 ♗e2, which gives Black an opportunity to grab the h4-pawn:

a) 9...♘d7 transposes to Line A12 in Chapter 1.

b) 9...♗f6 aims to accept the gift, but this line reminds me of a Hungarian saying: it is 'as brave as a rabbit that attacks with its hind legs'. 10 ♗h6 (by the way, 10 ♗xh5 can simply be met by 10...♗xh4, with a later ...♗g5) 10...♘g7 11 ♕d2 ♗xh4 12 0-0-0 ♗e7 13 ♔b1 ♘d7? (the knight intends to go quickly to the kingside; if Black had known what his opponent was intending, he would probably have chosen 13...h4, but then White could later

open the h-file by g3 anyway) 14 ♗xh5! ♘xh5 15 ♘xh5 gxh5 16 ♖xh5 f5 17 ♗xf8 ♗xf8 18 exf5 ♘f6 19 ♕g5+ ♔f7 20 ♕g6+ (20 ♖h7+ ♘xh7 21 ♕xd8?? ♗xf5+) 20...♔e7 21 ♖h7+ ♘xh7 22 ♕xh7+ ♔e8 23 ♕g6+ ♔e7 24 ♖h1 ♗xf5+ (24...♕e8 25 ♕g5+ ♔d7 26 ♖h7+ ♗e7 27 f6) 25 ♕xf5 ♗g7 26 ♕e6+ ♔f8 27 ♖h5 1-0 M.Kovacs-Haïk, Reggio Emilia 1977/8. This game was published in *Informator* and discouraged players from following up ...♘e8 with ...h5.

With the text-move, White does not sacrifice the h4-pawn.

9...♗f6 10 ♕d2 ♘g7 11 ♗d3

11 ♗e2 is also playable. In that case a later g4 advance could be White's plan.

11...♘d7 12 ♘ge2

White changes his plan. Now g4 or f4 can be prepared.

12...♘c5 13 ♗c2 a5 14 0-0-0 ♗xg5 15 hxg5 f6 16 gxf6 ♕xf6 17 ♖df1 b6 18 f3 ♗d7 19 ♔b1

Now the white king is safe, while the black one is less fortunate.

19...♔f7 20 g4! ♖h8 21 g5 ♕e7 22 f4

The black king was soon obliged to abdicate in Remlinger-Belakovskaya, Philadelphia 1991.

B)
8 ♗e2 *(D)*

This is also possible here, without h4.

At this point Black has two main continuations:

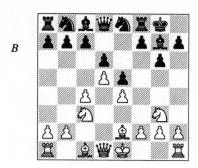

B

For 8...a5 see Line B of Chapter 4 (Classical Variation). Rarer are:

a) 8...♘d7 and then:

a1) Black's idea is to meet 9 f4 with 9...exf4, securing the e5-square for the knight.

a2) Better is 9 h4 f5 (it is also possible to play 9...h5, 9...a5 or 9...♗f6) 10 exf5 gxf5 11 ♗g5 (11 ♘h5 should be played first) 11...♗f6 12 ♕d2 a5 13 0-0-0 ♘c5 14 f4 ♕d7 15 ♘h5 with an advantage to White, Terdy-Besztercsenyi, Budapest 1959.

b) 8...c6 9 0-0 (White is satisfied with the fact that in the 7...c6 system, the retreat ...♘e8 does not have a good reputation) 9...cxd5 10 cxd5 f5 11 exf5 gxf5 12 f4 e4 (now we can see who the open c-file favours) 13 ♗e3 ♘d7 14 ♕d2 a5?! (it already seems clear that Black won't be able to defend on the queenside; 14...a6 15 a4 ♘df6 is better) 15 ♘b5 ♘c5 16 ♖ac1 b6 17 ♖c2 ♘c7 18 ♘d4 (the knight occupies the dominating d4-square) 18...♗b7? (in a difficult position it is easy to make a mistake; is it worth losing f5 to gain the d5-pawn? Hardly, since the king's bishop will be missing, and so the dark squares will be terribly

weak; better is 18...♗d7) 19 ♘dxf5 ♗xd5 20 ♘xg7 ♔xg7 21 f5 ♔g8 22 ♘h5 ♕c8 23 ♕d4 ♖f7 24 ♗h6 ♕d8 25 ♖f4 1-0 Forintos-Krisztian, Budapest 1967.

B1)
8...f5

White has a strong continuation here:

9 exf5! gxf5 (D)

Or 9...♗xf5, and now:

a) 10 h4 ♕f6 11 ♗g5 ♕f7 12 ♕d2 ♘d7 (Kozak-Sojka, corr. 1968) 13 h5 gives White a slight advantage.

b) Of course the strategy 10 0-0 is also good.

c) A good alternative was seen in Jakab-Tompos, Budapest 1998: 10 ♗e3 followed by ♕d2 and ♖ac1, making use of Black's position being somewhat paralysed by the need to keep an eye on the possible capture on f5.

W

10 f4

10 ♘h5 ♖f7 11 f4 ♗h8 (Black still does not concede his bishop; it is true that without this bishop ...e4 cannot be played, but it turns out that it is not playable with the bishop either) 12 0-0

e4 13 ♗e3 ♘f6 (13...♕h4 should be met by 14 ♔h1, as in the game, and not 14 g3 ♕h3) 14 ♔h1 ♘xh5 15 ♗xh5 ♖f6?! (the rook cannot reach the h6-square in time) 16 g4 fxg4 17 ♖g1! and White has a decisive advantage on the kingside, Plassmann-Mihalcz, Münster 1991.

10...♕h4!?

This is not so dangerous as it looks. Its main threat is psychological.

11 0-0 e4 12 ♗e3 ♘d7

12...♖f6 (Hanks-Haasse, Perth 1994) 13 ♘h5 leads quickly to an advantage for White.

13 ♖b1 ♘df6 14 ♘b5! ♗h6 15 c5 a6 16 ♘d4 ♘g7

The black pieces cannot really help the queen, so it will have to retreat soon. 17 cxd6 cxd6 18 ♖c1 ♘fe8 19 ♕b3 ♕e7 20 ♖c2 and White is active on the queenside, Dive-Abbasi, Wrexham 1994.

B2)

8...♕h4 9 0-0 *(D)*

9 ♗e3 can be met by 9...♗h6. Since ...♗f4 threatens to equalize, White has to exchange bishops. This way White would lose one tempo.

9...a5

Or:

a) 9...♘d7 10 ♗e3 f5 (10...♗h6 is better, as can be seen in several examples) 11 exf5 gxf5 12 f4 is a standard recipe, after which either a weak pawn is created on f5, or the e4-f5 pawn-structure can be attacked later by g4, and the black king will also be endangered. White is better. The continuation of Novikov-Nurkić, Cattolica 1993

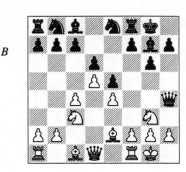

is quite instructive: 12...exf4 13 ♗xf4 ♘e5 14 ♘h5 ♘g6?! (the pride of the position was the e5-knight, and it is a pity to retreat it; 14...♗h8 is better) 15 g3 ♕e7 16 ♘xg7 ♘xg7 17 ♕d2 and White had a clear advantage.

b) 9...♗h6 10 ♗xh6 ♕xh6 and now:

b1) 11 ♕c1 ♕f4! 12 ♗d3 ♘d7 13 ♘ce2 ♕xc1 14 ♖axc1 ♘c5 15 ♗c2 a5 with level chances, Lida Garcia-E.Fabrega, Buenos Aires 1992.

b2) 11 ♗g4 ♗xg4 (11...f5 12 exf5 gxf5 13 ♗h3 planning 14 f4) 12 ♕xg4 ♘f6 13 ♕e2 a5 14 a3 ♘a6 15 ♖ab1 c5 (Raičević-Vukić, Cetinje 1990) 16 dxc6 bxc6 17 ♖fd1, and a later b4, gives White an advantage.

10 ♗e3 ♗h6 *(D)*

Now:

a) 11 ♕d2 and then:

a1) 11...♗xe3 12 ♕xe3 ♕f4 13 ♗d3 ♘d7 14 ♗c2 ♘c5 15 ♕e1 ♗d7 16 ♘ge2 ♕g5 17 ♕c1 ♕h4 = Fokin-Stoliarov, Russia Cup (Ekaterinburg) 1997. Exchanging queens, either now or earlier, would mean a slight advantage for White. It is more important to support the counterplay with ...f5.

a2) We propose 11...♗f4 *(D)* as better. It reaches a typical position where chances are about even:

a21) 12 ♖fe1?! can be met by 12...♗xe3!? and a later ...f5 ∓.

a22) 12 ♗xf4 exf4 13 ♘h1 f5 14 ♖fe1 is unclear.

a23) 12 ♖ae1 ♘a6 13 ♗d1 ♘c5 and now White can choose from various

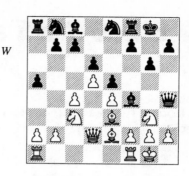

W

ideas: 14 b3 with a later a3 and b4; or 14 ♘ce2, eliminating the f4-bishop; or sacrificing a pawn by 14 f3!?. Black hardly can take the pawn: 14...♗xg3 15 hxg3 ♕xg3 16 ♘e2 ♕h4 17 ♗g5 ♕h5 18 ♘g3 wins the queen.

b) 11 ♗xh6 is best, and should be compared with other lines.

4 6...e5 7 d5 a5

1 d4 ♘f6 2 c4 g6 3 ♘c3 ♗g7 4 e4 d6 5
♘ge2 0-0 6 ♘g3 e5 7 d5 a5 *(D)*

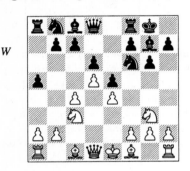

Now starts the shadow wrestling, as
the sides still avoid direct action. Their
plans are flexible for the moment.
White has two methods by which he
can seek an advantage in the opening:

1) 8 ♗e2 – the Classical Variation.

2) 8 h4, which we call the 'Future
Variation'. See page 56.

Classical Variation: 8 ♗e2

1 d4 ♘f6 2 c4 g6 3 ♘c3 ♗g7 4 e4 d6 5
♘ge2 0-0 6 ♘g3 e5 7 d5 a5 8 ♗e2

At this point Black has three major
moves:

A:	**8...♘a6**	38
B:	**8...♘e8**	52
C:	**8...c6**	53

A)

8...♘a6 *(D)*

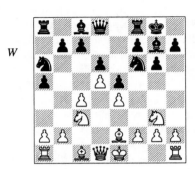

The natural method of development. Now:

A1:	**9 h4**	39
A2:	**9 ♗g5**	52

Or:

a) 9 ♗e3 is a natural way of developing, but it fails to exploit the main
strength of ♘g3, the support of the h-
pawn's advance. 9...♘c5 (9...h5 should
be compared with Line A13, while for
9...c6 see the note to White's 9th move
in Line C) 10 ♕d2 ♘g4 11 ♗xg4
♗xg4 12 f3 ♗d7 13 0-0-0 ♕b8!? 14
h4 h5, V.Johansson-Skripchenko, Mat-
inhos girls Wch 1994. Now 15 ♔b1 is
necessary, planning ♖dg1, ♘ge2 and
g4. Then 15...b5 could be countered
by 16 cxb5 ♗xb5 17 ♗xc5 dxc5 18
♕e3, when the pawns on the c-file
are weak.

b) 9 0-0 is a colourless continuation, after which Black can easily
equalize: 9...♘c5 10 b3 ♗d7 11 ♖b1

(preparing a3 and b4, but that is not a serious threat now; in addition, White cannot even carry it out) 11...h5 12 ♗g5 ♕e8 13 ♕d2 ♘h7 14 ♗h6?! h4 15 ♗xg7 ♔xg7 16 ♘h1 ♕e7 17 ♖be1 ♕g5! 18 ♕xg5 ♘xg5 19 f3 f5 and Black is better, G.Georgadze-Akopian, Tbilisi 1989.

A1)
9 h4
Now:

9...h6 can be strongly answered by 10 h5! and after 10...g5 the f5-square becomes weaker. Compare with Line A113.

A11)
9...♘c5 10 h5 *(D)*
10 ♗g5 is also playable:

a) 10...c6 transposes to Line C2.

b) We suggest 10...h6 11 ♗e3 h5!. Then 12 ♗g5 ♕e8 13 ♕d2 ♘h7 14 ♗h6 ♕e7 leads to balanced chances, since Black has a tempo more than in similar positions.

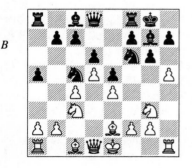

10...c6
Or:

a) 10...♗d7?! and now:

a1) The immediate 11 ♗g5 is a good reply. In the following example White castles on the queenside. 11...a4 12 ♕d2 ♖e8 13 0-0-0 ♕e7 14 ♖df1 (14 h6 ♗h8 15 ♖hf1!) 14...a3 15 b3 c6! 16 h6 ♗h8 17 ♖h4 ♖ec8 18 ♔b1! ♖ab8 19 f3 (the planned 19 f4 is answered by 19...b5 20 fxe5 ♕xe5!) 19...♗e8 20 ♖d1 (after some manoeuvring an instructive final position follows) 20...♖d8 21 ♖hh1 ♕c7 22 ♔a1! (preparing 23 b4 and setting a trap as well; in an inferior position Black falls into it) 22...♕a5? 23 dxc6! 1-0 Forintos-Gaber, Zalakaros 1999. Material loss is inevitable: 23...bxc6 24 ♗xf6 ♗xf6 25 ♘d5!.

a2) 11 h6 is another good move. 11...♗h8 12 ♗g5 ♕c8 13 0-0 ♗g4?! (13...a4 14 ♖b1) 14 f3 ♗d7 15 ♕d2 a4 16 f4! Z.Szabo-Igaz, Budapest 1996.

b) 10...♖e8 makes room for the bishop on f8. Why it is not a good idea for White to advance the h-pawn will be clear in a few moves: 11 h6?! ♗f8! 12 ♗g5 ♗e7 threatened ...♘xd5 in Jakab-Pataki, Paks jr 1995. Better is 11 ♗g5 instead.

c) 10...♘e8 11 hxg6 fxg6 12 ♗e3 ♘f6 13 ♕d2 (the flexible 13 ♗g5 is stronger, and only later ♕d2 and 0-0-0) 13...♘g4 14 ♗xg4 ♗xg4 15 f3 ♗d7 16 0-0-0 a4 17 ♗h6 ♕e7 18 ♖h2 ♗xh6 19 ♖xh6 ♖ab8 20 ♘b5!? ♗xb5 21 cxb5 and now, rather than the slow 21...♖a8 (Eichorn-Kell, Binz 1995), 21...c6! offers Black some counterchances.

After the text-move (10...c6) White can choose between:

A111: 11 ♗e3   40
A112: 11 hxg6   42
A113: 11 ♗g5!   42

Or 11 h6 ♗h8 12 ♗g5, and now:

a) 12...♕c7 13 0-0 ♘e8 14 ♕d2 ♗f6 15 f4 exf4 16 ♗xf4 ♘d7 and now, rather than 17 ♔h1 (Z.Szabo-Starostits, Budapest 1997), a rook move would have secured an advantage for White, e.g. 17 ♖ad1 ♘e5 18 c5! dxc5 19 d6 with activity for White.

b) 12...♗d7 13 0-0 cxd5 14 cxd5 ♕b6 15 ♕d2 and now:

b1) 15...a4 16 ♔h2 (planning f4) 16...♘g4+ (Jakab-Flumbort, Paks jr 1996) 17 ♗xg4 ♗xg4 and here we suggest a new motif: 18 ♗e7! ♖fe8 19 ♕g5! with the main threat of ♗f6. White is clearly better.

b2) 15...♖ac8 16 ♔h2 ♘g4+ was played in the game Jakab-Grabics, Hungary 1999, and now White could use the same motif as in line 'b1': 17 ♗xg4 ♗xg4 18 ♗e7 ♖fe8 19 ♕g5! with an advantage.

c) We suggest playing 12...♕b6, when ...♕xb2 is a serious threat. 13 ♖b1 (13 dxc6 bxc6; 13 ♕d2 is met by 13...♘g4! planning ...f6) 13...cxd5 14 cxd5 ♗d7 and Black has nearly equalized.

A111)
11 ♗e3 cxd5

Or 11...♕b6 12 ♕d2 a4 13 ♖b1 cxd5 14 cxd5 ♕b4 15 f3 ♗d7 and now instead of 16 hxg6 (Chilingirova-Grabics, Timisoara wom Z 1993), 16 h6 is

necessary, to force the bishop into the corner.

12 cxd5 *(D)*

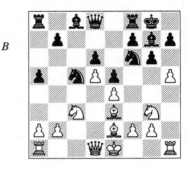

B

12...♕b6

We may call this Nunn's variation. It is regarded as better than 12...♗d7, by those who contributed to the development of the line. After 12...♗d7 White has two main options (13 ♕c2 is not logical, while 13 hxg6 fxg6! and 13 ♖b1 are worthless):

a) 13 ♕d2 and now:

a1) 13...♖c8 gives White time to play ♗h6, but is it a problem for Black now?

a11) 14 ♗h6 ♕b6 15 ♗xg7 ♔xg7 16 h6+? (giving up the h-file for the sake of playing f4, but there is an instructive tactical refutation) 16...♔h8 17 f4 and now instead of 17...♗g4 (Szekeres-A.Forgacs, Hungarian Cht 1997), 17...exf4! is best.

a12) We suggest 14 h6 ♗h8 15 ♗g5. After 15...♕b6 16 0-0 Black's pieces (the f8-rook, f6-knight and the h8-bishop) obstruct each other.

a2) 13...♕b6 was played in Duijn-De Vries, Dutch Cht 1994, and now 14 h6 ♗h8 15 ♖b1 is best since 15...♘g4 can be met by 16 &xg4 and ♘a4 with a slight advantage for White.

b) 13 a4 and here:

b1) 13...♕b6 14 ♖a3 and now:

b11) Not 14...♕xb2? 15 &xc5 dxc5 16 ♖b3.

b12) 14...♖ac8 transposes to Line A122.

b13) 14...♕b4 15 f3 ♘e8 (the beginning of a dubious plan; it is better to put one of the rooks on c8) 16 hxg6 hxg6 17 ♘f1 f5 18 ♘d2 ♘f6 19 exf5 gxf5 20 ♘c4 e4 21 0-0 threatens ♘a2. In Novikov-O.Popovych, New York 1993 Black did not find anything other than the pawn sacrifice 21...♘d3, but it proved insufficient.

b2) 13...♘e8 14 ♖a3 ♘c7 15 ♕d2 ♘7a6? (15...♕e7 is necessary) 16 ♘b5 ♕e7 17 hxg6 hxg6 (17...fxg6 18 ♕xa5) 18 &h6 f6 19 &xg7 ♕xg7 20 ♘xd6 ♘xa4 21 ♘gf5 gxf5 22 exf5 and the a3-rook came into play, and White won in Hort-R.Schöne, German Ch 1991.

13 b3

Others:

a) After 13 ♕d2, 13...&d7 transposes to note 'a2' to Black's 12th move, while 13...a4 14 ♖b1 should be compared with line 'b'.

b) 13 ♖b1 (a well-balanced move, but it does not give Black problems equalizing) 13...&d7 14 ♘f1!? (an important experiment: the knight is aiming for the c4-square) 14...a4 15 ♘d2 ♕a5!? (a provocative move; the threat is ...♘fxe4) 16 hxg6 (according to Gelfand 16 ♔f1 and 16 a3 lead to balanced chances; the tempting 16 ♘c4 would be met by 16...♕c7, when

both ...b5 and ...♘fxe4 are threatened) 16...hxg6 17 f3 (this closes the bishop's diagonal; Gelfand considers 17 ♔f1 superior) 17...b5 18 a3 ♘h5 and Black is better, Lutz-Gelfand, Horgen 1994.

c) 13 0-0 is interesting, not because it sacrifices the b2-pawn, but because it makes it possible for White to save a tempo.

c1) 13...♕xb2? 14 &xc5 dxc5 15 ♘a4! with an advantage.

c2) 13...&d7 and here White has a choice of transpositions (14 ♖b1, 14 b3 or 14 ♕d2), but there is also an independent line: 14 h6!? &h8 15 ♕d2 a4 (15...♕b4 is met by 16 f4 exf4 17 ♖xf4) 16 ♖ac1 ♖fe8 (16...♖fc8? 17 f4 exf4 18 ♖xf4 ♘e8 19 ♖cf1 ± and 19...&e5? can be met by 20 ♖xf7!) 17 &xc5!? dxc5 18 ♘b1 planning ♘a3 gives White better chances.

13...&d7

13...♕b4?! 14 &d2 ♕d4? 15 ♘b5 ♘d3+ 16 &xd3 ♕xd3 17 ♘xd6 and White is better – Nunn.

14 0-0

We think this is a moment when 14 h6 might come in handy, because the only possible answer is 14...&h8.

14...♕b4

Quieter is 14...♖fc8, but the brave advance with the queen cannot be refuted.

15 ♕d2 ♖fc8 16 a3

This chases the queen back, as taking on b3 is forbidden.

16...♕b6 17 ♖ab1 ♕d8 18 h6!? &f8!

Nunn prepares counterplay, either with ...&e7-g5, or by means of a later ...♕h4.

19 ♖fc1 ♘g4 20 ♗xg4 ♗xg4 21 b4 axb4 22 axb4 ♘a4 23 ♘xa4 ♖xa4

Chances are even, Korchnoi-Nunn, Wijk aan Zee 1992.

A112)

11 hxg6 fxg6 12 ♗g5

This pin is stronger than exchanging the passive g7-bishop: 12 ♗h6 ♗xh6 13 ♖xh6 cxd5 14 exd5 ♛b6 gave balanced chances in Evans-Horowitz, Havana 1952.

12...a4

A better move is 12...♛b6, which also threatens ...♘g4.

13 ♛d2 ♛a5 14 0-0 cxd5 15 exd5!

Avrukh-Drenchev, Mamaia U-14 Wch 1991. The e4-square is secured for White, because Black no longer has an f-pawn. White has the upper hand.

A113)

11 ♗g5! *(D)*

This is Szabo's variation.

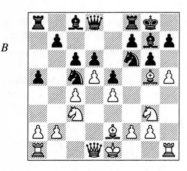

The pin is unpleasant; Black is generally provoked into chasing the bishop.

11...h6

Other possibilities:

a) 11...♛d7 12 ♛d2 cxd5 13 cxd5 a4 14 ♗h6 ♗xh6 15 ♛xh6 ♛e7 16 f3 (planning the following knight manoeuvre) 16...♗d7 17 ♘d1 ♔h8 (the pawn sacrifice is a tricky idea, which ends up rebounding on Black) 18 hxg6 fxg6 19 ♘e3! b5? (the pawn can be taken now) 20 ♛xg6 ♖g8 and now the *zwischenzug* 21 ♘gf5! left White a clear pawn up in Pähtz-B.Haider, Finkenstein 1993.

b) 11...cxd5 and now 12 hxg6! is our novelty. It is an important and typical *zwischenzug*, with the following ideas:

b1) 12...hxg6 can be met by 13 cxd5! with later ♛d2 and ♗h6.

b2) 12...fxg6 13 exd5! and the e4-square will be important for White.

b3) 12...d4 13 gxh7+ ♔h8 14 ♘d5 ♗e6 15 f3 ♗xd5 (15...♘xd5 16 ♗xd8 ♘e3 17 ♗g5! ±) 16 cxd5 ♛b6 17 ♘f5! gives White good tactical chances, e.g. 17...♛xb2 18 ♘xg7 ♔xg7 19 ♖b1 ♛c3+ 20 ♗d2 ♛a3 21 ♗h6+ ♔h8 22 ♛d2 d3 23 ♗g7+!.

12 ♗e3 cxd5 13 cxd5 g5

There is nothing better, as after 13...gxh5 14 ♗xh5! the h6-pawn is weak.

14 0-0 ♗d7 15 ♗xc5! dxc5 16 a4! ♘e8 17 ♗g4! *(D)*

A key moment. The f5-square becomes even weaker after the exchange of light-squared bishops. Szabo established two weaknesses (f5 and b5) with three excellent moves. The consequences of this can be seen.

17...♘d6 18 ♗xd7 ♛xd7 19 ♛e2 c4

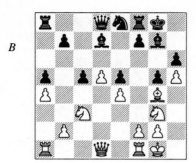

B

19...f5 is a good example of the spreading of weaknesses. After 20 exf5 ♘xf5 21 ♘xf5 ♖xf5 22 ♖ad1, White has obtained the e4-square, instead of f5, and this is ideal for the knight.

20 ♖fc1 ♖fc8 21 ♘d1!

The knights are strong in a closed position.

21...♖c5 22 ♘e3 ♖ac8 23 ♘ef5 ♘xf5 24 ♘xf5 ♗f8

24...c3 25 bxc3 ♖xc3 26 ♖xc3 ♖xc3 27 d6! is also unpromising for Black.

25 ♖c3

The good knight wins over the bad bishop.

25...♔h7 26 ♘e3 b5 27 axb5 ♕xb5 28 ♖ac1 a4 29 ♖xc4 ♖xc4 30 ♖xc4

1-0 Szabo-Klundt, Bamberg 1968.

Laszlo Szabo unfortunately died while this book was written at the age of 80, so we were not able to ask him personal questions about the 6 ♘g3 system, which he often favoured and employed with great success. This game was left to us among the material being prepared for his biography to come out later. Although modern grandmasters favour 11 ♗e3, we find

11 ♗g5, as chosen by Szabo, to be more promising.

A12)
9...c6 *(D)*

W

Rather than blocking the advance of the white h-pawn, Black intends to counter in the centre.

10 h5 cxd5

Not 10...gxh5? 11 ♗g5 ±. 10...♘c7 prepares ...b5 but it is slow. Forintos-Venegas Campo, Mexico 1999 continued 11 ♗g5 ♖b8 12 ♕d2 cxd5 and now the *zwischenzug* 13 hxg6! was an important novelty. The natural reply 13...fxg6 was met by 14 exd5!, when White controlled the central e4-square, while the counterattack ...b5 was delayed.

11 cxd5 ♘c5

The basic position of the 9...c6 defence. White now can choose:

A121: 12 ♗g5 44
A122: 12 a4 46

Or:

a) For 12 ♗e3 see Line A111.

b) 12 hxg6 transposes to Line A112.

c) 12 h6 ♗h8 13 ♗g5 ♕b6 (Black frees himself easily from the ♗g5 pin, and the queen goes on to the attack immediately) 14 ♖b1 (14 ♕d2) 14...♗d7 15 0-0 a4 (better is 15...♖fc8) and now:

c1) 16 ♕d2 ♖fc8 17 ♔h1 (since the f7-pawn became weak 18 f4 is the threat now) 17...♗e8 18 f4! (White continues his plan regardless) 18...exf4 (there was no other choice) 19 ♕xf4 ♘fd7 (now comes the surprise) 20 ♘f5!! ♗e5 (20...gxf5 21 ♗e7!) 21 ♘e7+ ♔f8 22 ♕h4 (Black is lost; the rest is instructive) 22...♗h8 23 ♘xg6+! hxg6 24 h7 (threatening mate) 24...f6 25 ♗xf6 ♘xf6 26 ♕xf6+! 1-0 Jakab-Berkes, Paks 1998.

c2) 16 ♔h1 and then:

c21) 16...a3 (Kaposztas-Gladyszew, Gyongyos 1995) can be answered by 17 bxa3 ♕a5 18 ♕d2 ♖fc8 19 ♖fc1 ♕xa3 20 ♖b6 with slightly better chances to White.

c22) 16...♕b4 17 ♕c2 ♖fc8 (nothing is threatened) 18 f4! (a typical solution when the f7-pawn is weak) 18...♘e8 (if 18...exf4, then 19 ♖xf4 ♘e8 20 ♖bf1 f6 21 e5! wins) 19 f5 f6 20 ♗d2 a3 21 b3 and in Kaposztas-Kerek, Eger 1995 Black missed the help of the h8-bishop.

A121)

12 ♗g5 *(D)*

Black now has three options:

A1211)

12...♕b6

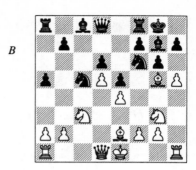

The same queen move as in note 'c' to White's 12th move in Line A12. The main difference is that the h-file can still be opened and ♕d2 followed by ♗h6 is also possible.

13 ♕d2

13 ♖b1 is also good, planning b3 and a3.

13...♗d7 14 ♖b1 a4 15 ♗h6

That is what White aimed for, but in this position the exchange of the bishops does not increase White's chances, since Black's bishop is out of play for the moment. Here White should transpose by 15 h6 ♗h8 16 0-0 into note 'c1' to White's 12th move in Line A12. 15 0-0 is another good alternative.

15...♕b4 16 ♖h4

This kind of move can only be good if the attack succeeds. In case of 16 ♗xg7 ♔xg7 17 0-0 ♕d4 18 h6+ ♔h8 19 ♕g5 ♘g8 20 ♖fd1 f6 the difficult part of the opening is over for Black.

16...♗xh6 17 ♕xh6 a3 18 ♕d2 axb2 19 ♖xb2 ♕d4

Black can be satisfied since the rook on h4 is out of play, Belozerov-Zakharevich, St Petersburg Chigorin mem 1997.

A1212)
12...a4 *(D)*

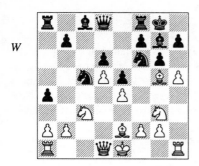

Black is going for a plan other than ...♕b6. He puts his queen on a5 and reserves the possibility of a quick ...b5.

13 ♕d2 ♕a5 14 0-0

Black's attacking chances will be less here than when White plays f3 and ♔f2. An example of that: 14 f3 ♗d7 15 ♔f2 (an interesting idea; it threatens to attack along the h-file) 15...b5 (15...a3 also comes into consideration) 16 b4 axb3! (a surprise) 17 axb3 ♕b6 18 ♗e3 b4 19 ♘a4 ♗xa4 20 bxa4 ♗h6! (Black shows a problem of the set-up with ♔f2; now ...♘b3 is the threat) 21 ♖hb1 (21 hxg6? ♗xe3+ 22 ♕xe3 fxg6!) and now instead of 21...♗f4 (Novikov-J.Polgar, Pamplona 1990/1), the simple 21...♘xa4 gives Black a decisive advantage.

14...a3

Or:

a) For 14...♗d7 see Line A1213.

b) 14...♕b4 (Kaposztas-Salai, Slovakian Cht 1998) can lead to incalculable complications.

15 h6!

White gains time until the bishop gets out from h8. That time can be used to strengthen the attack on the queenside.

15...♗h8 16 bxa3 ♗d7 17 ♖ab1 ♖fc8 18 ♖b4 ♕xa3 19 ♖fb1

An instructive position. White has made progress on the b-file, and the question is whether Black can counter this with his two open lines. Curiously enough, he cannot; the reason for this lies in the h6-pawn, which restricts the black king. There may be problems on the back rank in the case of mutual breakthroughs. This turns the game in White's favour.

19...♘e8 20 ♗e3 ♗f6 21 ♗xc5 ♖xc5 22 ♖1b3 ♕a5 23 ♖xb7 ♕d8 24 ♘f1!

24...♗g5 is prevented since it can be met by 25 ♖xd7!.

24...♘c7 25 ♕b2 ♖c8 26 ♖b8

White's strategy has been carried out: he has managed to penetrate to the 8th rank. Black could win the h6-pawn, but that would only mean restoring the material balance. The action is happening on the queenside. After 26...♘e8 27 ♖xc8 ♖xc8 28 ♗a6 ♖c7 29 ♖b8 ♕e7 30 ♗b7 White advanced the a-pawn in Forintos-Cvitan, Amantea 1992.

A1213)
12...♗d7 *(D)*
13 ♕d2 ♖b8

With 13...a4 Black plans ...♕a5. Now the white king should flee:

a) 14 0-0-0 ♕a5 15 ♔b1 b5 16 ♗d3 ♖fc8 17 hxg6 hxg6 18 ♗h6 ♘b3! 19 ♕g5 ♘h7 (Matulović-Bednarski,

W

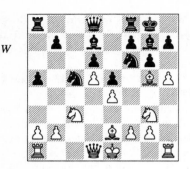

Palma de Mallorca 1967) and now 20 ♕e7! is very unclear – many lines end in a draw by perpetual check!

b) 14 0-0 ♕a5? (better is 14...b5; if White accepts the sacrificed pawn Black has the bishop-pair and activity as compensation) 15 f4! ± Billen-kamp-Wokura, corr. 1989.

14 f3

14 0-0 b5 15 h6 ♗h8 (threatening ...b4 and ...♘cxe4) 16 f3 ♕c7 (after 16...♕b6 17 ♔h1 a knight can arrive on c4 with tempo) 17 ♖ac1 b4 18 ♘d1 (Black had planned to exchange the dark-squared bishops, but now 18...♘e8 does not work, so he prepared it with his next move) 18...♗c8 (this move leads to some quite instructive play, but 18...♖fc8 is more natural) 19 ♘e3 ♘e8 20 ♘c4 ♗f6 (del Rey-Llanos, Montevideo 1992) and now White has the tactical possibility 21 ♗xf6 ♘xf6 22 ♕e3!, with a decisive advantage, in view of his three threats.

14...b5 15 ♘d1 b4 16 ♗h6 a4 17 ♗xg7 ♔xg7 18 ♘e3 ♕e7 19 0-0-0 ♖fc8 20 ♔b1

After securing the king's position, White now has to open the h-file and double rooks.

20...♔g8 21 hxg6 fxg6 22 ♖h6 ♕g7 23 ♖dh1 ♖d8 24 ♘c4 ♗b5 25 ♘a5 ♗xe2

25...♗e8 is met by 26 ♗c4.

26 ♕xe2

With the exchange of bishops White has secured the c6-square. Now he returned to the queenside with his pieces and won in Novikov-Sidelnikov, New York 1991. An excellent performance.

A122)

12 a4 *(D)*

Novikov's idea.

B

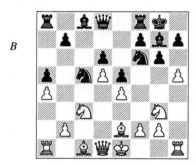

Igor Novikov has enriched the theory of the ♘ge2 King's Indian with several valuable ideas, including experimenting with this radical move. He must have been fed up with Black playing ...a4 (either before or after ...♗d7) in answer to 12 ♗g5, as this gives Black counterplay. The text-move prevents that, and at the same time controls the b5- and c4-squares. Still, it cannot be perfect, as Black's position is harmonious.

12...♗d7 13 ♖a3 ♖c8

13...♕b6 14 ♗e3 ♕b4 (14...♕xb2?? is a typical blunder; it is worth knowing the follow-up: 15 ♗xc5 dxc5 16 ♖b3 and the queen is captured) 15 f3 ♘xh5 (an unusual move, but later ...f5 is feasible and Black nearly gets an equal position) 16 ♘xh5 gxh5 17 ♖xh5 f5 18 ♕c2. Now in case of 18...fxe4?! Black has to count on 19 ♗xc5! dxc5 20 ♕xe4, when White is active.

14 ♗e3 ♕b6 15 hxg6 fxg6 16 f3

Novikov thinks White is slightly better in this complicated position. Now:

a) 16...♕b4 is tempting, but not really good, because if the king leaves e1, then the black queen can be surrounded by ♗b5. 17 0-0 ♕b6 (preventing f4) 18 ♖f2 ♖f7 19 ♗b5 h5 20 ♘f1 ♗f8 21 ♗xd7 ♘fxd7 22 ♘b5 ♗e7 23 ♘d2 and White is slightly better, just because of the difference of two bishops – almost all White's pawns are on light squares, Novikov-Gi.Hernandez, Pamplona 1991/2.

b) Our suggestion is 16...♖f7, preparing for several continuations. It is worth observing that the white queen stays longer on d1. The reason is, that later on, after the possible sequence ♗b5 ♗xb5, ♘xb5, Black would not be threatening ...♘xa4.

c) 16...♕xb2!? (at least somebody risks the queen sacrifice) 17 ♗xc5 ♖xc5 18 ♖b3 ♕xc3+ 19 ♖xc3 ♖xc3. Now, instead of 20 ♕a1 ♖fc8 21 ♔f2 h5 22 ♖b1 ♗h6 23 ♘f1 (½-½ Novikov-Cvitan, Forli 1993), White has a better plan. Our improvement is 20 ♕b1 – tactics help again to improve the position. The a4-pawn is taboo because of 21 ♕a1, while 20...♖c7 can be met by 21 ♕b6. Nevertheless although

White has the slightly better chances, the position is complicated.

A13)
9...h5 *(D)*

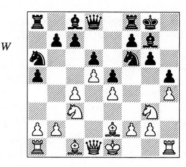

This move stops White's h-pawn but Black must consider the unpleasant pin ♗g5 in reply.

10 ♗g5
Now:
A131: 10...c6   47
A132: 10...♕d7   48
A133: 10...♕e8   49

10...♗d7? is too casual. Since the bishop occupies the retreat-square of the a6-knight from c5 to d7, a piece sacrifice on h5 is strong: 11 ♗xh5! gxh5 12 ♘xh5 and now Black cannot free himself of the pin because of the ♕f3 threat.

A131)
10...c6 11 ♗xh5!?

White is quick with the piece sacrifice here too.

11...♕b6?!

Here White can choose between two ways:

a) 12 ♘a4!? (those who like complications should choose this continuation in the hope of gaining a material or positional advantage) 12...♕b4+ 13 ♗d2 ♕xc4 14 ♘b6 and now:

a1) 14...♕b5 15 ♘xa8 gxh5 (after 15...♘xh5, White plays 16 ♘xh5 gxh5 17 ♕b3!, etc.) 16 ♕b3! with an advantage for White.

a2) 14...♕d4 15 ♗xa5! ♕c5 (or if 15...♕xd1+ then 16 ♗xd1) 16 ♕d2 gives White a clear advantage.

b) 12 ♗e2 leads to a positional advantage and involves less calculation. 12...♕xb2 13 ♘a4 ♕d4 (Iglesias-Vidal, Mar del Plata 1992) and now White should play 14 ♕b1 threatening ♗e3 and ♘b6.

All in all, the disadvantage of 10...c6 is that Black has to reckon on the sacrifice on h5.

A132)

10...♕d7

This has similar ideas to 10...♕e8 (Line A133), but also has ideas of ...♕g4 in case of White sacrificing on h5. However, it makes natural development more difficult.

11 ♕d2

11 ♗xf6 ♗xf6 12 ♗xh5 gxh5 13 ♘xh5 ♕e7 14 ♕f3 ♗g7 15 g4 f6 16 0-0-0 is also playable, but we should not attach much hope to it.

11...♔h7

A mistake, but not an obvious one. Black aims to play ...♘g8 and ...♗h6. Better is 11...♘h7, followed by ...♕e7 or first ...♗f6, an idea that proved successful in Line A133.

12 ♗xf6 ♗xf6 13 ♗xh5 gxh5

13...♕e7! 14 ♗f3 ♔g7 15 h5 ♗g5 16 ♕e2 is only slightly better, as it does not give enough compensation for the pawn.

14 ♘f5! *(D)*

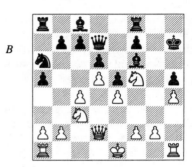

The thematic point, which can easily be overlooked as in other positions it was out of the question because of ...♗xf5. Here this attacking piece has to be put up with, and shows a great disadvantage of 10...♕d7. What is more, other surprises are also coming!

14...♗g7

14...♕d8 15 ♕h6+ ♔g8 16 ♖h3 ♗xf5 17 exf5 ♗xh4 loses to, e.g., 18 f6! ♕xf6 19 ♖g3+.

15 ♕g5!

Not 15 ♘xg7 ♕g4!.

15...f6 16 ♕xh5+ ♔g8 17 ♕g6 ♖f7

The otherwise usual 17...♕f7 is not possible here because of 18 ♘h6+; the also typical 17...♔h8 is refuted in a nice way: 18 h5! ♕f7 19 h6!! ♕xg6 20 hxg7++ ♔g8 21 ♖h8+ ♔f7 22 ♖xf8#.

18 h5! ♔h8

18...♔f8 19 h6 ♗h8 20 h7! ♖g7 21 ♕xf6+ ♕f7 22 ♕d8+ ♕e8 23 ♕xe8+ ♔xe8 24 ♘xg7+ ♗xg7 25 h8♕+.

19 h6 ♗f8 20 ♖h3

This thematic continuation wins, which is why White did not find the nice queen sacrifice: 20 ♕g7+! ♖xg7 21 hxg7++ ♔g8 22 ♖h8+ ♔f7 23 g8♕+ and mate.

20...♕e8 21 ♖g3
21 ♕g7+.
21...♗e7 22 ♕g7+!
This is still good.
22...♖xg7 23 hxg7+ ♔g8
23...♔h7 24 ♔d2 ♗xf5 25 g8♕+!.
24 ♘h6+ ♔h7 25 g8♕+ ♕xg8 26 ♘xg8 ♗d8

Black resigned at the same time in Forintos-Freisler, Budapest 1987.

A133)
10...♕e8 *(D)*

W

11 ♕d2
11 ♘f1 also can be considered, e.g. 11...♘h7 12 ♗e3 f5 13 exf5 ♗xf5 14 ♘g3! e4 (14...♗d7 15 ♘ge4) 15 ♘xf5 ♖xf5 16 g4! and the light squares in Black's position are too weak.

Black now has three main possibilities:

Or:
a) 11...♘d7 does not seem to be soundly based, as White can sacrifice a piece immediately.

a1) 12 0-0-0 is a good, solid continuation. After 12...♘dc5 the right plan is 13 ♘b5 (instead of 13 ♗h6, Liardet-Smolović, Leon U-26 Wch 1996) with a later ♖df1 and a slight advantage to White.

a2) 12 ♗xh5 and now:
a21) 12...gxh5 13 ♘xh5 and the f8-rook cannot be saved. The threat is 14 ♘xg7 followed by ♗h6. The remaining two pieces against the white rook and two pawns would give equality in theory, but because of the closed pawn-structure and the chance to open a file later we have seen White winning in similar positions.

a22) 12...f6! and then:
a221) 13 ♗h6 (after this Black can draw if he plays well) 13...♗xh6! 14 ♕xh6 gxh5 15 ♘f5 ♕f7 16 ♖h3 ♕h7!! 17 ♘e7+ ♔h8 18 ♘g6+ with perpetual check.

a222) 13 ♗g4!? leads to almost incalculable complications.

b) 11...♘c5 12 0-0-0 (12 ♘b5 is also a good move) 12...♘a4 (12...♗d7 or 12...♘g4 is better) 13 ♘b5 (this move is the way to refute Black's plan) 13...♕d8 14 ♖hf1 ♗d7 15 f4 and White has the better chances, Vandevoort-Lindam, Eupen 1993.

A1331)
11...♘h7 12 ♗e3 ♗d7 13 a4
This concedes the b4-square, but secures b5. In addition, the rook may help the attack on the king via a3.

13...♕e7

13...♘c5 14 ♖a3!? ♘xa4 15 ♘xa4 ♗xa4 16 ♗h6! is M.Gurevich's idea, intending a sacrifice on h5.

14 ♘b5 f5

Black is not willing to defend his pawns with ...b6. Instead he makes a positional pawn sacrifice, but on the other side of the board. 15 exf5 gxf5 16 ♗g5 ♘xg5 17 ♕xg5 ♕xg5 18 hxg5 e4 19 0-0-0 and now:

a) 19...♘c5 20 ♘xh5 ♘xa4 21 ♘xg7 ♔xg7 22 ♘xc7 ± followed by ♘e6+ (M.Gurevich).

b) 19...♗xb5 20 axb5 ♘c5 21 ♘xh5 a4 22 ♖h3 was slightly better for White in M.Gurevich-Nijboer, Holland 1992. Taking into account the opposite-coloured bishops, Black has almost enough compensation for the pawn.

A1332)

11...♔h7 *(D)*

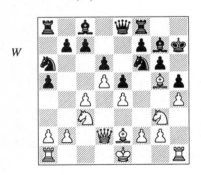

Black prepares ...♘g8, and prevents 12 ♗h6.

12 0-0-0

12 ♘b5 is Serper's plan, based on a combination.

a) The routine defence 12...b6 can be met by 13 a4 ♗d7 14 ♖a3 (after M.Gurevich), and the immediate threat is ♗xf6 followed by ♗xh5. White can also play for f4, after castling kingside, as the knight on b5 makes Black's defence more difficult.

b) 12...♗d7 13 ♕xa5 ♘xe4 14 ♘xe4 ♘c5 15 ♘xc7 (15 ♕xc7 is at least as strong) 15...♖xa5 16 ♘xe8 ♘xe4 17 ♘xg7 ♔xg7 18 ♗e3 and after the fireworks White is a pawn up and won later on in Serper-Panzer, Krumbach 1991.

12...♗d7

Or 12...♘g8, and now:

a) 13 ♔b1 ♘h6 (13...♗h6 is also good) 14 ♖de1 ♘c5 (14...f6 15 ♗e3 ♘g4!) 15 ♗e3 b6 16 f3 ♗d7 17 ♗d1 a4 18 ♘f1 b5? (18...f5 gives Black the best chance of counterplay) 19 cxb5 ♗xb5 20 ♘xb5 ♕xb5 21 ♗e2 ♕b6 22 ♕c2 ♖fb8 23 ♘d2 and the plan ♘c4 and g4 gives White the advantage, Kaposztas-Berecz, Hungary 1999.

b) 13 ♖dg1 is the first move of a long plan. White can surely achieve some advantage, but in Gokhale-Sziva, Manila wom OL 1992 Black defended badly and quickly found herself in trouble: 13...a4 (13...♗h6 is more urgent, either with or without ...f6) 14 ♕d1 (an unexpected regrouping to strengthen the sacrifice on h5) 14...f6 15 ♘xh5! gxh5 (15...fxg5 16 hxg5!) 16 ♗xh5 ♕e7 17 ♗e3 ♗d7 18 g4 a3 19 b3 ♖ac8 20 g5 f5 21 ♗f7! and White won.

13 ♔b1 ♘c5 14 ♖dg1 c6

Black starts his queenside activity by sacrificing a pawn.

15 dxc6 bxc6

15...&xc6 16 &xf6 &xf6 17 ♕xd6 ♘e6 18 ♘d5!.

16 ♕xd6 ♘e6 17 ♖d1!

The situation on the board has changed, and instead of continuing the kingside attack, White concentrates his forces in the centre, the rook goes back and the d7-bishop finds itself in danger. After 17...♖a7, White sacrificed the pawn back by 18 f4!? in Forintos-V.Gurevich, Koszalin 1999, but after 18...exf4 19 e5 ♘g8! 20 ♘g4 the chances were equal in this complicated position. White should have played 18 &e3 ♖b7 19 ♘a4 instead, with a clear advantage.

Thus we conclude that 11...♔h7 is hardly playable.

A1333)

11...&d7 *(D)*

Black waits for a move, partly to prevent ♘b5. White can choose first &h6 and only then castle queenside, or else castle immediately.

12 &h6

Castling kingside cannot be recommended as 12 0-0?! can be met by

12...♘h7, when there are problems with the h4-pawn, while the sacrifice does not work: 13 &xh5? f6!, Blakemore-Senff, Bratislava jr Wch 1993.

12 0-0-0 ♘c5 13 ♖dg1 (13 ♖df1 is also good) 13...a4 14 f3 (the preparatory moves 14 ♔b1 and &d1 are better; then White will only later start activity on the kingside) 14...♘h7 15 &h6 a3 16 b3 ♕e7 (16...f5 17 exf5 gxf5 18 &xg7 ♔xg7 19 f4!) 17 &xg7 and a draw was agreed in Novikov-Tsariov, Tuzla 1989. After 17...♔xg7 White could have fought for the advantage by 18 ♔b1, &d1 and later ♘f1.

12...♕d8

12...&xh6 13 ♕xh6 ♕d8 14 0-0-0 ♘c5 15 ♖df1 followed by f4 will be most awkward. That is why luring the queen to h6 is not desirable.

13 0-0-0 ♘c5 14 ♔b1 a4 15 ♖de1 c6 16 &g5 cxd5 17 cxd5 ♕a5

Both sides are attacking, but on different sides.

18 &xf6 &xf6 19 &xh5! ♘b3

19...b5 is the alternative. 19...gxh5 could be met by 20 ♘xh5 &h8 21 ♕h6 and ♖e3!.

20 ♕e3 ♘d4 21 a3 ♖a6 22 &d1 ♖b6

A sharp position has been reached, where White must be careful. 23 ♔a2 ♖c8 24 h5?? loses to 24...&g5!, while 23 ♘f1 ♖c8 24 ♘a2 ♖b5 25 ♕d2 (M.Gurevich-Geurink, Gent 1995) is more than adequately answered by 25...♖xd5!. 23 ♘ge2 ♖c8 24 ♔a2 &b5 gives Black counterplay, but 23 ♘a2 might be White's best continuation, for example 23...♖c8 24 h5 ♖c4 25 hxg6.

A2)

9 ♗g5 *(D)*

B

9...h6!

For 9...c6 see Line C2.

10 ♗e3 h5

Other possibilities:

a) 10...♘xe4 is an interesting motif. It is possible when a pawn is on h6. However, nobody has yet played it, probably since 11 ♘gxe4 f5 12 ♕d2 f4 13 ♗b6! gives White an advantage.

b) 10...♘c5 can be met by 11 0-0 and later ♕d2 with a small advantage for White.

c) 10...♗d7 and now:

c1) 11 h4 is met by 11...h5!.

c2) 11 0-0 c6 12 dxc6! ♗xc6 13 ♕d2 h5 14 ♗g5 (slightly better is 14 f3) 14...h4! 15 ♘h1 (15 ♗xh4 can be met by 15...♘xe4) 15...♘c5 16 f3 ♘e6 and Black equalized in Fokin-Nalbandian, Pardubice 1996.

c3) 11 ♕d2 h5 12 ♗g5 ♘c5 13 f3 ♕e8! 14 0-0 ♘h7 15 ♗e3 h4 16 ♘h1 ♕e7 and Black has good play with ...♗f6-g5 or ...f5.

d) 10...♘e8 (this opens the route towards h4 and prepares ...f5) 11 ♕d2 (11 h4 can be answered by 11...f5!)

11...♕h4!? 12 0-0-0 ♘c5 13 ♖df1 and then:

d1) 13...♗d7 14 ♗d1 (14 f4 exf4 15 ♖xf4 ♕e7 16 ♖f2 h5 leads to a complicated game) 14...♘f6 15 f3 ♔h7, Svela-Mork, Stavanger 1991. Now White could advance the g- and h-pawns, after the preparatory moves 16 ♗c2 and ♘ge2.

d2) In case of 13...♘xe4 14 ♘gxe4 f5 15 g3 ♕h3 16 f3! fxe4 17 ♘xe4 White has a clear advantage, planning ♘f2 or g4.

e) After 10...h5 White has to prefer long castling.

11 ♕d2

11 ♗g5 (although this move loses a tempo, it is also playable) 11...♕e8 12 ♕d2 ♘h7 13 ♗h6 h4 14 ♗xg7 ♔xg7 15 ♘f1 ♘c5 16 g3 ♕e7 17 ♕e3 ♗d7 18 ♘d2 with about equal chances, Rohde-J.Polgar, New York 1992.

11...♘g4 12 ♗xg4 ♗xg4 13 f3 ♗d7 14 0-0-0 ♕e7 15 ♔b1 ♖fb8 16 ♘ge2 f5 17 ♘b5 b6 18 ♘ec3 f4

With even chances, Novikov-Loginov, Tashkent 1986.

B)

8...♘e8 *(D)*

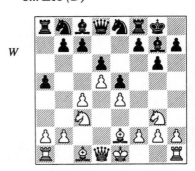

W

Black prepares ...f5 or ...♕h4. White must decide whether to allow ...♕h4.

9 h4

A logical continuation. The alternative is 9 0-0 ♘a6 10 ♗e3 f5?! (better is 10...♘c5) 11 exf5 gxf5 12 f4 ♕e7 (12...♕h4 can be met by 13 ♘h1, planning g3) 13 ♕d2 ♗d7 14 ♖ae1 e4 15 ♔h1 (making room for the rook) 15...♘f6 (15...♕h4 16 ♘h5) 16 h3 ♕e8 17 ♖g1 ♘c5 18 ♘f1 h5 19 g3 ♕g6 20 ♘h2 ♕h7 21 ♖g2 ♔f7 (Vasallo-Perez Candelario, Caseres 1995) 22 ♗xc5 dxc5 23 d6 with promising but sharp play.

9...h5

9...♘a6 is an inferior form of Line A2, while 9...♘d7 gives White extra options compared with lines in Chapter 3.

Or 9...f5 10 exf5 (the piece sacrifice 10 h5 f4 11 hxg6 is not correct) 10...gxf5 and now 11 f4? (Kramer-Evans, New York 1954) should be met by 11...♗f6! 12 h5 ♗h4 13 ♕d3 ♘a6 with the initiative. Instead, 11 ♘h5! and 11 ♗g5 should be compared with lines in Chapter 3.

10 ♗g5 ♗f6

Now:

a) 11 ♗h6 should be compared with the game Kovacs-Haïk in note 'b' to White's 9th move in Line A4 of Chapter 3.

b) 11 ♕d2 is also good. Then 11...♘a6 12 0-0-0 ♘c5 (12...♗g7 is more accurate) 13 ♗xh5! gxh5 14 ♘xh5 ♗xg5 15 hxg5 ♗d7 16 ♖h4 gives White a heavy attack.

c) 11 ♗xf6 ♕xf6 12 ♘f1 ♘g7 13 ♕d2 c6 14 ♘e3 ♖d8 15 0-0-0 ♘a6 16

g3 ♘c5 17 ♖df1 ♕e7 18 g4! gives White the advantage, Svela-Eriksson, Sweden 1990.

C)

8...c6

Sometimes this position is reached via the move-order 7...c6 8 ♗e2 a5. White now has two main developing moves:

C1: 9 h4!   53
C2: 9 ♗g5   55

After 9 ♗e3 ♘a6 White has the interesting idea 10 ♘a4!:

a) 10...c5 can be met by 11 ♘c3! with a lasting advantage, due to the weakness of b5. White can even castle queenside later on.

b) 10...♗d7 11 ♘b6 ♖b8 12 ♕d2 ♘c5 (Bern-Harestad, Norway 1991) and now White should play 13 ♗xc5! dxc5 14 ♕xa5, e.g. 14...cxd5 15 cxd5 ♕c7 16 ♖c1 ♖a8 (16...♖fc8 17 b4 +−) 17 ♖xc5! with an overwhelming advantage.

c) 10...cxd5 11 cxd5 ♘d7 is best.

C1)

9 h4! *(D)*

C11: 9...cxd5 54
C12: 9...h5 55

For 9...♘a6, see Line A12.
Or 9...♗d7?!, and now:

a) 10 ♗g5 h6 11 ♗e3 cxd5 12 cxd5 a4 13 h5 g5 14 a3 ♕a5 15 ♕d2 ♔h7 16 ♖c1 ♖c8 17 0-0 ♘a6 18 ♘b5! ♕xd2 19 ♗xd2 ♗f8 (Bönsch-Volke, Munich 1992) and now 20 ♗e3 is best, in order to exchange the knight on c5, with a white advantage on the light squares.

b) 10 h5 is the most promising continuation.

C11)
9...cxd5 10 cxd5 h5 11 ♗g5 ♘bd7
(D)

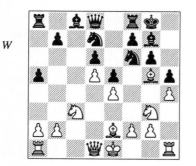

The position is very similar to Line A3 of Chapter 1, where the ♗xh5 sacrifice is very promising for White. However, the c-file is open here, and this is thought to make Black's defence easier. For example, after a later ...♘d3+, following ...♘xb2, the c3-knight can be attacked by the c8-rook. This assumption is difficult to prove. Ideas for White:

a) 12 ♔f1!? ♘c5 13 ♗xh5! (the time for the piece sacrifice, which is correct here, has come) 13...gxh5 14 ♘xh5 ♔h8. As we saw in Chapter 1, this is the best defence. It prepares the bishop move to g4. White can seek the advantage in three ways, depending on which is more to his liking. He has, however, more than sufficient compensation for the piece.

a1) 15 f3!? is an adventurous continuation, after which Black can choose an interesting idea, i.e. 15...♘xh5!? 16 ♗xd8 ♘g3+ 17 ♔g1 ♖xd8 18 ♖h2 ♗h6! 19 ♔f2 ♗f4 and, as Black had closed the kingside, he stands a good chance of fighting with his three pieces against the white queen, Pazos-Ovalles, Manzanillo 1991. The next two continuations are more promising for White.

a2) 15 ♕f3! (it is advisable for both sides to know the following typical combination) 15...♗g4 16 ♕xf6! (an important pattern) 16...♗xh5 17 ♕xd8 ♖fxd8 18 ♗xd8 ♖xd8 19 f3 leads to an endgame that is better for White.

a3) 15 ♘xg7! ♔xg7 and now both 16 ♕f3 and 16 h5 give White the better chances. See lines 'b' and 'c'.

Thus we may conclude that 12 ♔f1 is not an obstacle to playing the standard ♗xh5 sacrifice.

b) 12 ♖c1 is our suggestion:

b1) The standard move 12...♕b6? is hardly feasible now in view of 13 ♘a4! ♕b4+? 14 ♗d2 ♕d4 15 ♖c4 ♕a7 16 ♗e3, with advantage to White.

b2) 12...♘c5 13 ♗xh5 gxh5 14 ♘xh5 ♔h8! (14...♗g4?? 15 ♘xf6+) 15 ♘xg7! ♔xg7 16 ♕f3 ♖h8! 17 h5

♖h6! (the move h6+ must be prevented) 18 ♗xh6+ ♔xh6 19 ♕e3+! ♔h7 20 f3! (planning g4) 20...♕b6 21 ♖c2 ♕b4 22 ♕g5 and White wins.

c) 12 0-0 (another waiting move) 12...♘c5 (12...♕b6 is again met by 13 ♘a4!) 13 ♗xh5 (this is promising even now) 13...gxh5 14 ♘xh5 ♔h8 and then:

c1) 15 ♘xg7 ♔xg7 16 f4 ♕b6 17 ♗xf6+ ♔xf6 18 fxe5+ with a difficult endgame, which favours White.

c2) 15 ♕f3 also leads to a favourable endgame after 15...♗g4 16 ♕xf6! ♗xh5 17 ♕xd8 ♖axd8 18 ♗xd8 ♖xd8 19 f3.

C12)
9...h5 10 ♗g5 ♕b6 *(D)*

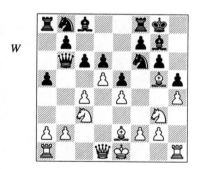

It is far better to get rid of the pin than suffer the consequences of ♗xh5. And this has to be done actively.

11 ♕d2 ♘bd7

11...♕d4? is risky. After 12 ♕c2 ♘g4 13 ♘d1 (Moutousis-Makropoulou, Komotini 1993) White is planning f3 and ♗e3, and this should be taken seriously.

12 ♗e3 ♕c7 13 0-0-0

13 ♖d1 is simple but good. True, after the text-move the rook gets there anyway, but the king can be a source of problems.

13...cxd5 14 ♘xd5

Better is 14 ♘b5 and exd5.

14...♘xd5 15 ♕xd5 ♖a6 16 ♔b1 ♖c6 17 ♕d2 ♘f6 18 ♗h6 ♗e6 19 ♗xg7 ♔xg7 20 ♘f5+

This motif is possible when only the king defends the f6-knight. However, there is a snag...

20...gxf5

After 20...♗xf5? 21 exf5 ♖d8 22 g4! White's attack arrives sooner.

21 ♕g5+ ♔h7 22 exf5 ♗xc4 23 ♗xc4 ♖xc4?

23...♖g8! is good for Black, as 24 ♕xf6 is met by 24...d5.

24 ♕xf6 ♕d8 25 ♕g5!

White won in Serper-Mestel, Hastings 1990/1.

C2)
9 ♗g5 *(D)*

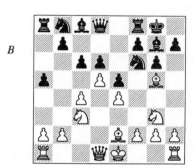

9...♘a6 10 h4

Or 10 ♕d2:

a) 10...♕c7?! 11 ♖d1! ♘e8 12 h4 ♘c5 13 h5 a4 14 ♗h6 ♕e7 with a slight advantage to White, Barczay-Ivkov, Sarajevo 1968.

b) 10...♘c5 11 ♖d1 (this is not necessary here; the immediate 11 0-0 is better – it can save one tempo for White as we can see later) 11...cxd5 12 cxd5 ♗d7 13 0-0 ♕b6 (R.Pavlović-Muktić, Pula 1992) and now retreating by 14 ♗e3 and ♖c1 is necessary, with balanced chances.

c) 10...cxd5 and after 11 ♘xd5, 11...♗e6! offers a correct pawn sacrifice.

10...♘c5

10...h5 transposes to Line A131.

11 ♕d2 cxd5 12 cxd5 *(D)*

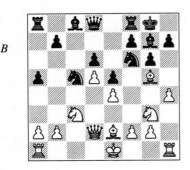

An important and typical position! White is ready to play h5, or after 12...h5 to sacrifice by 13 ♗xh5 – compare with Line C1.

12...a4

12...♗d7 and now instead of 13 f3 (Dive-Abdennabi, Thessaloniki OL 1988) we suggest 13 h5 with a minimal advantage.

13 f3 ♗d7 14 0-0 ♕b6 15 ♔h1 ♖fc8

When too many pieces go to the queenside White's kingside attack can

quicken as the f-file has been weakened.

16 f4! a3 17 ♖ab1 h6 18 fxe5 ♘e8

With this pawn sacrifice Black is planning to take the initiative after 19 ♗xh6 ♗xe5. However...

19 e6!

Black's king position is undermined by this move. 19...hxg5 (19...fxe6 20 ♗xh6 ♗f6 21 ♘h5 is also a win for White) 20 exf7+ ♔h7 21 h5! (a quick attack is worth more than a piece) 21...g4 22 ♕g5 and White won in Forintos-Mercier, Val Maubuée 1988.

Future Variation

1 d4 ♘f6 2 c4 g6 3 ♘c3 ♗g7 4 e4 d6 5 ♘ge2 0-0 6 ♘g3 e5 7 d5 a5 8 h4 *(D)*

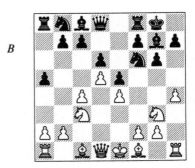

As usual, Black must make a choice: prevent h5, or put up with it. The latter is not recommended. Choosing 8 h4 against 7...a5 is also good because it simplifies the amount to be learned.

8...h5

Or:

a) 8...c6 9 h5 and now 9...♘a6? is line 'b', while 9...cxd5 is feeble because of 10 hxg6.

b) 8...♘a6?! (now that White has saved the move ♗e2, Black should not waste time on ...♘a6; if he does not want to defend with ...h5, then he should play ...c6 right away) 9 h5 (do not give up this move for all the tea in China, even for the sake of 9 ♗e2, although that is also good; this position is already good for White) 9...c6? (Black still follows the plan that proved good after ♗e2, but 9...♘e8 is better) 10 ♗g5! cxd5 11 h6! ♗h8 12 ♕f3! (this stratagem is impossible after 8 ♗e2) 12...♘b4! 13 ♘xd5 ♘bxd5 14 cxd5 a4 15 ♗e2 ♕a5+ 16 ♗d2 ♕b6 17 ♕a3! ♘e8 (the better 17...♘g4 can be met by 18 0-0!) 18 ♖c1 ♗f6 19 ♖c4 ♗d8 20 ♖b4 ♕a7 21 ♗e3 with an advantage for White, followed by a quick victory in Serper-Watzka, Eupen ECC 1994.

9 ♗g5 *(D)*

Black now has two ways to develop:

A: 9...c6 57
B: 9...♕e8 58

A)
9...c6

This is Smejkal's defence, and has a double aim: it opens the c-file and enables ...♕b6 to be played.

10 ♗e2 ♕b6

After 10...cxd5?, 11 ♘xd5 White exploits the strengthened pin to carry out the sacrifice on h5. 11...♗e6 12 ♗xh5! ♗xd5 13 cxd5 gxh5 14 ♘xh5 ♘bd7 15 ♕f3 (Black cannot break the pin) 15...♖c8 16 0-0 (16 ♖h3 ♖c4 17 ♖g3 is less clear due to 17...♘xh5) 16...♖c2 17 ♖fc1 ♖xb2 18 ♖c3 a4 19 ♖ac1 ♖xa2 20 ♕f5 a3 21 ♘xg7 ♔xg7 22 ♖g3 ♔h8 23 ♗xf6+ ♘xf6 24 ♖c8! 1-0 Liardet-Peng Xiaomin, Geneva 1997. A pretty and instructive finish.

11 ♕d2 ♘bd7 12 ♖b1

Now 13 dxc6 is the threat. Nevertheless, 12 ♗e3 is the right move, preventing 12...♘c5, since it can be met by 13 ♘a4!. On the other hand, it is not easy for Black to decide where to put the queen. If it goes back, it loses time, while going ahead is risky: 12...♕b4?! 13 a3 ♕b3 14 ♗d1! ♕xc4 15 b3 ♕a6 16 ♗e2 b5 17 dxc6 ♕xc6 18 ♗xb5 ♕c7 19 ♖c1 with better chances for White.

12...cxd5 13 cxd5 ♘c5 14 0-0 ♗d7 15 ♗e3

Now:

a) 15...♖fc8 comes into consideration. In the long run, however, the rook's support is not necessary for playing ...f5.

b) 15...♖ac8 and now:

b1) 16 f3?! is the wrong path, and is immediately exploited by Black: 16...♘h7! 17 ♗f2? (17 ♘h1 is the only acceptable reply, planning g3) 17...♗f6 18 ♘h1 ♗xh4! (White is lost after this awkward surprise) and now 19 g3 left White a pawn down in Dončević-Smejkal, Bundesliga 1983/4, while 19 ♗xh4 ♘xe4+ 20 ♗f2 ♕xf2+! is also hopeless.

b2) 16 ♖fc1 is necessary, planning b3 and a3 with balanced chances.

B)

9...♕e8 *(D)*

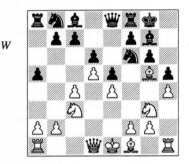

The queen steps out of the pin. It also defends h5 after a later ...f5.

10 ♗e2 ♘h7 11 ♗e3 ♕e7

Now ...♗f6 is threatened.

12 ♕d2!

In case of 12 ♘f1, 12...f5 is a promising pawn sacrifice, because only the bishop could take on h5.

12...♗f6 13 0-0-0 ♗xh4 14 ♘xh5

In the spirit of the variation!

14...♗g5

After 14...gxh5 15 g3 ♗g5 16 f4 ♗f6 17 ♖xh5 White has a decisive attack.

15 f4! exf4 16 ♘xf4 ♘d7

Black controls the e5-square, but this does not compensate for White's attack any more. Instead, 16...♘f6? is met by 17 ♘xg6.

17 ♖h2 ♖e8 18 ♖dh1 ♘df8

Formally, everything is defended. Still, the open h-file with the doubled rooks makes it easy for White to attack, and also poses defensive problems for Black.

19 ♔b1! ♗f6

The main problem is that Black cannot find any counterplay:

a) 19...♗d7 20 ♗d3 planning ♕f2-g3 with ever-increasing threats.

b) 19...f5 20 ♘xg6 ♘xg6 21 ♖xh7 ♗xe3 22 ♖xe7 ♗xd2 takes the queen without check, so White secures a decisive advantage after the sequence of captures by 23 ♖xe8+ ♔f7 24 ♘b5!.

20 ♗f3 a4 21 a3! ♗g7 22 ♘d3 ♗d7

22...b6 eases one of the problems, but White's advantage is still serious. If 22...f5?!, then 23 ♖e1!.

23 g4 ♗f6

Now the game Pähtz-Van Wely, Bad Mondorf 1991 concluded 24 e5?! dxe5 25 ♘e4 ♗g7 26 ♗c5 ♕d8 27 ♖h4 f5 28 ♕h2! ♘g5 29 ♗xf8 (29 ♖h8+! ♔f7 30 ♗xf8 is the best move-order) 29...♘xf3 (29...♔xf8!? 30 ♖h8+ ♔f7 is the only chance) 30 ♖h8+ ♔f7 31 ♕h7 ♘d2+ 32 ♔c2! ♖xf8 33 ♕xg7+ ♔xg7 34 ♖1h7# (1-0). A more clinical finish is 24 ♖xh7! ♘xh7 25 ♕h2 ♘f8 26 ♗g5!, threatening ♕h4.

5 6...e5 7 d5 c6

1 d4 ♘f6 2 c4 g6 3 ♘c3 ♗g7 4 e4 d6 5 ♘ge2 0-0 6 ♘g3 e5 7 d5 c6 *(D)*

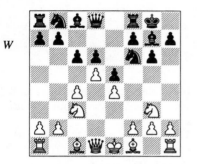

W

A popular system. Black first levers open the strong white pawn-centre, and only then continues his development. If possible, he seeks counter-play with ...a6 and ...b5, if not then with ...f5. The queen's knight generally heads for c5. However, this plan costs time. White may exploit this in two ways: with h4, before or after ♗e2, or by completing his development, preparing castling.

8 ♗e2

This is played almost exclusively. For 8 h4 see 8 ♗e2 followed by h4.

Black has three main responses:

A: 8...cxd5   59
B: 8...a6   70
C: 8...h5   72

For 8...a5 transposes to Line C in Chapter 4, 8...♘a6 leads to Line C in

Chapter 6 and finally for 8...♘e8 see note 'b' to Black's 8th move in Line B of Chapter 3.

A)

8...cxd5 9 cxd5

Now Black has the following plans:

A1: 9...♘bd7   59
A2: 9...a6   69

A1)

9...♘bd7

The most frequent treatment after 8...cxd5, aiming to play ...♘c5. Now:

A11: 10 h4   59
A12: 10 ♗e3   65
A13: 10 ♗g5   67
A14: 10 0-0   68

A11)

10 h4 *(D)*

B

A further advance by the h-pawn is threatened. Black can choose between:

A111: 10...a6   60
A112: 10...h5   62

Or:
a) 10...♕b6?! 11 a3 a5 12 ♗e3! and a later ♘a4 gives White an advantage.

b) 10...♕a5?! is not the best place for the queen either, as it can be forced back. 11 h5 (11 a3 is also good) 11...♘c5 12 ♗d2 (preventing the capture on e4, and also preparing b4) 12...♕b6 13 b4! and now:

b1) 13...♕xb4? 14 ♘b5 ♕a4 15 ♕xa4 ♘xa4 16 ♘xd6 gives White a clear advantage.

b2) 13...♘cd7 14 ♖b1 ♕d8 15 h6 ♗h8 16 ♗g5 (an unpleasant pin; the queen is bothered on d8, too) 16...a5 17 a3 with an advantage to White, V.Jensen-Ringsborg, corr. 1986.

b3) 13...♘a6 14 a3 ♗d7 15 ♗e3 ♕d8 16 ♖c1 ♘c7 (Everett-Ludwig, corr. 1992) 17 h6 followed by ♗g5 gives White a clear advantage.

c) 10...a5 11 ♗g5 (better is 11 h5 and only later developing the bishop) 11...♘c5 12 ♕c2 ♗d7 13 h5 a4 14 h6 ♗h8 15 0-0 ♕b6 16 ♖ab1 ♖fc8 with level chances, Forintos-Szuk, Hungarian Cht 1998. Now 17 ♔h1 and f4 was the right plan.

d) 10...♖e8 11 h5 ♘f8 and then White can play:

d1) 12 hxg6 (too hasty) 12...fxg6 13 ♗h6 ♖e7 14 ♕d2 ♗d7 15 ♗xg7 ♖xg7 16 ♕g5 ♘e8 with even chances, Jimenez-Toran, Havana 1952.

d2) 12 ♗e3 is more flexible, e.g. 12...♘xh5 13 ♘xh5 gxh5 14 ♖xh5 ♘g6 and now the simple 15 g3 ensures a clear advantage.

A111)
10...a6 (D)

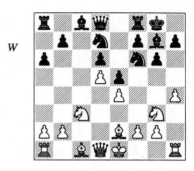

Black starts play on the queenside, which White prevents with his next move.

11 a4 h5
Or:
a) 11...♘e8 prepares ...f5 but White has a reply to counter that: 12 h5! ♗f6 (Vaughan-Jamieson, corr. 1990) and here we suggest the immediate 13 ♗h6 ♘g7 14 ♕d2 keeping the tension, and then advancing the pawn to h5.

b) 11...a5 secures the position of the knight on c5, although at the cost of a tempo; in return, the b5-square is weakened. After 12 h5 ♘c5 13 ♗e3 (aimed against ...♕b6) and now:

b1) 13...♕b6?! 14 ♘b5! ♗d7 15 ♖c1 ♖ac8 16 ♖c3 ♗xb5 17 ♗xb5 ♖c7 now instead of 18 f3 (Remlinger-Dannevig, Gausdal 1992), 18 h6 ♗h8 19 0-0 ♖fc8 20 ♕f3, planning ♖fc1, gives White a long-lasting initiative.

b2) 13...♘e8 (so that in the case of 14 ♗xc5 dxc5 the knight can occupy d6) 14 ♖a3 ♗f6!? 15 ♕d2 ♘g7?! 16 hxg6! fxg6 17 ♗xc5 dxc5 18 ♕h6 ♗g5 19 ♕xh7+ ♔f7 (Alber-Flögel,

Hessen Ch 1988) and now 20 ♘f5! gives White a convincing advantage.

b3) 13...♗d7 brings about the critical position. White may take on c5, especially if he likes fighting against weak squares. As for Black, there are some who like such positions, others not. 14 ♖a3 and now:

b31) 14...♕b6 can be met by 15 h6 – compare line 'b1'. Instead, 15 f3 cannot be recommended because of 15...♘xh5 and ...f5.

b32) 14...♕e7 (Forintos-Sandström, Malmö 1988) and now 15 h6 ♗h8 16 ♗g5 gives White a more comfortable position.

b33) 14...♖c8 15 f3 (the aim is ♕d2 and ♗h6, with the typical attack, or the exchange with ♗b5; that is why Black hurries with the freeing exchange on h5, but it is not that easy to get out of trouble) 15...♘xh5 16 ♘xh5 gxh5 17 ♖xh5 f5 18 ♗b5! (of the two black bishops, the one on d7 would be more effective without the exchange) 18...♗e8 (if 18...♗xb5, then 19 axb5 fxe4 20 fxe4 ♕f6 21 ♔e2! planning ♕h1) 19 ♗xe8 (19 ♖xf5 is also good) 19...♕xe8 and now instead of 20 ♖h3 ♕g6! (Pihajlić-Verőci, Jajce 1981), 20 ♖xf5! ♖xf5 21 exf5 gives White a clear advantage.

12 ♗g5 (D)

12...♕e8

The classical queen move, planning ...♘h7.

12...♕b6?! provokes the following advance, which is quite useful for White in any event: 13 a5!. Now the queen has to go back since it must not accept the poisoned pawn:

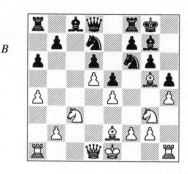

B

a) 13...♕xb2? 14 ♗d2 ♘c5 15 ♖a2 ♕b3 16 ♕a1 ♕b4 17 0-0 ♘b3 18 ♕b2 is winning for White, Remlinger-Shaw, New York 1991.

b) 13...♕c7 14 ♕d2 (after 14 ♗d2, we suggest 14...b6 rather than 14...b5?! 15 b4 ± Ye Naung Win-Ye Jiangchuan, Yangon 1999) 14...♘c5 15 ♖a3 b6 16 b4 (this is good for White) 16...♘cd7 17 0-0 bxa5 18 ♖xa5! ♘b6 19 ♖fa1 ♘c4 20 ♗xc4 ♕xc4 21 b5 with an advantage to White, Forintos-Udovčić, Titovo Užice 1966.

c) 13...♕d4 14 ♕c2 ♕c5 15 0-0 ♔h7 16 ♖fc1 (the following tactical and technical solutions are instructive) 16...♕c7 17 ♕d2 ♕b8 18 ♘a4 ♘g8 (Black tries to exchange bishops, but later follows a surprise) 19 ♖a3 ♗f6 (since the black queen is far away from the kingside a sacrifice must be successful) 20 ♗xh5! b5 (accepting White's sacrifice is not better either: 20...gxh5 21 ♕e2! with a heavy attack, in which the a3-rook can help if necessary) 21 axb6 ♘xb6 22 ♘xb6 (safer than 22 ♖b3 ♘xa4 23 ♖xb8 ♖xb8) 22...♕xb6 23 ♗e2 ♗d7 24 ♖ca1 ♗b5 25 ♗xf6 ♘xf6 26 ♗xb5 ♕xb5 27 ♕g5! (White is stronger on the kingside so he must attack there) 27...♘g8 28 h5 ♘h6 29 hxg6+ fxg6 30 ♘f5! (to make way for the a3-rook) 30...♘xf5 31 exf5 ♖xf5 32 ♖h3+ ♔g7 33 ♕e7+ ♖f7 34 ♖h7+! ♔xh7 35 ♕xf7+ ♔h6 36 ♖a3! mating, Forintos-Bogdanović, Sarajevo 1965.

13 ♖a3

13 a5 is an alternative; following 13...♘h7 14 ♗e3 ♕e7 15 ♘f1 Black's queenside is under pressure.

13...♘h7

Instead, 13...b6, followed by ...♖b8, and only then ...♘h7, should be taken into consideration.

14 ♗e3 ♘df6 15 ♕b3!?

White attacks via the b-file.

15...♕e7

After defending the b7-pawn Black plans ...♘g4 and ....♗h6, whereas the immediate 15...♘g4?! is not good because of 16 ♗xg4 hxg4 17 h5!.

16 ♗d2!?

White prevents ...♘g4, which could now be answered by f3.

16...♘e8

Preparing a pawn sacrifice in the hope of obtaining some counterplay.

17 ♘f1 f5 18 exf5 gxf5 19 ♘g3!

Because it is better to take on h5 with the knight.

19...♘ef6 20 ♘xh5 ♘xh5 21 ♗xh5 ♗d7 22 ♗d1 ♗f6 23 ♕c4!? ♖ac8

Or 23...♖fc8 24 ♕e2.

24 ♕b4

The queen cannot now be chased by ...a5.

24...♔h8 25 g3

Black does not have enough compensation for the pawn, Forintos-Borocz, Hungarian Cht 1993.

10...h5 *(D)*

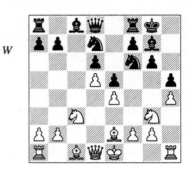

Black does not allow h5, but permits the ♗g5 pin to come with greater force.

11 ♗g5

11 ♗e3 is also good. Then 11...a6 (in case of 11...a5 we suggest 12 ♘a4 with a slight advantage to White) can be met by 12 b4, when 12...b5 13 a4 is to White's advantage.

11...a6

Black may also choose between the following options (11...♕a5 can be met by 12 a3 and b4, as in Pe.Wolff-Böhle, Hessen 1992, with an advantage for White):

a) 11...a5 and now:

a1) Here we suggest the solid 12 ♖c1, when 12...♕b6 (not 12...♘c5?, Breier-M.Roos, Binz 1995, since 13 ♗xh5! gxh5 14 ♘xh5 and then ♕f3 is inevitable) can be answered by 13 ♘b5!.

a2) 12 ♗xh5. This novelty is our other suggestion. As far as we can see, it makes no fundamental difference that the pawn is on a5 rather than a6 in this case. Compare the main line.

b) 11...♕b6 is a good and active move:

b1) 12 ♕d2 and then:

b11) 12...♕d4?! was played in Teyssou-Brito, Benidorm 1989 and now White should continue 13 ♘b5 ♕xd2+ 14 ♔xd2!.

b12) 12...♘h7? 13 ♗e3 ♘c5 14 ♘a4 +−.

b13) 12...♘c5 and here:

b131) This time 13 ♗xf6 is not advisable: 13...♗xf6 14 ♗xh5 (Alber-Scherer, German Cht 1994); for example 14...gxh5! (14...♕xb2?! is risky at best) 15 ♘xh5 ♕d8! and Black is better.

b132) 13 ♗e3! (threatening ♘a4) 13...♗d7 14 0-0 ♖ac8 15 ♖ab1 a5 16 f3 a4?! (this will prove weak later on; better is 16...♘h7) 17 ♘h1 ♘h7 18 ♗f2 (a tricky move, but 18 ♘f2 f5 19 ♘d3 is the right continuation) 18...f5?! (18...♗f6, planning ...♗xh4 or ...g5, equalizes) 19 exf5 gxf5 20 ♘g3! with an advantage for White, Vegh-Krebs, Zalaegerszeg 1992, since 20...f4 can be met by 21 ♘ge4.

b133) 13 ♖b1 ♗d7? (the better 13...a5 14 ♗e3 should be compared with line 'b132') 14 b4 ♘a4 15 ♗e3 ♕c7 16 ♘b5 ♗xb5 17 ♗xb5 ♘b6 18 ♖c1 ♕d8 19 f3 is favourable for White, Vaassen-Verolme, corr. 1987.

b2) 12 ♖b1 a5 13 a3 (13 ♗e3 ♘c5!) 13...♘c5 14 b4 axb4 15 axb4 ♘a6 (here we can see that it is advisable to move to c5 only if the b4-square is also secured) 16 ♘a4 (Sielaff-Idler, corr. 1994) 16...♕d4 17 ♕xd4 exd4 18 ♘b6 is only slightly worse for Black.

We return to 11...a6 *(D)*:

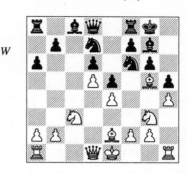

White now has to decide between the quiet way (A1121) and a complicated path (A1122):

A1121: 12 a4   63
A1122: 12 ♗xh5!?   64

Similarly solid, but rare, is the 12 ♘f1 ♕e8 13 ♘d2 knight manoeuvre. After 13...b5 14 a3 ♘h7 15 ♗e3 f5 16 f3 (16 exf5?! gxf5 17 ♗xh5 ♕e7 and Black takes the initiative) 16...♘df6 17 ♖c1 (Novikov-Xie Jun, Helsinki 1992) Black should play 17...♗d7!, keeping the balance.

It is basic knowledge that 12 0-0 is not recommended, because after ...♕e8 and ...♘h7 the h4-pawn may get into trouble.

A1121)
12 a4

The most frequent continuation, but is also has some drawbacks. Black now has a choice between three queen moves, and one rook move:

a) 12...♕c7?! 13 ♕d2 ♘h7 (or 13...♘c5 14 ♖a3) 14 ♗e3 ♗f6! 15 ♘f1 ♕d8 16 g3 ♗g7 (16...b6!?) 17 ♕c2!

makes room for the knight, Meleg-hegyi-Rye, corr. 1978.

b) 12...♕e8 and now:

b1) 13 a5! has the idea of ♘a4, and also frees the a4-square for a future ♕a4-b4. Now the best move, 13...b6, can be answered by 14 b4; for example, 14...♖b8 15 b5! with a slight advantage for White.

b2) 13 ♕d2 ♘h7 14 ♗h6! ♗xh6 15 ♕xh6 ♕e7 16 ♘f1 ♘c5 17 ♖a3 a5 18 ♘d2 ♗d7 19 ♘c4 ♔h8 20 g3 f5!? (a necessary pawn sacrifice for the initiative) 21 ♘b6 ♖ad8 22 ♘xd7 ♕xd7 23 ♕xg6 ♖f6 24 ♕xh5 fxe4 25 ♘d1! ♖df8 26 g4 ♘d3+ 27 ♗xd3 exd3 28 ♖xd3 ♖f4 29 ♖g3 ♕xa4 30 0-0 ♕d4 31 ♘e3 a4 32 ♕g6 and White took the upper hand in Forintos-d'Amore, Lugano 1984.

c) 12...♕a5 13 ♗d2 (here we suggest instead 13 ♖b1 and only after 13...♕b4 to play 14 ♗d2) 13...♕d8 and then:

c1) 14 b4 a5! (14...b6, Bozinović-Muhvić, Croatian Cht 1997, can be met by 15 a5) 15 ♘b5 (15 bxa5 ♖xa5 16 ♘b5 ♖a6) 15...axb4 and now:

c11) 16 ♘xd6 ♘c5 17 ♘xc8 ♖xc8 18 ♗xb4 ♘cxe4!? 19 ♘xe4 ♘xe4 20 ♗xf8 ♕a5+! 21 ♔f1 ♗xf8 and Black has compensation for the exchange in this unclear position.

c12) 16 ♗xb4 ♘c5 17 ♗xc5 dxc5 18 ♕d2 ♗d7 and Black equalized in Hurme-V.Mäki, Finnish Cht 1991.

c2) 14 a5!? is more promising as 14...b5?! can be met by 15 b4 with advantage. After the superior 14...b6 15 b4 bxa5 16 ♖xa5 White is slightly better.

d) 12...♖e8 prepares the manoeuvre ...♘f8-h7. White can now play:

d1) 13 ♘f1 ♘f8 (13...♕b6 14 ♖a3!) 14 ♕b3 ♕a5 (better is 14...b6) 15 ♘d2 b5 16 0-0 bxa4 17 ♖xa4 ♕d8 18 ♘c4 ± Elliston-Embrey, corr. 1992. ♕a3 is the main threat.

d2) 13 b4 is best. Then 13...a5 14 ♘b5! ♘f8 15 ♖c1 gives White the initiative, while 13...♘f8 is strongly met by 14 a5.

A1122)

12 ♗xh5!?

We recommend this for those who like complications. Apart from the psychological effect, Black has to negotiate his way through some minefields. Even if he manages to do that, he may only get a position with chances for both sides.

12...gxh5

12...♕b6 is feeble: 13 ♘a4! ♕b4+ 14 ♗d2 ♕d4 15 ♗f3 and White is a pawn up.

13 ♘xh5 (D)

13...♕e8!

It is best to keep the queen near the king. Other moves:

a) 13...♛a5 14 ♘xg7 ♚xg7 and now:

a1) 15 ♕f3 ♖h8 (Hanks-Cuellar, Tel Aviv OL 1964) 16 h5 gives White chances.

a2) 15 ♕d2! (threatening ♗xf6+) 15...♘g8 16 ♖h3 f6 (16...♘df6?? 17 ♗xf6+ and 18 ♕g5+ wins) 17 ♖g3!. These two attractive rook moves demolish Black's defence:

a21) 17...♚h7? 18 ♕e2.

a22) 17...fxg5 18 ♕xg5+ ♚f7 19 ♕g6+ ♚e7 20 ♕e6+ ♚d8 21 ♖xg8 and White is better with his kingside pawns.

a23) 17...♚f7! 18 ♗h6 ♘xh6 19 ♕xh6 b5 (19...♚e8 is the alternative, but the march of the h-pawn and the threats on the 7th rank, as can be seen in the game, are impossible to counter) 20 ♖g7+ ♚e8 21 ♕h7 b4 22 ♘d1 ♕c5 (22...♚d8 is a bit tougher) 23 h5 ♕d4? 24 ♖c1! (White's attack is unstoppable; now ♖xc8+ is the mate threat) 24...♘c5 25 ♖xc5! (White has created his own evergreen game, so it was worth playing 13 ♘xh5 in any case) 25...dxc5 26 ♖c7 1-0 Duchesne-N.Saeed, Biel 1986.

b) 13...♕b6 can be answered by 14 ♘xg7 followed by ♖h3!.

14 ♘xg7 ♚xg7

Devaud-Baron, Paris 1993. Now 15 ♕d2! is correct, with the double threat ♗xf6+! and ♗h6+. In the complicated position after 15...♘g8 White can play 16 g4 planning f3, ♘e2 and ♘g3, with better chances.

A12)
10 ♗e3 *(D)*

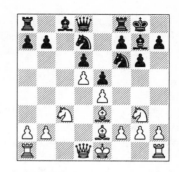

The intention of this line is different from that of the h4 or ♗g5 construction. Now ♘b5 is the threat.

10...a6

This is correct. Others:

a) After 10...a5? (Paldanius-Franssila, Tampere 1988) our recommendation is 11 ♘a4 giving White queenside pressure, e.g. 11...♖b8 12 ♖c1 b5 13 ♘c3 b4 14 ♘a4 with an advantage for White.

b) 10...b6? 11 ♘f1! ♘c5 12 ♘d2 ♗a6 (exchanging the bishops favours White) 13 ♗xa6 ♘xa6 14 0-0 ♕d7 15 f3 ♖ac8 (15...b5 16 ♕e2 ♘c7 is just slightly better) 16 ♕e2 ♘c5 17 ♖fc1 ♘a4 18 ♘c4 ♘xc3 19 ♖xc3 ♖fd8 20 ♖ac1 ♘e8 21 ♘a3 ± Novikov-Deutsch, Graz 1996.

11 0-0

Other possibilities:

a) 11 ♕d2 b5 and now:

a1) 12 ♗h6 ♕b6 13 ♗e3 ♕d8 just repeats.

a2) 12 b4 (H.Steiner-E.Pedersen, Dubrovnik OL 1950) and now with 12...♘b6! Black can equalize if he plays accurately.

a3) 12 f3 h5 13 ♗g5 ♕b6 14 ♘f1 ♘h7 15 ♗e7 (or 15 ♗e3 ±) 15...♖e8

16 ♗h4 f5 17 ♗f2 ♕d8 18 exf5 gxf5 19 ♘e3 ♕f6 20 0-0 ♕g6 21 ♔h1 ♘df6 22 a4 f4 23 ♘c2 ♗f5 24 ♘b4 with better chances to White in a complicated position, Petrosian-Geller, USSR Ch 1973.

b) 11 a4 h5 12 ♘f1 (12 h4 can be met 12...♔h7 planning ...♘g8 and ...♗h6 – Vogt) 12...♘c5 13 ♘d2 ♘g4 14 ♗xc5 dxc5 15 ♘c4 b6 16 a5 b5 17 ♘b6 ♖a7 now instead of the exposed 18 d6?! (Ru.Rodriguez-Vogt, Thessaloniki OL 1988), 18 ♘xc8! ♕xc8 19 ♗xg4 hxg4 20 h3 is necessary, with slightly better chances to White.

11...h5 *(D)*

The best. Others:

a) 11...b5 12 b4 (blockading the queenside) 12...♘b6!? (as White lost time with castling, Black may play for exchanges; 13...♗d7 is the plan) 13 a4 and now:

a1) 13...♘c4? 14 axb5! ♘xe3 15 fxe3 ♕b6 16 ♕d3 ♗g4 17 ♖xa6 ♖xa6 18 bxa6 ♕xb4 19 ♗xg4 ♘xg4 20 h3 ± Szabo-R.Byrne, Havana OL 1966.

a2) 13...♘xa4 14 ♘xa4 bxa4 15 ♖xa4 (the right move) 15...♘d7 (15...h5 can be met by 16 ♗g5 and after 16...♕e8 or 16...♕b6, 17 b5 is strong) 16 ♕d2 ♘b6 17 ♖a5 f5 18 exf5 gxf5 19 f4 e4 20 ♘h5 ♗h8 21 ♗d4 ♖f7 22 ♗xh8 ♔xh8 23 ♖a3! with the traditional attack on the kingside. The rook appearing on the 3rd rank decided the fight in Meleghegyi-Tengely, Hungary 1991.

b) 11...♘e8 (Black's plan is original: he brings his knight to g7, and only then plays ...f5) 12 ♖c1! ♗f6 13 ♕d2 ♘g7 14 a4 h5 15 b4 ♗e7 16 a5

h4 17 ♘h1 f5 18 exf5 ♘xf5 (the plan has been accomplished; the price is that White controls the e4- and g4-squares) 19 ♗g4! ♘f6 and now instead of 20 ♗h3 (Dely-Hort, Moscow 1962), 20 ♗b6 ♕e8 21 f3! ± is best, further controlling the h5-square.

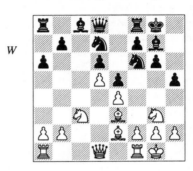

After the text-move, White has to decide where to go with the g3-knight.

12 ♖e1

This move makes room for the g3-knight to retreat to f1. Others:

a) 12 ♗g5 is not too effective now: 12...♕e8 13 ♕d2 ♘h7 14 ♗h6 h4 15 ♘h1 ♕e7 16 ♗xg7 ♔xg7 17 ♖ac1 ♘df6 and Black had nearly equalized in Zsu.Polgar-Brustman, Thessaloniki wom OL 1988.

b) 12 b4 h4 13 ♘h1 ♘h7 14 f3 ♗f6 15 a4 ♗g5 16 ♕d2 ♗xe3+ 17 ♕xe3 ♔g7 (after the exchanging of queens by 17...♕g5, the c7-square would become weak in the ending) 18 ♖fc1 ♘df6 19 a5 ♘h5 20 ♗f1 ♘g5 21 ♘f2 ♕f6 22 ♘a4 h3 23 ♘b6 hxg2 24 ♗xg2 ♖b8 (Forintos-Sznapik, Ljubljana 1981) 25 ♖c7 gives White the better chances.

12...♘h7 13 ♕d2

13 ♘f1 ♗f6! 14 a4 ♗g5 15 a5 (15 g3 =) 15...h4, Chekhov-Ye Jiangchuan, Beijing 1991. Now 16 ♕d2 ♘c5 17 ♖a3 f5 18 exf5 gxf5 19 b4 is necessary, with chances for both sides.

13...h4 14 ♘f1 f5

It is better first to play ...♗f6-g5, as we saw in the previous note.

15 exf5 gxf5 16 f4 ♕e8 17 fxe5!?

An interesting and promising plan, but not without risk. The solid 17 ♔h1 and 17 ♖ac1 are also playable.

17...dxe5 18 d6 ♘df6!

18...f4? 19 ♗c4+ ♔h8 20 ♗xf4! or 18...♘hf6 19 ♗g5.

19 ♘d5

Changing plan by 19 ♗f4! is also strong, e.g. 19...♔h8 20 ♗d1 ♘g4 21 ♘d5 with better chances in a complicated position.

19...♘xd5 20 ♕xd5+ ♗e6 21 ♕xb7 ♕g6 22 d7

Avrukh-Van den Doel, Duisburg U-14 Wch 1992. Now Black should try 22...h3 23 ♖ad1 ♕xg2+ exchanging queens with a complicated position.

A13)

10 ♗g5 *(D)*

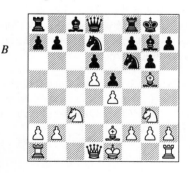

White hopes for 10...h6 11 ♗e3, with an improved version of Line A12 (10 ♗e3), as the h6-pawn is a target.

10...h6

10...a6 is possible, though after 11 ♕d2 the move ...h6 is now impossible.

11 ♗e3 a6

Other, less direct, lines:

a) 11...a5?! 12 ♕d2 (12 ♘a4! is worth consideration here, as in Line A12) 12...h5 13 h4 ♘c5 (Carlton-Podlofsky, Chicago 1994) 14 0-0-0 gives balanced chances.

b) 11...♔h7?! 12 h4! ♘g8 (Black is right to be frightened of the ♗xh5 sacrifice after 12...h5 13 ♗g5, but this is hardly any better) 13 h5 a6 14 hxg6+ fxg6 15 ♕d2 and the opened h-file was very unpleasant for Black in A.Garcia-Frick, Moscow OL 1994.

c) 11...♘e8 has been under-rated. 12 ♕d2 ♔h7 and now:

c1) 13 h4?! (an error, for if ...f5 has already been prepared and it threatens a fork with ...f4, then h4 in reply is already too late!) 13...f5! 14 f4 and here, instead of 14...♘c5?! Rasztik-P.Bauer, Zalakaros 1996, Black should play 14...exf4! 15 ♗xf4 fxe4 16 ♘cxe4 ♘e5 with better chances to Black, since after 17 h5 g5 a sacrifice can be refuted, while 17 0-0-0 can strongly be met by 17...♗g4.

c2) Better is 13 0-0, when 13...h5 can be met by 14 ♗d3, as 14...h4 15 ♘ge2 f5? does not work because of 16 exf5 gxf5 17 ♗g5!.

12 0-0

There are other moves; in short:

a) 12 ♕d2 h5 13 ♗g5 b5 14 0-0 b4?! 15 ♘a4 ♕a5 16 b3 ♖e8 and now

17 a3 left White better in Hanks-Canfell, Adelaide 1990, though 17 ♖fc1 is even more precise.

b) 12 h4 h5! 13 ♖c1! (13 f3, 13 ♘f1 and 13 a4 have no individual significance, each transposing into other lines) 13...b5 14 a3 ♖b8 (Fittante-V.Smith, Manila wom OL 1992) 15 ♘a2 heads for c6, while 15...a5 can be answered by 16 ♘c3 b4 17 ♘a4 with an advantage.

12...b5

Or:

a) 12...♘h7 and now:

a1) 13 a4 h5 14 a5 h4 15 ♘h1 f5 16 exf5 gxf5 17 f4 exf4 18 ♗xf4 ♘e5 19 ♘f2 ♗d7 20 ♕b3 ♕e7! (Jenei-Udovčić, Budapest 1960) 21 ♖ae1 and only later ♕b4 keeps a slight advantage for White.

a2) 13 ♕d2 comes into consideration. For 13...h5 14 ♖fe1 see Line A12 (at move 13).

b) 12...h5! is possibly best, and transposes to Line A12 (at move 11).

13 b4

A long time ago this plan, which originates from the Hungarian master Jenei, impressed us. Its fame has faded since, as Black's play has been improved. However, we have a novelty, as you can see later on.

13...♘b6 14 a4! ♘xa4!

14...♘c4?! 15 axb5 ♘xe3 16 fxe3 ♕b6 should be compared with note 'a1' to Black's 11th move in Line A12.

15 ♘xa4 bxa4 16 ♖xa4! h5!

White played 17 f3 in the game Szabo-Yanofsky, Winnipeg 1967 and after 17...h4 18 ♘h1 ♘h5! Black got a certain amount of counterplay. Instead

we suggest 17 ♗g5 planning ♕a1 or ♗xh5; for example, 17...♕b6 18 b5 a5 (18...♗b7 19 ♗e3!) 19 ♕d2 favours White. The a5-pawn is in danger.

A14)

10 0-0 *(D)*

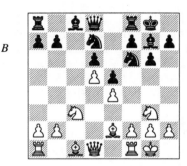

B

White will decide upon his set-up depending on his opponent's answer.

10...a6

Or:

a) 10...a5 and now:

a1) 11 ♗g5 h6 12 ♗e3 ♘c5 13 ♖b1 (13 ♕d2 and 13 ♖c1 are more promising) 13...♗d7?! (13...h5 is more precise, because it stops the g3-knight moving to e2) 14 f3 h5 15 ♗b5! h4 16 ♘ge2 ♘h5 17 a3 ♘f4 18 ♗xd7 ♕xd7 (18...♘xe2+ 19 ♕xe2 ±) 19 ♘xf4 does not give Black enough compensation for the pawn, Formanek-Rizzati, Cattolica 1992.

a2) 11 ♗e3 and then:

a21) 11...h5 (Balazs-Borriss, Dresden 1989) should be answered by 12 ♖e1 in order to make room for the manoeuvre ♘f1-d2-c4.

a22) 11...♘c5 12 ♖c1! (12 a3 was met by 12...h5! in Levin-P.Popović,

Belgrade 1992) 12...♗d7 13 a4 ♖c8 14 f3 ♕e7?! (better is the immediate 14...h5, and if 15 ♗g5, then 15...♕b6) 15 ♗b5! h5 16 ♗g5 ♕e8 17 ♘ge2 ♘h7 18 ♗e3 f5 19 exf5 gxf5 20 ♗xd7 ♕xd7 21 ♘b5 b6 22 f4! ♘f6 23 fxe5 dxe5 24 d6! ± Arkhipov-Harestad, Gausdal 1991.

b) 10...♘e8 11 ♗e3 and then:

b1) 11...a6 12 ♖b1 f5 13 exf5 gxf5 14 f4 exf4 15 ♗xf4 ♘e5 16 ♕d2 ♕b6+? (better is 16...♗d7) 17 ♔h1 ♗d7 18 ♗h6 and White won quickly in Dive-Reid, British Ch (Norwich) 1994.

b2) 11...♘b6 (Bilek-Smailbegović, Sarajevo 1962) is not advisable. White should answer 12 a4, with an opening advantage.

c) In case of 10...h5?! the bishop can get to g5 in one move: after 11 ♗g5 a6 12 ♖c1! White is better developed.

We return to 10...a6 *(D)*:

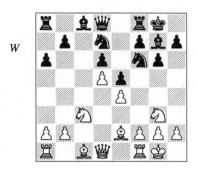

This can be regarded as the critical position. Black, before doing anything else, secures himself against ♘b5 or ♗b5.

11 a4 h5

Better than 11...♘e8 or 11...b6.
12 ♗g5 ♕e8

The immediate 13 ♕d2 is not best, as 13...♘h7 14 ♗e3 h4 15 ♘h1 f5 16 exf5 gxf5 17 f4 ♘c5! exploits the momentary lack of harmony between the a4-pawn and the queen on d2. Black has nearly equalized, Tempone-Correa, São Paulo 1989.

We suggest 13 a5, planning pressure on the queenside.

A2)
9...a6 *(D)*

10 h4
Or:

a) 10 ♗e3 h5 (planning ...♘g4 and ...f5) 11 h3 ♘bd7 12 ♘f1 b5 13 ♘d2 ♘h7 14 ♘b3?! (better is 14 0-0 f5 15 exf5 gxf5 16 f4 with chances for both sides) 14...f5 15 exf5 gxf5! 16 ♗xh5 b4 17 ♘a4 (17 ♘e2 is better) 17...f4 with activity for Black, Szabo-Z.Bašagić, Sarajevo 1972.

b) 10 0-0 b5 11 b4 ♘bd7 12 a4! (this must be played before Black puts his knight on b6) 12...bxa4 13 ♕xa4 ♗b7 (13...♘b6? 14 ♕c6) 14 ♗e3 (14 ♕a5!?) 14...h5 15 ♗g5 ♔h7 16 ♕a5!

with an advantage to White, Serper-Murrey, North Bay 1997.

c) 10 a4 can transpose to various other lines depending on Black's reply.

10...h5

Or:

a) 10...♘bd7 transposes to Line A111.

b) 10...b5 can be strongly met by 11 ♗e3 ♘bd7 12 a4!.

11 ♗g5 ♕e8 12 ♕d2 ♘bd7 13 ♗h6 ♕d8 14 a4 ♖e8

After this Black loses space, and has no counterplay. 14...b6 should be tried.

15 a5 ♘f8 16 ♗xg7 ♔xg7 17 ♘a4 ♖b8 18 ♖a3! ♗g4 19 f3 ♗d7 20 ♘b6 ♕e7 21 ♖c3

± Hort-Wahls, Munich 1991.

B)

8...a6 *(D)*

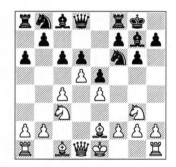

This is an original system, deserving serious attention. It keeps the possibility of transposing into Line A by a subsequent ...cxd5, depending on White's move.

9 a4

Or:

a) 9 h4 b5 10 h5 (10 dxc6 bxc4 11 ♗xc4 ♘xc6) 10...cxd5 11 cxd5 ♘bd7 12 ♗e3 ♘b6 13 b3! with a small advantage, Ermenkov-Topalov, Šumen 1991.

b) 9 ♗g5 also keeps the advantage: 9...h6 10 ♗e3 cxd5 11 cxd5 h5 and now 12 ♗g5 (Comas Fabrego-Xie Jun, Pamplona 1998/9) or 12 a4.

The text-move prevents ...b5.

9...a5 *(D)*

9...cxd5 10 cxd5 ♘bd7 should be compared with Line A1.

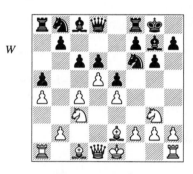

This is the real point of 8...a6. Black makes use of not having moved his queen's knight, so it may still go to a6. Still, it loses a little time compared to 7...a5 8 ♗e2 c6 (Line C of Chapter 4).

10 h4

Now Black can choose:

B1: 10...♘a6   70
B2: 10...h5   71

B1)

10...♘a6 11 h5

11 ♗g5 ♘c5! (Black is not fooled into playing ...h6, as that would only be a weakening) 12 ♕c2 ♕b6 13 ♖a3

♗d7 14 h5 cxd5 (the complications start here) 15 ♗xf6 ♗xf6 16 ♘xd5 ♕d8 17 ♘f1 ♘e6 ½-½ Forintos-Hazai, Hungarian Cht 1991. The game could continue 18 ♘fe3 ♘d4 19 ♕d1 ♗g5 20 hxg6 fxg6 (20...hxg6 can be met by 21 ♘g4 planning ♖ah3) 21 ♘c2 with chances for both sides.

11...♘c5

Or:

a) In case of 11...♘e8, 12 hxg6 fxg6 13 ♗e3 is best.

b) 11...cxd5 12 cxd5 and here after both 12...♘c5 and 12...♗d7, 13 ♗e3 is best.

c) 11...♕b6 12 ♖a3 ♘c5 transposes back to the main line.

12 ♖a3 ♕b6 13 ♗e3!

Or:

a) 13 dxc6 is not advisable because of 13...bxc6! 14 hxg6 fxg6 15 ♕xd6 ♖d8!, when Black gains a substantial initiative.

b) 13 h6 ♗h8 14 ♕c2 cxd5 15 cxd5 ♘g4 (threatening ...♘xf2) 16 f3! ♘f6 (16...♘f2 17 ♖f1) 17 ♗e3 ♗d7 (now White has managed an interesting plan) 18 ♘b5 ♖ac8 19 ♖c3! (intending ♘xd6) 19...♗xb5 20 ♗xb5 and although White's position is favourable, the game Dieu-Gallagher, Royan 1989 was later drawn.

The text-move tends to surprise those who see it for the first time: White abandons the b2-pawn just when it is attacked. However, it is based on a simple trick: 13...♕xb2?? 14 ♗xc5 dxc5 15 ♖b3, making use of ♖a3.

13...♕b4

A risky move but it is hard to find anything better.

14 h6

Better is 14 hxg6, which leads to complications:

a) 14...♘cxe4 15 gxh7+ ♔h8 16 ♘gxe4 ♘xe4 17 ♕c1! planning ♗h6 or ♔f1 and ♘a2; e.g., 17...cxd5 18 ♔f1! d4 19 ♘d5 ♕c5 20 ♗h6 ♗f5 21 ♗xg7+! ♔xg7 22 ♕h6+ ♔h8 23 ♗d3 ♖ac8 24 ♔g1! and White wins.

b) 14...hxg6 fully opens the h-file, which can be dangerous. It can be met by 15 ♕c2, e.g. 15...♘g4 16 ♗d2 ♕b6 17 ♘d1 cxd5 18 ♗xg4 ♗xg4 19 ♘e3!.

c) 14...fxg6 15 dxc6 bxc6 (alternatively, 15...♘cxe4 16 ♘gxe4 ♘xe4 17 ♖b3! ♘xc3 18 bxc3 +−) 16 ♕xd6 ♘cxe4 17 ♘gxe4 ♘xe4 18 ♕xc6 ♗b7 (18...♕xb2 19 ♘xe4 and White wins) 19 ♕e6+ ♖f7 20 ♖xh7 with activity for White.

14...♗h8 15 0-0 cxd5 16 cxd5 ♗d7

Now 17 ♗d2? (Spies-Riemersma, Houten 1988) is weak, because Black can take on b2 without any problem, as there is no ♗xc5 in reply. Better is 17 f3 ♖fc8 18 ♗b5, with a slight advantage.

B2)

10...h5 *(D)*

W

11 ♗g5

Now:

a) 11...♘a6 12 ♗xh5! ♕b6 13 ♗e2 ♕xb2 14 ♖c1 cxd5 15 exd5!? (taking with the e-pawn seems better than 15 cxd5 ♗d7 16 0-0 ♘c5 17 ♗b5 with an unclear position, Meleghegyi-Hausner, Balatonbereny 1980; 15 ♗xf6 ♗xf6 16 ♘xd5 ♗d8 is also unclear) and now Black cannot contemplate 15...♗d7?? 16 ♗xf6! ♗xf6 17 ♘ge4 ♗e7 18 ♖b1 ♕a3 19 ♖b3 +-.

b) 11...♕b6 is better:

b1) 12 ♕d2 (it is worth knowing the coming important motif) 12...♘a6 13 0-0 ♘h7!? 14 ♗e7 ♖e8 15 ♗xd6 (15 ♗g5? ♘xg5 ∓ Bowerman-Yoos, Winnipeg 1997) 15...c5 16 ♘b5 ♗d7 17 f4! with complications.

b2) 12 ♖a3 and now:

b21) 12...♘a6? 13 ♗xf6! ♗xf6 14 ♗xh5! gxh5 15 ♘xh5 with an attack – Bologan.

b22) 12...♘bd7 13 ♕c2 ♘c5 14 ♗e3 (White loses a tempo) 14...♗d7 (14...♘g4!) 15 ♘f1 ♖ac8 16 ♘d2 ♕b4 17 ♘a2 ♕b6 18 ♘c3 ♕d8 ∓ Ionov-Bologan, USSR Ch (Moscow) 1991.

C)

8...h5 *(D)*

9 ♗g5 ♕b6

This was Black's aim. However, as in other cases the queen does not stand well on b6, and it has to run away soon. Other moves:

a) 9...♕c7 and now:

a1) 10 0-0 ♘h7 11 ♗e3 h4 12 ♘h1 f5!? 13 dxc6 bxc6 14 c5! (14 ♘b5

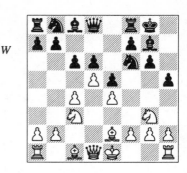

W

cxb5 is unclear) 14...f4 15 cxd6 favours White, Biriukov-Soloviov, Russia 1996.

a2) 10 h4 also comes into consideration, for after the typical 10...♘h7 11 ♗e3 c5, even 12 ♗xh5 is conceivable.

b) The delayed 9...cxd5 can be met by 10 exd5!?, e.g. 10...♕e8 (10...♕b6 11 ♕b3) 11 ♘b5 ♕d7 12 ♗xf6! ♗xf6 13 ♘e4 ♗e7? (13...♗d8!?) 14 ♘bxd6! with an extra pawn.

10 ♕d2 ♕d4 11 ♕c2! *(D)*

B

After the compulsory retreat of the black queen White gains a tempo, Formanek-Abbasi, Philadelphia 1993.

6 6...e5 7 d5: Other Moves

1 d4 ♘f6 2 c4 g6 3 ♘c3 ♗g7 4 e4 d6 5 ♘ge2 0-0 6 ♘g3 e5 7 d5

Besides the popular systems there are the following rarely played lines:

A: 7...c5   73
B: 7...h5   77
C: 7...♘a6   81

A)

7...c5 *(D)*

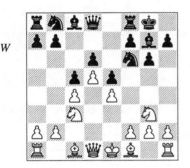

Black wants to limit White's prospects on the queenside in this line. His plan is to prepare ...f5 or ...b5. If the centre opens he will try to secure the d4-square, even at the cost of a pawn sacrifice, by ...e4. White can often prepare a3 and b4. The position can also be reached by the move-order 6...c5 7 d5 e5. White now has a choice of moves:

A1:   8 h4   73
A2:   8 ♗d3   73
A3:   8 ♗e2   74

A1)

8 h4

As Black can no longer put his knight on c5, activity on the kingside is more justified than ever. White's plan is to make it impossible for Black to play ...f5.

8...h5

This is best. Allowing White to play h5 would mean submission on the kingside. For 8...♘e8 see Line A2 in Chapter 3.

9 ♗g5 ♕a5

Other possibilities:

a) 9...♘a6 10 ♗e2 ♕b6 11 ♕d2 ♗d7 12 0-0-0 with a slight advantage to White, Rettedal-Gretarsson, Norway 1988.

b) 9...♕d7 10 ♗e2 ♘h7 should be compared with Line A31.

c) 9...a6 10 ♗e2 ♘bd7 11 ♕d2 ♔h7 12 0-0 (12 0-0-0 could be met by 12...b5, while 12 ♗xh5 is premature) 12...♕e8 13 a3 ♘g8 14 b4 ♘h6 15 ♘a4 and White has gained the initiative on the soon-to-be-opened b-file, Jenei-Gasztonyi, Budapest 1958.

Now (after 9...♕a5):

a) 10 ♗e2 ♘bd7 transposes to Line A34.

b) 10 ♕d2!? is also good, planning ♘b5.

A2)

8 ♗d3 *(D)*

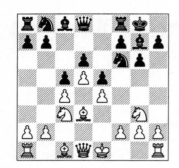

Not the best way to develop, although it is true that the manoeuvre ...♘a6-c5 is no longer to be feared.

8...♘e8

Or:

a) 8...♘a6 9 a3 ♘c7 10 0-0 ♘fe8 11 ♗d2 and then:

a1) 11...♗d7 12 ♕c2 a5 (12...a6 can be met by the strong 13 b4 with a queenside initiative) 13 b3 ♖b8 14 ♖ab1 with a slight advantage to White, Bertok-Milić, Yugoslav Ch 1962.

a2) 11...f5 12 exf5 gxf5 13 ♕h5 ♘f6 14 ♕h4 e4 15 ♗c2, with the idea of f3, gives White a slight advantage – Gufeld.

b) 8...a6 9 0-0 h5!? 10 ♗g5 ♕e8 and now:

b1) 11 ♕d2 ♘h7 12 ♗h6 ♘d7 13 ♗xg7 (13 a3, followed by b4, is more precise) 13...♔xg7 (Tempone-Zapata, Mar del Plata 1996), and now the plan of a3 and b4 gives White slightly the better chances.

b2) 11 ♖b1 is worthy of attention. Then 11...♘h7 12 ♗d2 h4 13 ♘ge2 f5 14 f4 exf4 15 exf5 ♗xf5 16 ♗xf5 ♖xf5 17 ♗xf4 is to White's advantage.

c) 8...♘g4 should be compared with Chapter 2.

9 h4 h5 10 ♗g5 ♗f6 11 ♕d2 ♘d7 12 f3

12 0-0-0, planning ♖df1, is a good alternative.

12...♗e7 13 ♘f1

Van der Morel-Pel, Groningen open 1997. Now 13...♘g7, planning ...f5, is best, and nearly equalizes.

A3)
8 ♗e2 (D)

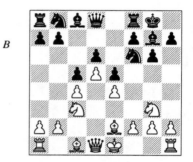

As usual, ♗e2 is also playable. Now there is another split:

A31: 8...a6   75
A32: 8...♘a6   75
A33: 8...♘e8   76
A34: 8...♘bd7   77

Or 8...h5 9 ♗g5 (the immediate 9 h4 is the alternative), and now:

a) It is good to know that 9...♕b6 does not really threaten the b-pawn, e.g. 10 h4 ♕xb2 11 ♘b5 ♘a6 12 a3 ♗d7 13 ♖b1 ♕a2 14 ♕c1! and White is much better.

b) 9...♕d7 and here:

b1) Quiet and good is 10 0-0 ♘h7 11 ♗e3 h4 12 ♘h1 ♕e7 13 ♕d2 f5 14 exf5 gxf5 15 f4.

b2) 10 h4 ♘h7 11 ♗d2 (11 ♗e3 is
more natural) 11...♕e7! (...♗f6xh4 is
threatened so White has to regroup) 12
♘f1 ♘a6 13 a3 (this keeps the knight
on a6, and threatens b4) 13...♗d7 and
now White can choose from three
plans:

b21) 14 ♘e3 (14 ♖b1 is met in the
same way too) 14...f5!? 15 exf5 gxf5
16 ♗xh5 f4 17 ♘f1 e4 with some initiative for the sacrificed pawn.

b22) 14 g3 f5 (or 14...♘c7 15 b4
b6 16 ♘h2 ±) 15 exf5 ♗xf5 16 ♘e3
leads to sharp play, in which White's
chances are to be preferred.

b23) 14 ♕b3!? (this distracts the
rook, so that it can no longer support
...f5) 14...♖fb8 15 ♘b5 ♖c8 16 ♕g3?!
(White should play 16 g3, intending
♘h2) 16...♘c7 17 a4 ♘a6! and Black
has solved his opening problems,
Forintos-Djurić, Forli 1989. The position is level.

A31)
8...a6 9 a4
Or:

a) 9 h4 h5 10 ♗g5 ♕c7 (10...♕a5
11 ♕d2 a6 transposes to Line A34) 11
♕d2 ♔h7 and now 12 f4?! exf4! 13
♗xf4 ♘g4! gave Black good chances
in Klein-Heyne, Germany 1996/7. 12
♘f1 is the right plan, preparing g4.

b) 9 ♗e3 ♘e8 10 ♕d2 f5 11 exf5
gxf5 12 f4 e4 13 ♘h5 ♗h8 14 ♖g1!?
(short castling is also good, although
long castling could be met by a ...b5
pawn sacrifice) 14...♘f6 (14...♕h4+?
15 ♗f2 ♕xh2 16 0-0-0 +−) 15 ♘xf6+
♗xf6 16 g4 ♔h8 (16...♗h4+ 17 ♔d1
gives White a clear advantage) 17

0-0-0 (better than 17 g5, Paszcwyk-
S.Steel, Durban 1995) 17...b5 18 gxf5
♗xf5 19 ♗g4 gives White attacking
chances.
9...b6
9...♘bd7 10 0-0 ♖b8 11 ♗g5 h6 12
♗e3 ♘e8 13 ♕d2 ♕h4! (Soby-O.Jak-
obsen, Danish Ch 1963) 14 ♕c2 and
White has just a minimal advantage.
10 h4
10 0-0 is a superior alternative.
10...h5 11 ♗g5 ♕d7 12 ♕d2 ♘h7
12...♔h7 would prevent ♗h6.
13 ♗h6 f6
Liardet-Neuenschwander, Geneva
1991. Here we suggest the surprising
retreat 14 ♗e3 since now that Black
has played ...f6, White's bishop will
be better in the coming middlegame.

A32)
8...♘a6 *(D)*

9 h4
9 0-0 is also good. Then 9...h5 10 a3
♘h7 11 ♗e3 h4 12 ♘h1 f5 13 exf5
gxf5 14 f4 (Adianto-Gi.Hernandez,
Manila OL 1992) 14...e4 with a slight
advantage for White.
9...♘c7

Or 9...h5 10 ♗g5 ♕a5 11 ♕d2 ♔h7 12 0-0 ♗d7 13 a3 ♖ae8 14 b4! ♕c7 (14...cxb4 15 axb4 ♕xb4 16 ♗e3!) 15 ♘b5 ♕b8 16 ♖ab1 and White has a clear advantage, Jenei-Cs.Laszlo, Budapest 1960.

10 a3

10 h5 is also good. Then 10...♕e7 11 ♗g5! ♗d7 12 ♗g4! a6 13 ♗xd7 ♕xd7 14 ♕f3 ♘ce8 15 a4 gave White an advantage in Krueger-Cummerow, Bargteheide 1989.

The text is a preparatory move, so that b4 can be played when appropriate.

10...a6 11 ♗g5 ♗d7 12 b4!

Now that Black cannot play ...♘d7 any more, this is the right time to play this.

12...b6 13 b5

13 ♖b1 is also good.

13...a5 14 ♕d2 ♕c8 15 h5 ♗g4 16 f3 ♗d7

16...♗xh5? 17 ♗xf6 ♗xf6 18 ♘xh5 gxh5 19 ♕h6! +−.

17 0-0-0

This is a logical continuation since the queenside has been closed.

17...♘ce8 18 ♖h4 ♕c7 19 ♖dh1

Forintos-Krähenbühl, Reykjavik 1982. White is clearly better on the kingside, and plans ♗d3, ♔c2, ♕c1, ♖1h2 and ♕h1.

A33)

8...♘e8 *(D)*

This position sometimes occurs by transposition from 7...♘e8 8 ♗e2 c5. White does best to return to the treatment with h4.

9 h4 f5 10 exf5 ♗xf5

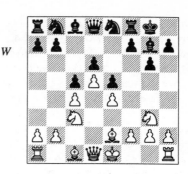

10...gxf5 11 ♘h5! gives White the advantage, as we can see in other games, with the difference that instead of ...c5 Black played something else.

11 h5 ♘d7

In case of 11...g5? White could control the light squares; e.g., 12 h6 ♗h8 13 ♘xf5 ♖xf5 14 ♘e4! and ♗g4 followed by ♗xg5 is inevitable.

12 hxg6 ♗xg6 13 ♘ge4

White is better since the position of the black king is not safe enough. The continuation is quite instructive.

13...♘df6 14 ♘g5 ♘c7 15 ♗e3

The knight on g5 is very unpleasant for Black; in addition it is not advisable to chase it away.

15...a6

15...h6 can be answered by 16 ♘e6!.

16 a4

Not only preventing ...b5, but also preparing a later ♖a3-g3.

16...♖b8 17 ♕d2 ♕d7

Planning ...♘g4 in order to exchange a piece.

18 ♖h4 ♖fe8 19 ♔f1!

The king looks for a safe place.

19...b6 20 ♔g1 ♖e7 21 ♖a3! ♕e8

The plan is ...♘h5-f4.

22 ♕d1 ♕f8 23 ♗c1

The third rank is being cleared.

23...e4 24 ♗f4 ♖ee8 25 ♕c1 ♕e7

Now the h4-rook is in danger.

26 ♖h1 ♖f8 27 ♘d1

27 ♕e3 is better, but it is almost impossible to play a whole game without mistakes.

27...♗h8

The only chance is 27...b5.

28 ♕e3 b5?

Too late!

29 ♕g3! +– ♘ce8 30 axb5 axb5 31 ♘xh7! ♘xh7 32 ♕xg6+ ♕g7 33 ♕e6+ ♕f7 34 ♖g3+

White won in the game Forintos-Karl, Zurich 1984.

A34)

8...♘bd7 *(D)*

W

9 h4

When the centre is closed, it is logical to attack on the kingside.

9...h5

9...♘e8 10 h5 a6 11 a4 ♖b8 and now 12 ♖a3 ♘c7 led to chances for both sides in Forintos-Gligorić, Belgrade 1961. Instead, 12 ♗d2 planning ♕c1 or ♗d3 is ±.

10 ♗g5 ♕a5 11 ♕d2 a6

The alternative is 11...♖e8, planning ...♘h7 but there is a problem: 12 ♘b5! ♕b6 and now:

a) 13 ♖b1 a6 14 ♘c3 is a good option for White.

b) 13 a4 and here:

b1) 13...♘f8?! 14 ♖a3?! (14 a5 is more logical) 14...a6 15 a5 ♕d8 16 ♘c3 ♗d7 17 ♘a4 ♗xa4 18 ♖xa4 b6 and Black has nearly equalized, Kupka-Boukal, Czechoslovak Cht (Harrachov) 1968.

b2) 13...a6 is better, since 14 a5 can be strongly met by 14...axb5, when Black has more then enough compensation for the queen.

With the text-move, Black prevents ♘b5.

12 a3!?

This move is more cunning than 12 0-0.

12...♖b8 13 0-0 b5?

13...♕c7 is better, when Black is only slightly worse.

14 b4! cxb4 15 axb4 ♕xb4 16 ♖fb1 ♕c5 17 cxb5 axb5 18 ♗e3 ♕c7 19 ♘xb5

+– T.Szekeres-Galgovics, Hungarian Cht 1993.

B)

7...h5 *(D)*

This move anticipates White's h4-h5 advance, keeping the possibility open to choose between ...a5, ...♘a6, ...♘bd7, etc., according to White's reply. This is a clever idea, the only problem being that the move ...h5 cannot be taken back later. White now has three ways to develop:

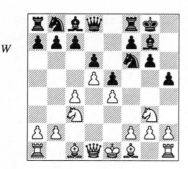

W

B1: 8 ♗g5   78
B2: 8 h4   79
B3: 8 ♗e2   80

B1)

8 ♗g5

This is the most natural line.

8...♕e8

This is the only logical reply.

9 h4 *(D)*

The most natural line. Other moves:

a) 9 ♕d2 (the start of an inaccurate plan) 9...♘h7 10 h4? (an instructive mistake) 10...♘xg5 11 hxg5 f6! (just in time, when the sacrifice on h5 is not good yet) 12 ♗e2 ♕e7 13 gxf6 ♕xf6 14 ♗xh5 (this sacrifice cannot be successful since the black queen defends the king properly; anyway, Black already has the upper hand) 14...gxh5 15 ♘xh5 ♕g6 16 ♘xg7 ♔xg7 17 0-0-0 ♘a6 18 ♖de1 ♗d7 19 ♖e3 ♖f4!. White's attack has lost its dynamism, and he remained with a material disadvantage in the game Vigh-Loginov, Budapest 1992.

b) 9 ♗d3 (the disadvantage of this bishop move can be that White does not threaten the sacrifice ♗xh5 any more) 9...♘h7 (9...♘a6 is also possible)

10 ♗e3 (White's threat is 11 ♘b5, to win one of the pawns) 10...h4 (we suggest 10...♕e7 instead) 11 ♘f1 (in the case of 11 ♘ge2 h3 12 g3 ♗g4 13 0-0 ♗f3 14 ♕c2 the black bishop is unpleasant on f3) 11...♘a6 12 ♘d2 f5 (a logical continuation, but given the unfavourable outcome, Black should prefer 12...♕e7, and possibly the plan with ...♗f6-g5) 13 f3 ♗f6 (before White castles kingside, the threat of ...f4 is not serious) 14 a3! c5 15 exf5 gxf5 16 ♕c2 ♗g5 17 ♗xg5 ♘xg5 18 0-0-0 ♗d7 19 ♖hg1 ♔h8 20 ♖df1 b5 21 cxb5 ♘c7 22 f4 e4 23 fxg5 exd3 24 ♕xd3 ♗xb5 25 ♘xb5 ♕xb5 26 ♘c4 f4 27 ♖f3 1-0 Hort-Uhlmann, German Ch (Bad Neuenahr) 1991.

c) 9 ♘b5 ♘a6 10 ♗e2 ♘h7 11 ♗e3 is a good continuation.

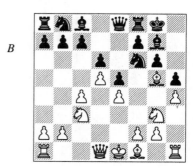

B

9...♘h7

9...a5 is best met by 10 ♗e2, transposing to Line B of Chapter 4 (Future Variation).

9...a6 10 ♗e2 ♘bd7 transposes to Line B of Chapter 1.

9...♔h7 (planning ...♘g8 and ...♗h6) cannot be recommended because of the sacrifice ♗e2xh5.

10 &e3

10 &d2 ♘d7 11 &e2 ♕e7 (threatening ...&f6) 12 ♘f1 ♘df6 13 g3 ♖e8 14 ♘e3 &h6 15 ♕c2 &d7 16 f3 c6 17 ♕d3!? (the game is made interesting by some unexpected queen moves) 17...♖ac8 18 ♘cd1 (the other plan is 18 ♖d1, when 18...c5 can be met by 19 ♖b1 with a later a3 and b4) 18...cxd5 (18...b5 19 cxb5 cxb5 20 ♕a3) 19 cxd5 a6 20 a4 ♖f8 (making room for the knight on e8) 21 ♕a3! ♘e8 22 ♕b3 ♖c7 (22...b5 23 axb5 axb5 24 &xb5 ♖b8 25 ♖a7) 23 &a5 ♖c5 24 ♕xb7! +− Forintos-Halasz, Balatonbereny 1984. 24...♖xa5 could be met by 25 b4.

10...♕e7 11 &e2 a6

In the case of 11...&f6 12 ♘f1 &xh4 13 &xh5 &g5 Black is on his way towards equalizing.

12 ♘f1 ♘d7 13 g3 ♘df6 14 ♘h2

Deciding over the position of the knight is riskier than 14 f3, preparing a later g4.

14...&d7 15 ♕b3 ♖fb8 16 a4 ♕f8!

16...b5 would be premature.

17 ♕c2! &h6 18 ♕d2 &xe3 19 ♕xe3 c5 20 ♖b1 ♔h8

20...♕d8, planning ...♕a5, is best. Most probably Black was afraid of 21 ♖g1 and g4.

21 b4 cxb4 22 ♖xb4 a5!

He is carving out the c5-square for himself, and finally manages to place a knight there, but in the meantime a lot of things could happen – and even more could have happened!

23 ♖b6 &e8 24 ♘b5 &xb5 25 ♖xb5 ♘d7

Forintos-Loginov, Budapest 1990.

Since two black rooks are busy on the queenside White should play 26 g4 hxg4 27 &xg4, planning h5. For example, 27...f5 28 h5! fxg4 29 hxg6 ♘hf6 30 ♘xg4+ ♔g8 31 ♘h6+ ♔g7 32 ♕g5!.

B2)

8 h4 *(D)*

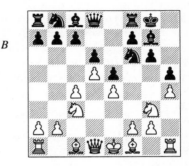

Beside 8 &g5 this is the other way to stop ...h4. Now Black has a choice:

B21: 8...♘h7 79
B22: 8...&g4 80

B21)

8...♘h7 9 &e2 ♘d7

Or 9...&f6, and now:

a) 10 &e3 (not the best) 10...♘d7! and now:

a1) 11 ♕d2 &xh4! 12 &xh5 &xg3 13 fxg3 gxh5 14 ♖xh5 f5 15 0-0-0 ♘df6 −+ Farrell-Rowson, Scottish Ch 1994.

a2) 11 ♘f1 is just slightly better. After 11...&xh4 12 &xh5 &g5 Black has nearly equalized.

b) 10 &h6! ♖e8 11 ♘f1 &xh4 12 &xh5 &g5 13 &g4 gives White the advantage.

10 ♘f1 ♘df6 11 ♘e3 c5 12 g3 ♗d7 13 a3 ♕c8 14 ♗d2 ♘g4 15 ♘xg4 hxg4 16 h5 gxh5 17 ♖xh5 f5

This is Black's plan, but he'll soon be disappointed. 18 exf5 ♗xf5 19 ♗e3 a6?! (19...♘f6 20 ♖h4) 20 ♗d3! e4 21 ♘xe4 ♗xb2 (presumably Black's plan was 21...♗xe4 22 ♗xe4 ♘f6 but he probably observed only now that it could be strongly met by 23 ♗f5 ♕e8 24 ♗e6+; it does not usually bode well when a plan has to be changed) 22 ♘xd6 ♗c3+ 23 ♔e2 ♗xd3+ 24 ♕xd3 ♕d7 25 ♖ah1 1-0 Kumaran-Britton, London Lloyds Bank 1988.

B22)

8...♗g4 9 ♗e2

9 ♕b3 and 9 f3 are at least as good.

9...♗xe2 10 ♘gxe2

10 ♕xe2 is also strong.

10...♘bd7 11 ♗g5

Now:

a) 11...♕e7?! (the continuation is quite instructive) 12 g4! (a typical move, which accelerates the attack) 12...♕e8 (12...hxg4 13 h5 gxh5 14 ♘g3 ♕e8 15 ♘f5 planning f3 with a strong attack on the kingside) 13 gxh5 ♘xh5 14 ♘g3 (first 14 ♘b5 is also strong) 14...♘df6 15 h5 f6 16 ♗xf4 exf4 17 ♘ge2 f5 (17...g5 18 h6) 18 ♕c2 and after castling queenside, White won in Berthelot-C.Thomas, corr. 1992.

b) 11...♕e8 12 ♘b5 ♕b8 is better.

B3)

8 ♗e2 *(D)*

White does not really bother about the possibility of ...h4, but he should not cry if he has cause to regret it later.

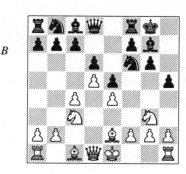

B

8...a5

Or 8...h4 9 ♘f1 ♘h7! 10 ♗e3 ♘d7 11 ♘d2 a5 12 f3 (other possibilities are 12 0-0 f5 13 exf5 gxf5 14 f4 and 12 ♕c2, planning 0-0-0) 12...♘c5, and now:

a) 13 ♘b3 b6 14 ♘xc5 (or 14 0-0) 14...bxc5 15 ♕d2 ♗d7 16 g3 ♕e7 17 0-0-0 ♖fb8 (Fokin-Loginov, Hungary 1992) and now 18 ♘b5! leads to balanced chances.

b) In case of 13 a3 a4! 14 ♗xc5 dxc5 15 ♘xa4 ♕g5 Black has good counterplay for the sacrificed pawn because White is missing his dark-squared bishop.

9 ♗g5

9 0-0 h4 10 ♘h1 ♘h7 11 ♗e3 f5 12 exf5 gxf5 13 f4 ♘d7 14 ♕d2 e4 15 ♘f2 ♘c5 16 ♔h1 ♔h8 and now in Vigh-P.Steiner, Oberwart 1992 White played 17 ♖ab1!?, planning a3 and b4. 17 ♖g1 could also be considered, to open the g-file by g3.

9...♕e8

This prevents the typical sacrifice on h5.

9...♘a6 10 ♗xh5!? (for 10 h4 see Line A13 of Chapter 4) 10...gxh5 11 ♘xh5 ♔h8 (threatening ...♗g4) 12 h3!

♘c5 13 ♕f3 ♘cd7 (there was no other choice) 14 h4 ♖g8 15 ♖h3 ♔h7 16 ♖g3 ♗h8 (now the only defence would be the move ...♖g6 but there is no time to play it) 17 ♘xf6+ ♘xf6 18 ♗xf6 ♗g4 19 ♖xg4 ♕xf6 20 ♔e2 and White is winning, Kras-Bachler, Orlando Park 1992.

10 ♕d2 ♘h7 11 ♗e3

The immediate 11 ♗h6 is better.

11...h4 12 ♘f1 ♘a6 13 0-0-0 ♗d7 14 ♗h6 ♗xh6 15 ♕xh6 ♕e7 16 g3 ♕g5+!

A typical solution for Black, to exchange both dark-squared bishops and queens.

17 ♕xg5 ♘xg5 18 ♘d2 ♘c5 19 f4

After 19 gxh4 ♘h3 20 ♖df1 f5 Black could take the initiative.

19...♘h3 20 ♖hf1 exf4 21 gxf4 ♖ae8 22 f5 gxf5 23 exf5 ♖e3 24 ♖f3 ♖fe8

With mutual chances, Oll-Uhlmann, Tallinn 1987.

C)

7...♘a6 (D)

This is a rare system because it has the drawback that the a6-knight cannot easily be brought into play.

Black, contrary to those lines where he has played ...♘bd7, leaves the diagonal of the c8-bishop open. This way he can gain counterplay, partly with the ...h5-h4 attack, and also controlling the g4-square. That is why we have only met 8 ♗e2 in reply.

8 ♗e2 c6 (D)

The best. Others:

a) 8...h5 (Black wins space on the kingside, and if possible will prod the g3-knight) 9 h4 (preventing ...h4) 9...♕e8 (Menadue-Britton, Hastings 1995) 10 ♗g5 (better than 10 ♗d2) 10...♘h7 11 ♗e3 ♗f6 12 ♘f1.

b) 8...♘d7 9 0-0 (9 h4 is more powerful) 9...h5 10 ♗e3 h4 11 ♘h1 f5 12 exf5 gxf5 13 f4 ♘f6 14 ♘f2 with a slight advantage for White, Dive-Britton, London 1994.

c) 8...♘e8 (supporting ...f5 or ...c6) 9 0-0 (9 h4 is also good) 9...c6 (here we suggest 9...♕h4, with a later ...♗h6) 10 ♗e3 f5 11 exf5 gxf5 (Degerman-Wikner, Sweden 1994) 12 dxc6! bxc6 13 ♘h5 f4 14 ♘xg7 ♘xg7 15 ♗c1 ♘c5 16 ♗f3 and White's chances are better.

d) 8...♕e7?! 9 h4 c5? (this worsens Black's chances further; the refutation is instructive) 10 h5 ♘c7 11 h6! (the aim of this thematic move is to create a strong pin from g5) 11...♗h8 12 ♗g5 a6 13 ♕d2 ♗d7 (Vandevoort-Brico, Huy 1991) and now 14 f4! is decisive, e.g. 14...exf4 15 ♕xf4 ♕e5 16 ♕xe5 and 0-0.

e) 8...♕e8 (preventing ♗g5) 9 h4 h5 10 ♗g5 ♘h7 (Breier-Balcerak, Binz 1995) and now 11 ♗e3 ♕e7 12 ♘f1 is necessary.

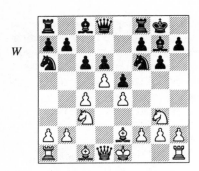

9 ♗g5

Other possibilities:

a) 9 h4 cxd5 10 cxd5 and now Black has two lines:

a1) 10...♗d7 is a position that can occur from 7...c6, but the knight is even less frequently placed on a6 there. 11 h5 ♕b6 (Gislason-Brendel, Reykjavik 1990) and now 12 ♖b1, planning ♗e3, is necessary.

a2) 10...h5 11 ♗g5 ♕e8? (this move is not advisable; 11...♕b6 is correct) 12 ♕d2 ♔h7 13 ♘b5 (this exposes the shortcomings of ...♕e8)

13...♕d7 (Liardet-Arakhamia, Geneva 1990) 14 ♖c1! favours White.

b) 9 0-0 ♕c7 (Black does not intend to move his c-pawn for a long time) 10 h3 h5 11 ♖e1 h4 12 ♘f1 ♘h7 13 ♖b1 f5 14 b4 (better is first 14 dxc6) 14...c5 15 b5!? ♘b8 16 exf5 gxf5 17 ♖b3! (the closure of the queenside can be understood now: White is going to use the rook in the attack on the king) 17...♔h8 18 ♗h5! (threatening ♗g6 and ♕h5, which cannot be allowed) 18...♖f6 19 f4! e4 Forintos-Van Wely, Metz 1988. Later the opening of the g-file would have decided.

9...h6 10 ♗e3 cxd5 11 cxd5 h5

This position can also be reached via 9 ♗e3 cxd5 10 cxd5 h5.

12 h3!? ♘h7 13 ♕d2 ♗f6

The ...♗g5 plan is not good here. Better is 13...h4 and ...f5.

14 0-0 h4 15 ♘h1 ♗d7 16 f4! exf4 17 ♗xf4 ♖c8 18 ♘f2

White won in the game Bönsch-Poldauf, Bundesliga 1991/2.

7   6...c5 7 d5 e6 8 ♗e2 exd5 9 exd5

1 d4 ♘f6 2 c4 g6 3 ♘c3 ♗g7 4 e4 d6 5 ♘ge2 0-0 6 ♘g3 c5 7 d5 e6 8 ♗e2 exd5 9 exd5 *(D)*

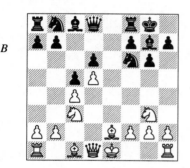

B

The d5-pawn and the g3-knight mean a slight advantage for White, partly because ....♗f5 and ...♘e4 will not be feasible for a while. White takes less risk in this system than in the case of 9 cxd5 (Chapter 8), where Black has several sources of counterplay. The choice is a question of style and preference.

Now Black has several moves:

A: 9...♖e8	83
B: 9...♘bd7	86
C: 9...♘e8	90
D: 9...♘a6	91

Less popular are:

a) 9...h5 10 ♗g5 ♕b6 11 ♕d2 (here 11 ♕b3 is the right reply since after exchanging queens the d6-pawn is more vulnerable) 11...♘h7 12 ♗f4 f5!? 13 h4?! (better is 13 ♘b5) 13...♘d7 14 ♖b1 ♘e5 and Black has the better chances, Reichmann-Kovaliov, Porz 1990.

b) 9...♘fd7 10 0-0?! (10 ♗e3 is necessary) 10...f5 11 f4 ♗xc3! 12 bxc3 (the c1-bishop is now closed in by its own pawns) 12...♘f6 13 h3?! ♘bd7 14 ♗d3 ♕a5! 15 ♗d2 ♘b6 and Black is slightly better, A.Hoffman-Barria, Cordoba Z 1998.

c) 9...♕e7 10 0-0 ♘bd7 11 ♖e1 ♖e8 12 ♗d2 a6 13 a4 ♕f8 14 ♕c1 ♘e5 (14...h5 is more precise) 15 h3 h5 16 f4 ♘ed7 17 ♕c2 h4 18 ♘f1 ♘h7 19 ♗f3 ♗d4+ 20 ♔h1! ♖xe1 (better is 20...f5) 21 ♗xe1! (Black has development problems because of the weak h4- and d6-pawns) 21...♘df6 22 ♘e2 and the d4-bishop is in danger, Forintos-Najbar, Poland 1997.

A)
9...♖e8

This move controls the e4-square. Now:

A1: 10 ♗f4!	84
A2: 10 0-0	85

10 h4 is not an effective idea. After 10...♘fd7!? (10...♘g4!?) 11 h5 f5 12

hxg6 hxg6 13 ♗h6 ♘e5 14 ♗xg7 ♔xg7 15 ♕d2 ♘f7! (a good place for the knight) 16 0-0-0 ♘d7 17 f4 a6 18 ♖de1 ♘f6 the chances are equal, because the black king is defended well by two knights, Szabo-Kavalek, Lugano 1970.

A1)
10 ♗f4! *(D)*

White threatens 11 ♘b5 and makes it difficult for Black to achieve the important manoeuvre with ...♘bd7-e5.

10...a6

Or:

a) 10...♘g4 11 0-0 (11 ♕d2 is also possible) 11...♘xh2 (this motif is good to know anyway) 12 ♖e1 ♘g4 13 ♗xg4 ♖xe1+ (thanks to this the knight can escape) 14 ♕xe1 ♗xg4 and now White should continue by 15 ♘ge4! with an advantage, instead of 15 ♘b5 (McCarthy-Hergott, British Ch (Swansea) 1987).

b) 10...h5!? aims to secure the e4-square. 11 0-0 (11 ♗g5 is better; the compensation for the lost tempo is that h5 may prove a weakness later on) 11...h4 12 ♘h1 ♘e4 and the aim of

...♖e8 has been achieved, i.e. the e4-square is secure. Black is better, Tawakol-Brendel, Dortmund 1993.

c) 10...h6 should be answered by 11 h4!, while 11 ♘b5 is a mistake: 11...g5! 12 ♗xd6?? a6 13 ♗c7 ♕d7 14 ♗xb8 axb5 −+.

11 0-0 *(D)*

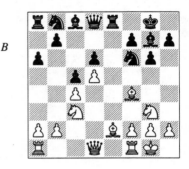

11...♕e7

Where shall we put the queen? On c7 or f8 via e7? It is slightly rarer in practice to put it on c7, and this is not without reason. 11...♕c7 12 ♕d2 (12 ♕a4!?) 12...♘bd7 and now:

a) 13 ♗h6 ♗h8 14 ♖ae1 ♘f8 15 h3 ♗d7 16 f4 favours White, Forintos-Daum, Heppenheim 1981.

b) 13 ♖fe1 ♘e5 and now:

b1) 14 ♗f1 (premature) 14...♗d7 15 ♗g5 ♔h8!? and in Kumaran-Arakhamia, Oakham 1990, 16 ♘ge4 was not good enough because of 16...♘g8! and the following pawn attack with ...h6 and ...f5.

b2) 14 h3 is more precise, so that after 14...♗d7 15 ♗g5 White might threaten f4.

12 ♖e1 ♘bd7 13 ♕d2 ♘e5 14 h3! **♕f8**

Black is planning to continue with ...h6 and ...g5.

15 ≗e3! h5 16 f4

After careful preparation the general idea is accomplished. Of course, concrete calculations were also necessary.

16...♘ed7

16...♘eg4 (White sometimes must take into account the sacrifice ...♖xe3) 17 hxg4 ♖xe3 18 ♕xe3 ♘xg4 19 ♗xg4! ♗d4 20 ♗xc8 ♖xc8 21 ♖ad1 ♗xe3+ 22 ♖xe3 means a clear advantage for White.

17 ♗f3

17 ♗d3 could also be considered, since after 17...h4 18 ♘f1 ♘h5, 19 ♕f2! ♗f6 20 ♘e4 is strong.

17...♘b6! 18 b3 ♔h8

After 18...♘h7 19 f5! White is a little better due to his extra space.

19 ♖ac1

The natural 19 ♖e2 is better. Then 19...h4 20 ♘f1 ♘e4? can be refuted by 21 ♗xe4 ♖xe4 22 ♘xe4 ♗xa1 23 ♕e1!.

19...♘g8 20 a4!

The a5 advance can sometimes be unpleasant. Now:

a) 20...♖xe3 21 ♖xe3 ♗d4 22 ♖ce1 (White intends to occupy the e-file) 22...♘h6 23 ♔h2 ♗xe3 24 ♕xe3! h4?! (the h-pawn can be weak later on, but White had the better chances in any case) 25 ♘ge4 ♘f5 26 ♕f2 ♕h6 27 ♗g4! (Black has problems with the d6- and h4-pawns) 27...♗d7 28 ♗xf5 (or 28 a5, winning material) 28...gxf5 29 ♘g5 ♔g8 30 ♖e7 and White soon won in Forintos-Tsimmerman, Hungarian Cht 1997/8.

b) After the better 20...f5 21 a5 ♘d7 22 ♗f2 White still has the upper hand.

A2)

10 0-0 *(D)*

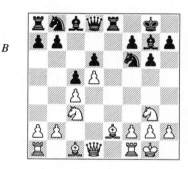

This allows Black to play the important move ...♘bd7.

10...h5

Or:

a) For 10...♘bd7 see Line B11.

b) 10...♘fd7? 11 ♘ge4! ♗xc3 (or 11...♕e7 12 ♗g5 ♕f8 13 ♗f4 ♗e5 14 ♗xe5! with advantage) 12 ♘xc3 f6 13 b3 ± Alber-Kopp, Hessen 1990. On b2, the bishop will be very powerful, providing support for the f4 advance.

c) 10...a6 can be met by 11 ♗f4!.

d) 10...♘a6 and now:

d1) 11 ♗f4 ♘c7 and then:

d11) 12 a4 is directed against ...b5. Now the queen manoeuvre 12...♕e7 13 ♕d2 ♕f8 did not help in Comas Fabrego-Silva, Elista OL 1998 because White can expect a slight advantage after 14 ♘b5 ♘xb5 15 axb5 a6 16 ♖a2 planning b4.

d12) 12 ♕d2 ♕e7 13 a3! ♕f8 14 b4 b6 15 bxc5 bxc5 16 ♖ab1 ♘d7 17

♘ce4 and the way for the queen has
also opened towards a5, with advantage for White in Taimanov-Silva, Paz
e Amizade 1985.

d2) 11 h3 ♘c7 and here:

d21) 12 f4 should be answered by
12...h5! here as well. Instead, 12...b5!?
13 cxb5 ♘fxd5 14 ♘xd5 ♗d4+ 15
♔h2 ♘xd5 16 ♗f3 ♗e6 17 f5! ± shows
an interesting motif.

d22) 12 ♗f4 (hindering the manoeuvre ...♘d7-e5) 12...a6 13 a4 b6
14 ♕d2 ♖b8 15 ♖ab1! (it is a good
plan to counter ...b5 with b4) 15...♕e7
(Pnevmonidis-Hua, Quebec 1997) 16
♖fe1 gives White a slight advantage.

e) 10...h6 11 ♗f4 (White need not
be afraid of ...g5) 11...b6 12 ♖e1 a6 13
♕d2 g5?! 14 ♗e3 ♖a7 15 h3 ♖ae7 16
♗d3 and White controls the important
f5-square, Pazos-Juarez Flores, Novi
Sad OL 1990.

11 ♗g5 ♕b6 12 ♕d2 ♘bd7 13 a4!

Threatening ♘b5 and a later a5.

13...a6 14 ♖fe1 ♘f8

Black's plan is 15...♘8h7 16 ♗f4
h4 17 ♘h1 ♘e4. But here follows a
surprise and this is not a coincidence
when the knight is on the back rank.

15 ♗xf6! ♗xf6 16 ♗xh5 *(D)*

White's domination of the e-file
strengthens the attack.

16...♖xe1+ 17 ♖xe1 ♗d7

17...gxh5 18 ♘xh5 ♕d8 (18...♗g7
19 ♕g5) 19 ♖e8!.

18 ♗d1!

A strong move, and there is a trick
behind it.

18...♕b4 19 ♘ge4 ♗e5 20 h4!

The initiative must be sought where
we are strong. The bishop-pair is not
enough compensation for Black. The
position has a tactical point again, that
is why it is instructive.

20...♕xc4?

20...f5 21 ♘g5 ♕xc4 22 g3 is good
for White

21 ♘xd6! ♕d4

21...♗xd6? loses material after 22
♖e4.

**22 ♕xd4 ♗xd4 23 a5 ♖b8 24 ♘c4
♗b5 25 ♘b6 ♘h7 26 ♗f3**

White won with his extra pawn in
Forintos-Kindermann, Budapest 1986.

B)

9...♘bd7 *(D)*

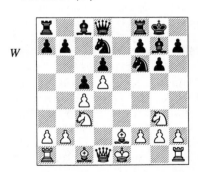

This is thought to be the best. It aims
for both ...♘e5, and after the ...b5

pawn sacrifice the knight may attack the d5-pawn from b6. Now:

B1: 10 0-0 87
B2: 10 ♗f4 89

10 ♗e3 promises less: 10...a6 11 a4 b6 (an old-fashioned concept, but it is still played in our time) 12 ♕d2 ♖e8 13 0-0 ♖a7 (it cannot be foreseen when the plan can be continued) 14 h3 ♕e7 15 ♖fe1 ♕f8 16 ♔h1 (preparing f4; 16 a5 could also be considered) 16...h5 17 f4 ♗h6 18 ♗f3 and White is only slightly better, Forintos-Sapi, Hungarian Ch 1976.

B1)
10 0-0
Now:

B11: 10...♖e8 87
B12: 10...♘e8 88

Black has some less significant defences:

a) 10...a6 is useful mainly if it encourages the response a4. Otherwise it may lose time: 11 ♗g5! (11 ♗f4 ♘e5 12 ♕d2 is also good; compare Line B2) 11...h6 12 ♗f4 ♘e5 13 ♕d2 ♔h7 14 ♗xe5! dxe5 (Pukropski-Porubszki, Badenweiler 1995) and now 15 ♖ad1 gives White an advantage.

b) 10...♘e5 11 h3! (11 ♗g5 h6! was equal in L.Horvath-Medl, Zalakaros 1993) 11...♘e8 (planning ...f5; inserting 11...a6 12 a4 does not alter things either – see line 'b3'; what is more, 12 a4 is not even necessary) 12 f4 ♘d7 13 f5!? and now:

b1) 13...♗d4+ 14 ♔h1! ♕h4 15 ♖f4 ±.

b2) 13...♕e7 14 ♗f4 ♘e5 15 ♕d2 gxf5 16 ♗g5 ♗f6 and now instead of 17 ♗xf6 (Züger-Barlov, Lugano 1988) we suggest 17 ♘xf5 ±.

b3) 13...♘e5 14 ♘ce4 h6 15 ♗e3 ± (in Behle-Funke, 2nd Bundesliga 1988/9 this occurred with the moves ...a6 and a4 moves inserted). Now 15...♕h4 is refuted by 16 f6!.

B11)
10...♖e8 11 ♗f4 *(D)*
Or:

a) 11 f4 (this is premature here too) 11...h5! 12 h3 a6 13 f5 h4 14 ♘h1 ♘h7! with chances for both sides, Rubio-de la Riva, Saragossa 1994.

b) 11 ♗g5 (a good alternative for White) 11...h6?! 12 ♗e3 ♘e5 13 h3 ♔h7 14 ♕d2 ♕e7 15 ♖ae1 ♖b8 (J.Rodrigues-Durão, Portuguese Cht 1993) and now 16 f4 ♘ed7 17 ♗d3 gives White an advantage.

11...♘e5 12 ♕d2 a6 13 h3!?
White does not mind the ...b5 sacrifice.

a) 13 a4 (White decides to prevent ...b5) 13...♕a5!? (the alternatives are 13...♕c7 and 13...♕e7) and now:

a1) 14 h3 ♕b4 (a bold move) 15 b3! h5?! (admitting the error by 15...♕a5 is the only chance) 16 a5! ♗d7 17 ♕c2! (Black is helpless) 17...b5 (17...h4 also gives some practical chances as White has to find 18 ♘ce4 hxg3 19 ♘xd6!) and now instead of 18 ♖fb1?! (Navarovszky-Jansa, Tbilisi 1965) White should play 18 ♘xb5!, threatening ♗d2, with a clear advantage.

a2) 14 ♖fe1 ♗g4 (an interesting idea, but 14...h5 is better) 15 ♗f1! ♘h5!? 16 ♘xh5 ♗xh5 17 ♘e4 ♕d8 18 h3 f6! 19 ♗xe5! ♖xe5 20 f4 ♖e8 (Serper-Fishbein, New York 1996) and now White should not be afraid of the rook sacrifice: after 21 g4 ♖xe4 22 ♖xe4 f5 23 gxf5 White is better.

b) 13 ♗g5 and then:

b1) 13...♕c7 14 a4 h5 15 f4! ♘eg4 (planning ...♘e3 or ...♘h6) 16 f5 ♘h7 17 ♗xg4! hxg4 18 f6! ♗h8 19 ♘ce4 (White is clearly better, but the rest is also instructive) 19...♗f5 20 ♘xf5 ♖xe4 21 ♘e7+ ♔f8 22 ♗h6+ ♔e8 23 ♗g7!! ♗xg7 24 fxg7 ♔xe7 25 ♕h6 ♕d8 26 ♕h4+! g5 27 ♕xh7 ♖e5 28 ♖xf7+ 1-0 Serper-Kotronias, Gausdal 1991.

b2) 13...♕b6!? is Serper's suggestion. After 14 ♖ae1 White has just a minimal advantage.

13...♖b8 14 a4 ♕a5?! 15 ♕c2!

This makes room for the bishop on d2.

15...h5

After 15...♕b4 16 a5! the queen is in danger; for example, 16...♗d7 17 ♘d1!, 16...♘xc4 17 ♗xc4 or 16...b5 17 ♘xb5 ♖xb5 18 ♗xe5 with a clear advantage to White.

16 ♗g5! ♘h7 17 ♗d2 ♕d8

17...h4 does not equalize either: 18 ♘ge4 ♗f5 19 f4 ♘d7 20 ♗d3!.

18 f4 ♕h4

18...♘d7 19 f5! is also good for White.

19 fxe5 ♗xe5 20 ♘ge4 ♗d4+ 21 ♔h1 ♗xh3 22 ♖e1!

1-0 Forintos-Manhardt, Austrian Cht 1998.

B12)

10...♘e8

To prepare ...f5 and make room for the ...♘e5-f7 manoeuvre.

11 ♗f4

This allows ...♗xc3, as while the way is clear for the c1-bishop, this is not a serious threat. Other moves:

a) 11 ♗e3 (to free the f-pawn to advance; a future ♕d2 and ♗h6 can be prepared this way too) 11...h6 12 ♕d2 ♔h7 13 f4 f5 14 h3 ♘df6 15 ♗f2 ♗d7 16 ♖ab1 h5?! (Black should overcome this kind of temptation!) 17 ♖fe1 ♘g8 18 ♘f1! ♘h6 19 ♘h2 ♗f6 20 ♘f3 ♘f7 21 a3 a5 (Forintos-Masić, Vršac 1973) and now 22 ♗d3 and ♕c2 keeps the advantage.

b) 11 ♗d2 is more passive than the other bishop moves, but is still playable:

b1) 11...♕h4 12 ♘ge4 h6 13 g3 ♕e7 14 f4 f5 15 ♘f2 ♘c7 16 a4 b6 and Black has nearly equalized, A.Hoffman-G.Mohr, Elista OL 1998.

b2) 11...f5 12 ♕c1 ♘e5 13 h3 ♘c7 14 ♖e1 ♕f6 (Barkhagen-Degraeve, Hilversum ECC 1993) 15 ♗g5 followed later by f4 means a slight advantage for White.

c) 11 ♕c2 does not lead to an advantage either: 11...f5 12 f4 ♕h4 13 ♗d2 (13 ♗e3 ♘c7 planning ...♖e8xe3 is equal) 13...♘df6 14 ♗e1 ♕h6 15 h3 ♘c7 16 a3 ♗d7 with balanced chances, Portisch-Uhlmann, Budapest 1962.

d) 11 f4 ♗d4+ 12 ♔h1 ♗xc3 (taking the knight is logical only when f4 has been played, and so the c1-bishop is hindered by White's own pawns) 13 bxc3 f5 14 ♗d3 ♘b6 15 ♗d2 ½-½ Comas Fabrego-Watanabe, Santiago jr Wch 1990.

11...f5

11...h6 12 ♕d2 ♔h7 (a more leisurely approach) 13 ♖ae1 (13 ♗e3 and f4 can be considered, preventing the manoeuvre ...♘e5-f7) 13...f5 14 ♗d3 ♘e5 is equal, Ker-Grivas, Novi Sad OL 1990.

12 ♕d2 ♘e5 13 ♖fe1 ♘f7

This is the ideal defensive set-up for Black.

14 ♗e3 ♘f6 15 h3 ♗d7 16 f4 ♖e8

Black threatens ...♖xe3 and ...♘g4.

17 ♗d3 a6 18 a4

18 a3 is more active.

18...♕a5 19 ♕c2 ♖e7 20 ♗d2 ♖ae8!

Nedobora-Striković, Candas 1992 soon ended in a draw.

B2)

10 ♗f4 *(D)*

This move restricts Black's options, because the d6-pawn has to be defended.

10...♘e8

Or:

a) 10...♘e5 and now:

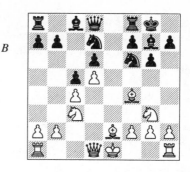

a1) 11 ♕d2 ♖e8 (11...♘e8 transposes to the main line) 12 0-0 a6 13 ♗g5 ♕b6 planning ...♕b4, Serper-Van Wely, Krumbach 1991. White should now continue by 14 f4 ♘eg4 15 f5! with an advantage, e.g. 15...h6 16 ♗xf6 ♘xf6 17 fxg6 fxg6 18 ♗d3.

a2) 11 0-0 h5?! 12 ♗g5 ♕b6 13 ♕b3! ♕c7 (the d6-pawn would be in trouble after an exchange of queens) 14 f4 ♘eg4 15 h3 ♘h6 (15...♘e3? 16 ♘b5) 16 ♗d3 ♘h7 17 ♖ae1 (17 ♘b5 is even better) gave White a clear advantage in Flear-Van Wely, Bad Mondorf 1991.

b) 10...♕b6?! is not recommended, because the ...♕b4 plan is difficult to achieve: 11 ♕d2 ♖e8 12 0-0 ♘e5 13 ♗g5 and now if 13...♕b4, then 14 a3 ♕b3 15 ♘ce4!, while 13...a6 transposes to line 'a1'.

11 ♕d2 ♘e5

Or:

a) 11...f5 is also good:

a1) 12 ♗h6 ♘e5 13 ♗xg7 ♘xg7 14 f4 ♘d7 15 0-0 ♘f6 with equality, Szabo-Ciocaltea, Hamburg Echt 1965.

a2) 12 h4 h5 (12...♗f6 13 ♗h6! ±) 13 ♗g5 with the more comfortable position for White.

b) 11...a6 12 a4 ♖b8 13 0-0 ♘e5
14 ♗h6 f6 15 ♗xg7 ♔xg7 16 f4 with
an advantage for White, Taimanov-
Bertok, Vinkovci 1970.
12 h4!? ♕e7!
The ...♘xc4 threat makes the white
king decide on a location.
12...f5 is the alternative: 13 h5 ♘f7
14 hxg6 hxg6 15 ♗e3! a6 Forintos-
Tringov, Ljubljana 1969. Now 16 ♗d3
planning ♘ge2-f4 is a flexible plan for
White; only later will he decide where
to put his king.
13 ♔f1
13 0-0-0 is braver and more critical.
13...h5! 14 ♘ge4 a6 15 a4
15 ♖e1 is better, planning ♕e3 and
♘xd6.
15...♗d7
= Mäki-Yrjölä, Finnish Cht 1998.

C)
9...♘e8 *(D)*

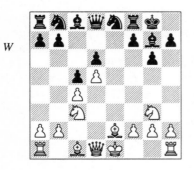

W

Black aims to establish control over
the e4-square with a quick ...f5. He
also opens the way for the queen and
the g7-bishop. Now:
C1: 10 ♗e3   90
C2: 10 h4   90

C1)
10 ♗e3
It is reasonable not to be in a hurry
with castling since there are more important moves to play first.
10...♘d7
In case of 10...♕h4, 11 ♕d2 is unpleasant.
11 ♕d2 f5
This move prepares the regrouping
...♘e5-f7, but White can prevent it.
12 f4 ♘c7
Now only one of the black knights
remains on the kingside. In case of
12...♘ef6 13 0-0 ♖e8 14 ♖fe1 White
is slightly better.
Now (after 12...♘c7):
a) 13 a4 (too cautious) 13...♖e8 14
♗f2 (not 14 0-0?? ♖xe3! – one must
always pay attention to this motif!)
14...♘f6 15 0-0 a5! ½-½ Forintos-
G.Mohr, Austrian Cht 1999. Since the
queenside is closed, the only chance to
do something is on the kingside by
♗f3, h3, ♘h1, ♗h4 and ♘f2 preparing
g4. In the meantime Black may occupy
the e-file. Then White's attack would
lose power after exchanging the rooks.
b) The other and more flexible
possibility is 13 0-0 b5!? (13...a6 14
a4; or 13...♖e8 14 ♗f2) 14 cxb5 ♘b6 15
♗f2 ♗b7 16 a4! and White is better.

C2)
10 h4
This move lessens the effect of ...f5,
but does not prevent it.
10...f5
Or 10...h5 11 ♗g5 (here we suggest
11 ♘ge4, when 11...f5 can be met by
12 ♘g5) 11...f6 12 ♗f4 ♘d7 (also

possible is 12...f5) 13 ♘ge4! ♕e7 14 ♕d2 ♘e5 15 0-0-0 a6 16 ♖de1 ♗d7 17 ♔b1 ♘c7 18 ♘xc5 dxc5 19 d6 ♗f5+ 20 ♔a1 ♕d7 21 dxc7 ♕xc7 (Remlinger-Formanek, Philadelphia 1992) and now 22 f3, planning g4, is best, and yields an advantage.

11 h5 ♘d7

11...g5?! can be met by the standard 12 f4.

12 hxg6 hxg6 13 ♗h6 ♗xh6

Better is 13...♘e5 planning ...♘f7.

14 ♖xh6 ♕g5 15 ♕d2 ♕xd2+ 16 ♔xd2

It is instructive how Topalov undermines Black's solid pawn-structure.

16...♔g7 17 ♖ah1 ♘df6

Now ...♘h5 is the threat.

18 ♖6h2 ♗d7 19 a3! ♘c7 20 b4 ♖h8 21 ♖xh8 ♖xh8 22 ♖b1!

He still needs one of the rooks. Some more moves are instructive: 22...b6 23 f4! ♖e8 24 ♗f3 ♔f7 25 ♘ge2 ♔g7 26 bxc5 dxc5 27 ♘c1! and the knight is heading towards e5, which gave White an advantage in Topalov-Danailov, Candas 1992.

D)

9...♘a6 (D)

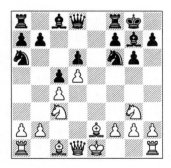

Sometimes 5...♘a6, and often 6...c5 7 d5 ♘a6, can transpose to this position. The aim is to prepare ...b5 after ...♘c7 even with a sacrifice to weaken the d5-pawn.

10 0-0

Or:

a) 10 ♗e3 ♘c7 11 ♕d2 ♖e8 12 0-0 ♖b8 13 ♖ab1 ♘g4 (this could have been played earlier) 14 ♗f4 ♘e5 (much better than 14...♗e5? 15 ♗xe5 ♖xe5 16 h3 ♘f6 17 f4 ♖e8 18 f5 with an attack for White, Strenzke-Klotzki, Bargteheide 1989) 15 ♗h6 f5 16 ♗xg7 ♔xg7 17 a3 ♕h4 18 f4 ♘f7 19 b4 is slightly better for White.

b) 10 ♗g5 h6 11 ♗e3 ♘c7 12 ♕d2 ♔h7 and then:

b1) 13 h4?! (White is trying too hard to exploit the weakness of h6) 13...♘g4! 14 ♗f4 ♘e5 and Black equalized in Forintos-Karl, Imperia 1992, since the h4-pawn gave problems sooner for White.

b2) Better is 13 0-0; for example, 13...♘g4 14 ♗xg4 ♗xg4 15 f4 ♖e8 16 ♔h1 ♕h4 17 ♖ae1 with a slight advantage.

c) 10 ♗f4 ♘c7 11 0-0 is also good – see note 'c' to White's 11th move.

10...♘c7 (D)

Or 10...♗d7 11 ♗f4 ♖e8 12 ♕d2 (12 ♗xd6 ♕b6!) 12...♕b6 and now instead of 13 ♖ab1?! (Garcia Palermo-J.Fernandes, Rio de Janeiro 1999), when 13...h5! equalizes, White should play 13 h3.

For 10...♖e8, see note 'd' to Black's 10th move in Line A2.

After the text-move White must decide whether he is afraid of ...b5.

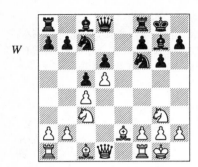

W

D1: 11 a4   92
D2: 11 ♖e1   93

Or:

a) 11 f4? can be met by 11...h5! (and not 11...a6?! 12 f5!, as happened in Quaresma-Bonaveri, Szeged jr Wch 1994).

b) 11 ♗g5 h6 12 ♗f4 ♖e8 13 ♕d2 g5 (this can be regretted later because of f4) 14 ♗e3 ♘g4 (14...b5? 15 cxb5 ♗b7 16 ♗c4 ♖e5 17 f4 favours White, B.Vigh-Szlovak, Hungary 1977) 15 ♗xg4 ♗xg4 16 ♔h1, planning f4, leaves White just slightly better.

c) For the better 11 ♗f4 ♖e8 see note 'd1' to Black's 10th move in Line A2.

d) 11 h3 a6 12 a4 ♖b8 13 ♗f4 ♘fe8 14 ♕d2 f5 (this is similar to the best defensive position, but it lacks a black knight on e5) 15 ♖fe1 ♗d7 16 ♗g5 ♘f6 17 ♕f4 ♗e8 18 ♗d3 b5 19 axb5 axb5 20 b3 (a typical and simple solution) 20...bxc4 (after the slightly better 20...b4 21 ♘d1 ♖a8 22 ♖b1 ♗f7 23 ♘e3 White has almost a free hand on the kingside) 21 ♗xc4 ♗b5 22 ♘xb5 ♘xb5 23 ♖e6, Bozinović-Bosković, Zadar 1997. White occupies the two open files, with a clear advantage.

D1)
11 a4
This does not allow the ...b5 pawn sacrifice.
11...♘fe8
Other possibilities:

a) 11...♘d7 12 ♗f4 ♘e5 13 ♕d2 ♖e8 14 ♖fe1 f5 15 ♗g5 ♗f6 16 ♗xf6 ♕xf6 17 f4 with a slight advantage for White.

b) 11...b6 12 h3 a6 13 ♗f4 (partly to lure the g-pawn forward; objectively better is 13 ♗e3 with a later f4) 13...h6!? 14 ♕d2 ♔h7 15 ♗d3 (the immediate 15 ♖ab1 is better) 15...♖b8 16 ♖ab1 b5 17 b3 with equal chances, Forintos-Rukavina, Rijeka 1967.

c) For 11...♖e8 12 ♖e1 see Line D2.

12 ♗f4 ♘a6 13 ♕d2 ♘b4
This knight insertion is effective if there is an open line nearby. As it is not so now, White does not bother about the knight.
14 ♖fe1 a6 15 ♗f3!
As Black cannot oppose on the e-file.
15...h6?
Black hopes that White cannot take on h6 because of the ...♘c2 fork, but this is incorrect.
16 ♗xh6! ♗xh6 17 ♕xh6 ♘c2 18 ♖xe8! ♖xe8
18...♕xe8 loses to 19 ♘ce4 ♕e5 20 ♖c1 ♘d4 21 ♘h5!.
19 ♗e4! ♖xe4
19...♘xa1? 20 ♘h5.
20 ♘cxe4 ♘xa1 21 ♘h5

The whole attack is based on this.
21...gxh5 22 &f6+ &xf6 23 &xf6 &d7 24 &xd6

White has an obvious advantage, Meleghegyi-Perenyi, Balatonbereny 1980.

D2)
11 &e1 *(D)*

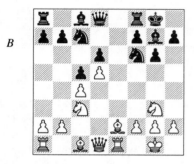

The development of the c1-bishop depends on the opponent's reply.

11...&e8

11...&fe8 12 a4 should be compared with Line D1.

12 a4

Preventing ...b5, cxb5 &b7. 12 h3 and 12 &f4 are alternatives.

12...&g4

12...&d7 is more natural.

When the text-move was played against me it was a novelty. Black seeks an exchange or to provoke a weakening. After thinking for ten minutes, but still unwillingly, I made a move with the pawn.

13 f3

White control over the e3-square is weakened, and the way for the e2-bishop gets blocked. Still, I thought it better to keep the bishops, because the black bishop is in the way on either c8 or d7.

13...&c8 14 &f4! a6 15 &d2

White has a slight advantage. There is harmony among his pieces, which makes it easy for Black to blunder.

15...b6 16 &g5

A standard and very unpleasant pin.

16...&e7 17 &f4! &e5! 18 &xe5 dxe5

18...&xe5? loses a pawn to 19 &f4.

19 &ce4! &xe4

19...&d7? 20 &d6 &f8 21 &e7.

20 &xe4

Now &d6 and a5 are the threats.

20...f5! 21 &f6+

Not 21 &d6?! &f8 22 &e7? &d7, when the d6-knight is in danger.

21...&xf6 22 &xf6 &f7 23 &g5

With his bishop-pair White has the better chances since there are pawns all over the board.

23...a5! 24 &ad1 &d7 25 b3 &a6 26 &d2 &g7 27 &d1 h6 28 &h4 g5 29 &f2 &b4 30 g4! f4 31 &e4 &f6 32 &e1! &e7 33 &de2 &ae8 34 &c3 &c8

34...h5 35 h4! hxg4 36 hxg5+ &xg5 37 &xe5+ wins for White.

35 h4! &b7 36 &h2 &g6 37 hxg5 hxg5

An instructive position. One way of using the bishop-pair can clearly be seen here; paradoxically White gives up one of his bishops at the right moment, exchanging it for the knight.

38 &xb4! axb4 39 &c2 &g7 40 &h5

The black pawns now started falling in Forintos-Hresc, Austrian Cht 1999.

8 6...c5 7 d5 e6 8 ♗e2 exd5 9 cxd5 (Benoni line)

1 d4 ♘f6 2 c4 g6 3 ♘c3 ♗g7 4 e4 d6 5 ♘ge2 0-0 6 ♘g3 c5 7 d5 e6 8 ♗e2 exd5 9 cxd5 *(D)*

B

Now the game transposes into the Modern Benoni. White's play has to be found on the kingside and in the centre because of his pawn-majority in this sector. Black usually prepares his counterplay on the queenside, and tries to slow down White's plans, so both players have to play on the whole board. There are considerable risks for both sides, and, owing to this, really serious blunders may be made even quite early on by both players.

A: 9...a6   94
B: 9...♘a6   97
C: 9...b6   101
D: 9...h5   103
E: 9...♖e8   104
Lines D and E are rare.

A)
9...a6

The most popular and best defence. Since ...b5 would give Black good chances, it really must be prevented:
10 a4 ♘bd7

For 10...♖e8 11 ♗f4, see Line E.

Or 10...h5 11 ♗g5 (11 f3 is also good – see Line D) 11...♕e8 12 ♕d2 ♘bd7 13 a5?! (it is better to play 13 0-0) 13...♖b8 14 ♕f4?! (the d6-pawn is tempting; White may have thought that in reply 14...♕e5 or 14...♕e7 was necessary) 14...b5! 15 f3 (15 ♕xd6? is met by 15...b4 16 ♗xf6 ♗xf6 17 ♘d1 h4) 15...♕e5 16 ♕d2 (16 ♕xe5 ♘xe5 17 f4 ♘c4!) 16...c4 17 f4 ♕e8 and the e4-pawn is weak, Egger-Istratescu, Duisburg jr Wch 1992.

Now:
A1: 11 0-0   95
A2: 11 f3   96

11 ♗f4 is also good, e.g.:

a) 11...♖e8 offers the d6-pawn:

a1) 12 0-0 transposes to note 'c' to White's 12th move in Line A1.

a2) However, 12 ♗xd6 is good: 12...♕b6 13 ♗f4 ♕xb2 14 ♖c1! ♘h5! (14...b5 15 ♗d2! ±) 15 ♗d2 ♘xg3 16 hxg3 ♕b6 17 ♕c2.

b) 11...♘e5 12 ♕d2 ♗d7?! 13 0-0 h5 14 ♗g5 h4 15 ♘h1 (15 ♗xh4 is also

good) 15...c4 16 ♕f4 h3 17 ♕h4 ♖e8
18 a5 hxg2 19 ♔xg2 ♗b5 20 f4 ♘ed7
21 ♖f3! ♕c7 22 ♘f2 ♘h7 23 ♘g4
♘xg5 24 fxg5 ♖e5 25 ♖af1 ♕d8 26
♖xf7 ♖xg5 27 ♖xg7+ ♔xg7 28 ♕h6+
♔g8 29 h4 1-0 Szabo-Velimirović,
Budapest 1973.

c) 11...♕c7 12 0-0 ♖e8 transposes
to Line E.

A1)
11 0-0 *(D)*

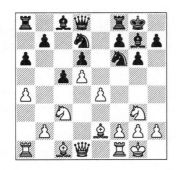

11...♖e8
Other possibilities:

a) 11...♕c7 12 ♗e3 and now:

a1) 12...♖e8 13 ♖c1!? ♘e5 14 h3
♕e7 15 ♕d2 ♖b8 16 ♖ce1 with a small
advantage, as f4 is threatened, Chern-
osvitov-Griasev, Dortmund 1993.

a2) 12...♖b8 13 h3 (better is 13 f4)
13...♖e8 14 ♕c2 b6 15 b3 h5 leads to
an equal position, Raičević-Krogius,
Genoa 1989.

b) 11...♖b8 and then:

b1) 12 ♗f4 ♘e8 13 ♕d2 ♘e5 and
Black has nearly equalized, Taima-
nov-Bertok, Vinkovci 1970.

b2) 12 ♗g5 h6 13 ♗e3 h5 (13...♔h7
14 f4 ± Simeonidis-Madl, Budapest

1995) 14 f3 ♘e5 15 ♕d2 ♘h7 16 ♖ae1
(P.Genov-Dochev, Bulgarian Ch 1994)
16...h4 17 ♘h1 f5 18 ♘f2 with better
chances for White.

c) 11...h5 12 ♗g5 ♕c7 13 ♕d2 ♖e8
(Dive-Kountz, Werfen 1994) and here
14 ♖fc1, intending ♖ab1 and b4, is the
right plan; then 14...♘h7 can be met
by 15 ♗h6!.

d) 11...b6 12 f4!? (sharper than the
usual ♗g5) 12...♕c7 13 ♗e3 ♖e8 14
♕d2 ♗b7 (better is 14...h5) 15 f5 ♘e5
16 ♗h6 with an attack, Burgerhoff-
Lammens, Vlissingen 1996.

12 ♗g5
Or:

a) 12 ♗e3 and now:

a1) 12...♖b8 13 ♕d2 ♕a5 14 ♗h6
± Zowada-Widera, Poland 1995.

a2) 12...♕e7 13 ♕d2 h5 14 f3 b6
15 ♘h1 ♗b7 16 ♘f2 ♖ac8 17 ♖ac1
♘e5 (Menadue-McFarland, British Ch
1995) and now 18 b3 is best, planning
♖ae1, h3 and f4.

b) 12 f3 can be suggested for those
looking for security. One example:
12...♖b8 13 ♗g5 ♘e5 14 ♕d2 c4?! 15
♖ab1, planning b4, leaves White better,
Mestel-Panzer, Hastings 1990/1.

c) 12 ♗f4 can also be chosen:

c1) 12...h5!? 13 ♗g5 ♘f8 (Kaposz-
tas-Blees, Harkany 1994) and here we
suggest 14 ♕c1 ♘8h7 15 ♗h4.

c2) 12...♕e7 13 ♕d2 and then:

c21) 13...b6 14 h3 ±.

c22) 13...♖b8 14 ♖ae1 ♕f8 15 h3
h5 16 ♗g5 ♘h7 17 ♗h4 with equality,
Von Hermann-Minasian, Berlin 1996.

c23) 13...♘e5 14 h3 ♖b8 15 ♗e3
♕f8 16 f4 ♘ed7 (Jakab-Prokopishin,
Gyongyos 1996), and now instead of

17 ♗f3, the more versatile 17 ♗d3 is an improvement.

d) 12 a5 b5 13 axb6 ♕xb6 led to equal chances in J.Mortensen-H.Mortensen, Copenhagen 1998.

12...h6

Or:

a) 12...♖b8 13 ♕d2 ♕a5 (Castellanos-Garriga, Olot 1992) and here we suggest 14 ♕f4; for example, 14...♕b4 15 ♖fb1!? and a5 followed by ♖a4 is threatened.

b) 12...h5 13 ♕d2 ♕a5 (13...♕c7 gave White a slight advantage in Tyrtania-G.Hartmann, Bundesliga 1988/9) and now:

b1) 14 ♗h6? (Liardet-Navrotescu, Biel 1994) can be met by 14...h4, intending ...♘xe4.

b2) 14 ♖fe1! ♘h7 (14...b6 15 ♕c2) 15 ♗f4 ♘e5 16 ♘f1! is slightly better for White.

13 ♗e3 ♖b8

13...h5 14 f3 ♘f8 15 ♘h1 ♗d7 16 ♘f2 ♕c7 17 ♖fc1 ± Navrotescu-Negulescu, Romanian Ch (Predeal) 1988.

14 ♕d2 ♔h7 15 ♔h1

Here we suggest 15 f4.

15...b5!? 16 axb5 axb5 17 ♗xb5 ♘g4 18 ♗xd7 ♗xd7 19 ♗f4 ♕h4 20 h3 ♘e5 21 ♗xe5 ♗xe5 22 ♖a7 ♗xh3!?

Black achieved a draw in Shemiakin-Moskalenko, Yalta 1995.

A2)

11 f3 (D)

Aiming to achieve the ♗g5 or ♗e3 with ♕d2 set-up even before castling. This way White keeps the f1-square free for the knight.

B

11...h5

Or:

a) 11...♘e5 12 ♗e3 (preparing a later plan of f4 and e5) 12...♗d7 13 h3 b5 14 f4 ♘c4 15 ♗xc4 bxc4 16 0-0 and now:

a1) 16...♖e8 17 ♕f3 h5 18 e5! ♘h7 was played in Nenashev-Tzermiadianos, Khania 1999, and now 19 ♖ad1! h4 20 ♘ge4 gives White a slight advantage according to Tzermiadianos.

a2) 16...♖b8!? 17 ♕d2 (17 e5 ♘e8 should be compared with lines below) and then:

a21) 17...♖e8? 18 e5!.

a22) 17...♖b3 and now 18 f5?! ♕e7! was OK for Black in Nenashev-Tzermiadianos, Nikea 1999. We suggest 18 e5 ♘e8 19 ♘ge4 with activity.

a23) 17...♘e8! is more accurate. Play is complex but level after 18 e5 dxe5 19 ♗xc5 ♘d6!.

b) The usual 11...♖e8 is also good.

12 ♗g5

The drawback of 11 f3 is that after ...h5-h4, ...♘h5 is possible. The text-move aims to hinder ...h4.

12...♖b8

Black prepares ...b5, which often involves a pawn sacrifice. Other moves:

a) 12...♕e8 13 ♕d2 ♘h7 14 ♗h6 h4 15 ♗xg7 ♔xg7 16 ♘f1 ± Renet-Sorin, Buenos Aires 1994.

b) 12...♕c7 13 ♕d2 and then:

b1) 13...♘h7 14 ♗h6 ± Akhsharumova-Xie Jun, Kuala Lumpur wom IZ 1990.

b2) For 13...c4 14 ♗h6! (14 0-0 ♖b8 nearly equalizes) 14...♖b8 see the main line.

b3) 13...♖e8 14 0-0 (14 ♗h6 is more accurate) and then:

b31) 14...♘h7! 15 ♗h6! (15 ♗e3 ♕a5!? = Hochstrasser-Suetin, Biel 1995) 15...♗h8! 16 ♖ac1 (better is 16 ♖fc1) 16...♕a5! with good counter-play for Black, Dreev-Kotronias, Las Vegas 1999.

b32) 14...♖b8 15 ♖fc1! ♘h7 16 ♗h6! ♗h8 (16...♗d4+ 17 ♗e3 ±) 17 ♖ab1 ♘e5 18 ♗e3, Yusupov-Kotronias, Bundesliga 1996/7, and here we would seek an advantage for White with the b4 advance.

13 ♕d2 ♕c7 14 ♗h6! c4 15 ♗xg7 ♔xg7 16 a5!?

Not 16 0-0?! h4 17 ♘h1 b5 18 axb5 axb5 19 ♘f2 and here instead of the hasty 19...b4? 20 ♘a4 ♘c5 21 ♘xc5 ♕xc5 22 ♖fc1 with a serious advantage for White, Christiansen-Fedorowicz, San Francisco 1991, Black should continue 19...♘c5, with slightly better chances.

16...h4 17 ♘f1 ♘c5 18 ♗xc4 ♘cxe4 19 fxe4

Sadler gives 19 ♘xe4 ♘xe4 (not 19...♕xc4? 20 ♘xf6! ♔xf6 21 ♘e3 ♖e8 22 ♔f2) 20 ♕d4+ ♘f6 21 ♘d2 ♖e8+ 22 ♘e4, but here 22...♔g8! questions White's advantage.

19...♕xc4 20 ♘e3 ♕c5 21 ♕f2

A versatile move, but according to Korchnoi 21 0-0 is objectively better.

21...b5

21...♗d7 can be answered by 22 e5!.

22 h3 ♘h5

22...b4 23 0-0 ♔g8! 24 ♘a4 ♘xe4 25 ♕f4 ♕d4 26 ♖ad1 ♕e5 27 ♕xh4 f5 with approximately equal chances (Sadler).

23 0-0 ♘g3?

The expected mistake. 23...f5! is correct according to Sadler.

24 ♕f6+ ♔g8 25 ♖f3 ♗d7?

25...b4 is necessary.

26 ♕xh4 b4 27 ♖xg3 bxc3 28 bxc3 ♕xc3 29 ♖f1 ♕e5 30 ♔h2

30 ♘f5! (Van der Wiel) is better.

30...♖b4 31 ♖f4 ♖e8 32 ♖g5 ♕e7?

32...♕g7 is tougher – Korchnoi.

33 ♕h6 ♖xe4 34 ♖xf7!

1-0 Korchnoi-Xie Jun, Arnhem 1999.

B)

9...♘a6 (D)

It is useful to know that 6...♘a6 7 ♗e2 c5 8 d5 e6 and 6...c5 7 d5 e6 8

♗e2 ♘a6 can also lead to this position.

10 0-0

This is the main line. Its importance is enhanced by the fact that the position can arise via various transpositions, as mentioned above. Now Black has a choice:

B1: 10...♖e8   98
B2: 10...♘c7   99

Here is a side-line: 10...♗d7 11 f4!? ♖e8 12 f5! (this is good now, as a knight can't reach e5) 12...gxf5 13 exf5! and the black kingside is vulnerable.

B1)

10...♖e8

Best. Black starts the fight against the e4-pawn; his plans also include ...h5 and ...b5. White now has two ways to develop:

B11: 11 ♗g5   98
B12: 11 ♗f4   98

Or:

a) 11 f3 ♘c7 12 ♗g5 should be compared with Lines B11 and B23.

b) 11 f4? is now dubious because of 11...h5!.

B11)

11 ♗g5 *(D)*
11...♕e7

Or:

a) 11...♘c7 12 ♕d2 ♕e7 13 f3 a6 14 ♖ae1! b5 and now 15 ♗d1! gave White a slight advantage in Korchnoi-Garcia Padron, Las Palmas 1981, but 15 e5!? is sharper.

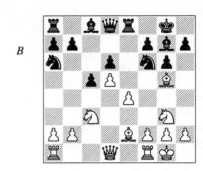

B

b) 11...♕b6 12 ♕d2 ♘d7 13 ♗f4 ♘e5 14 ♗b5! ♕f8 15 ♖fe1 ♘c7 16 ♗f1 and White has the initiative.

c) 11...h6 12 ♗f4 h5 13 ♗g5 ♕b6 14 ♕d2 ♘h7 and now White can play either 15 ♗h4 ± or 15 ♗h6!, as if Black accepts the sacrifice by 15...♗xh6 16 ♕xh6 ♕xb2 17 ♖fc1!, White threatens ♗xh5 and ♖ab1.

12 ♕d2 ♕f8

It would be a mistake to believe that the queen finds a good place on f8. For 12...♘c7, see note 'a' to Black's 11th move.

13 f4 h6 14 ♗h4 ♘d7 15 ♖ae1 ♗d4+ 16 ♔h1 ♘c7 17 ♗d3 a6 18 e5!?

White's central break comes in time, before the ...b5 counterplay. There is also a quiet continuation: 18 ♘ge2 ♗g7 19 ♘g1! and ♘f3.

18...dxe5 19 fxe5 ♘xe5 20 ♖xe5! ♖xe5 21 ♗xg6 f5 22 ♘h5

In Shemeakin-P.Demeter, Hlohovec 1995 Black defended badly: 22...♘e8? should have been met by 23 ♖f3! and ♖g3. Instead, 22...♘xd5 or 22...♖xd5 gives Black about equal chances.

B12)

11 ♗f4 *(D)*

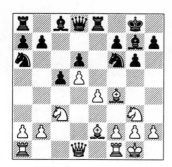

An important line, as after 6...c5 7 d5 e6 8 ♗f4!? exd5 the assessment of the transposition into the Benoni (9 cxd5) depends on it. It is promising in other cases as well, when it is against ...♘d7.

11...♘c7

Or:

a) 11...♘d7? is not recommended since after 12 ♗xd6! ♕b6 13 ♘b5 ♗xb2 14 ♖b1 White has a strong centre.

b) For 11...h5 see note 'c' to Black's 11th move in Line B11.

c) After 11...♕b6 12 ♕d2 ♘d7 (or 12...♗d7 13 a4 ±), 13 ♘b5 is awkward.

12 a4 ♖b8 13 ♕d2 a6 14 ♗h6!

This is better than 14 ♗g5 (Paronian-Molokin, Moscow 1994).

14...b5 15 ♗xg7 ♔xg7 16 axb5 axb5

Hanks-Kraidman, Grieskirchen seniors Wch 1988. Now White should play 17 ♕f4, e.g. 17...b4 18 ♘d1 (or 18 ♘b1) and the knight heads toward c4.

B2)
10...♘c7

Now:
B21: 11 ♖b1 99
B22: 11 a4 100
B23: 11 f3 101

Or:
a) 11 ♗f4 transposes to Line B12 after 11...♖e8 or 11...♖b8 12 a4 ♖e8.

b) 11 f4 is premature due to 11...b5! 12 ♘xb5 ♘xb5 13 ♗xb5 ♘g4!.

B21)
11 ♖b1 *(D)*

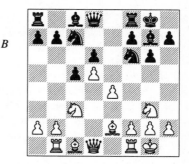

White's plan is to meet ...b5 with b4, weakening the c5-pawn.

11...♖e8

Other lines:

a) 11...h5 12 ♗g5 ♕d7 13 ♕d2 ♖e8 14 b4!? and now:

a1) 14...♘h7?! 15 ♗h6 h4 16 ♗xg7 ♔xg7 17 ♘h1 b6 18 bxc5 bxc5 19 f4 gives White the upper hand.

a2) 14...b6 15 ♖fe1 gave White a slight advantage in Dive-Olesen, London 1994.

b) 11...♘d7 12 ♗f4 ♘e5 13 ♕d2 h5 (13...♖e8 can be answered by 14 ♖fe1) 14 ♗h6 h4 15 ♘h1 f5 16 ♗xg7 ♔xg7 17 f4 ♘f7 18 ♘f2 with the better game for White, Dive-Cherniaev, London 1994.

c) 11...♖b8 can be met by 12 a4, transposing to the note Black's 11th move in Line B22. Instead after 12 a3 b5 13 b4 ♘h5 14 ♘xh5 ♗xc3, Black almost equalizes.

d) 11...a6 12 a3 (for 12 a4 see Line B22) 12...b5 13 b4 (Dive-Dowden, New Zealand Ch 1991) and now Black should continue 13...♘h5 14 ♗d2 ♘xg3 15 hxg3 f5 with even chances.

12 ♗e3

Or 12 ♖e1 ♘d7 13 ♗f4 ♘e5 14 ♕d2 h5 15 h3 (15 b4 is also good) 15...h4 16 ♘f1 f5!? (Dive-Hamdouchi, Moscow OL 1994) and here we suggest 17 ♘e3 fxe4 18 ♘xe4 ±.

12...b5 13 b4 c4

After this move White takes over the initiative on the queenside. The correct 13...cxb4 could be answered by 14 ♘xb5, with only a slight advantage to White.

14 ♗d4! h5 15 f3 h4 16 ♘h1 g5 17 ♘f2 ♘h5

Black intends to occupy the dark squares on the kingside.

18 ♗xg7 ♔xg7 19 ♕d4+ f6?!

Black should exchange queens by 19...♕f6.

20 a4 a6 21 axb5 axb5 22 ♖a1 ♗d7 23 ♕b6! ♘f4 24 ♕xd6 ♘xg2

The last trap: 25 ♔xg2?? ♗h3+.

25 ♖xa8 ♘xa8 26 ♖a1 ♘b6 27 ♖a7

With a double threat: ♔xg2 and ♖b7.

27...♖e7 28 ♖a6!

1-0 Jakab-Tsimmerman, Hungarian Cht 1999.

B22)
11 a4 (D)

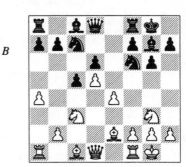

White does not fear ...♘a6-b4 because there is no open file on the queenside.

11...a6

11...♖b8 12 ♖b1! b6 13 ♗f4 ♖e8 14 ♕d2 ♗a6 15 ♗xa6 ♘xa6 (Szabo-Borik, Dortmund 1974) 16 ♖fe1 and White is better – Kapengut.

12 ♖b1

12 ♗g5 ♖e8 (better is first 12...h6) 13 ♕d2 ♗d7 (Bukhman-Shashin, Leningrad 1971) 14 ♕f4 planning ♕h4 and e5 gives White the advantage.

12...♘d7 13 ♗f4 ♘e5

Now:

a) 14 b4 cxb4 15 ♖xb4 a5 16 ♖b1 ♘a6 is unclear – Gufeld.

b) 14 ♕d2 and then:

b1) Black could play 14...b5!? 15 axb5 ♘xb5 16 ♘xb5 axb5 17 ♗xb5 ♕b6, with an unclear position according to Gufeld. But the question is whether Black has enough compensation for the pawn after 18 ♗xe5 ♗xe5 19 ♗c4 ♗d7 20 f4 ♗d4+ 21 ♔h1 planning f5 either immediately or after the e5 sacrifice.

b2) 14...h5 (Novikov-Gufeld, Tbilisi 1988) 15 a5 planning b4 leaves White slightly better.

B23)

11 f3

This move aims at securing the e4-pawn against ...b5 or ...h4. As there is no longer the possibility of ...♕b6, it can be played easily.

11...♖b8 12 ♗g5

12 ♗f4 b5 13 ♕d2 ♖e8 14 ♔h1 = Christiansen-Nunn, Munich 1991.

12...h6

After 12...b5 13 ♕d2 ♖e8 14 ♖fc1! White intends a3 and b4, and after 14...b4 the ♘d1-e3 manoeuvre is possible, unlike in positions where the bishop occupies the e3-square. Sometimes ♘d1-f2 is necessary. We recommend that Black play 12...h6 partly because of this, so that the bishop is forced to e3.

13 ♗e3 ♖e8

After 13...b5, 14 e5 is strong.

14 ♕d2 ♔h7 15 a4 a6

We have been following Czerwonski-Kaminski, Gdansk 1994. Instead of 16 f4?!, 16 ♖ab1 is better, with chances for a slight advantage. As there are a lot of pieces and the position is asymmetric, the better player may win. A story: Laszlo Szabo prepared for a candidates tournament with GM Gedeon Barcza. They analysed a new line in an opening for quite a long time, but even after days they did not decide over it. As they had a lot more to analyse, Barcza, closing the dispute sighed: "It must be tried out! And let the better player win!"

Szabo cried out: "That is exactly what I do not want to happen!"

C)

9...b6 *(D)*

Interestingly enough, a decade ago this was held to be the best. Its aim is ...♗a6 followed by exchanging the light-squared bishops. The opinion is different now.

10 0-0

This move questions the basic idea itself. It says that the exchange of the bishops does not mean such a great advantage that would compensate for the lack of ...♕b6 and the fact that the ...a6, ...b5 plan is also slowed down.

10 a4 is another important possibility, when ...♗a6 can sometimes be met by ♘b5. Then:

a) 10...♖e8! (preventing ♘b5) 11 0-0 ♗a6 and now:

a1) 12 ♗f4 (quiet and rather ineffective) 12...♗xe2 13 ♕xe2 a6 and now in Taimanov-Minić, Vinkovci 1970 Black equalized after 14 ♕d2 ♘g4!. This could be prevented by 14 f3, e.g. 14...♕c7 15 ♖fc1 planning ♖ab1 and b4 with chances for advantage.

a2) 12 ♗g5 (this bishop move is thought to be even better) 12...♗xe2 13 ♕xe2 a6 14 f4!? is similar to the main line.

a3) 12 f3 ♗xe2 13 ♕xe2 a6 14 ♖b1 (White's plan is in accordance with the pawn-structure) 14...♘bd7 15 ♗d2 intending b4.

b) 10...♗a6 11 ♘b5! h5 12 f3 h4 13 ♘f1 ♗xb5 14 axb5 ♘bd7 (the weak a7-pawn can cause trouble for Black in the ending) 15 ♗g5! h3 and now instead of 16 g4!? (Adianto-Benjamin, Horgen 1994) White can accept the pawn sacrifice, planning ♘g3 with advantage.

c) 10...h5?! 11 ♗g5 ♕e8 12 0-0 a6 13 ♖e1 ♘bd7 14 ♕d2 ♘h7 (Kaposztas-Zilahi, Harkany 1998) and now 15 ♗h6 keeps the upper hand.

10...♗a6
10...♖e8 should be compared with Line E.

11 ♗g5 *(D)*
This seems best. Other ideas:

a) In case of 11 f4!? (Prevenios-Witkowski, Switzerland 1997), Black should reply 11...h5!, planning ...♘g4. Then 12 h3 h4 13 ♘h1 ♘h5 is equal.

b) 11 ♗f4 (a quiet, constructive plan) 11...♗xe2 12 ♕xe2 ♖e8 13 f3 a6 14 ♕d2 ♕c7 (14...b5 15 a4 b4 16 ♘d1 ±) 15 ♗h6 ♗h8 16 h3 (preparing f4) 16...b5 17 a4 b4 18 ♘d1 ♘bd7 19 ♘e3 a5 20 b3 ♘b6 (20...♘h5? 21 ♘xh5! ±) 21 ♖ac1 ♖ac8 22 ♔h1 ♕b8 23 ♕d3! ♘fd7 24 f4 with an advantage for White, Taborov-Shtyka, Voronezh 1997.

c) 11 ♗xa6 ♘xa6 (this position can also arise from ♗d3 lines) 12 ♗g5

♕e8 (better is 12...h6, while 12...♕d7 13 ♕f3 ♘e8 has also been played) 13 ♕d2 (threatening ♕f4; 13 ♖e1 ♘d7! is equal) 13...♘d7 and now White can play 14 ♘b5; for example, 14...♘e5 15 ♘xd6 ♕d7 16 ♕e2! ♘c7 17 ♘c4 ♘xc4 18 ♕xc4 ♗xb2 19 ♖ad1 with strong central pawns.

11...♖e8 12 f4!?
12 ♖e1 ♗xe2 13 ♕xe2 a6 14 a4 ♘bd7 15 f3 ♕c7 is not clear (according to Shipov and Notkin), Fokin-Kotsur, Ekaterinburg 1997.

12...♗xe2 13 ♕xe2 h6?!
This move can be answered by an instructive plan. 13...♘bd7 is slightly better.

14 ♗xf6!? ♗xf6 15 e5!
A typical breakthrough in the Benoni set-up.

15...dxe5
15...♗g7 16 ♘ge4! dxe5 transposes to the main line.

16 ♘ge4 ♗g7
16...♘d7 is not better either: 17 f5! ♗g7 (17...g5 18 d6 and ♘d5) 18 fxg6 fxg6 19 ♕g4! ♘f8 20 d6 with a heavy attack.

17 f5!

This secures the position of the e4-knight. In this type of position the blockading knight can be very strong.

17...♕d7 18 g4

18 fxg6 f5! affords Black counter-chances.

18...a6 19 fxg6 fxg6 20 ♖f6! b5 21 ♖af1 b4 22 ♖xg6 ♔h8 23 ♘f6 ♕f7 24 ♖xg7! ♕xg7 25 ♘xe8 ♕e7 26 ♘e4

White won in Rowson-Bates, British League (4NCL) 1997/8.

D)

9...h5 *(D)*

W

10 f3

White maintains the possibility for the knight to retreat to f1, while the c1-bishop still waits to see where it should go.

10 ♗g5 is also good. After 10...♕b6 11 ♕b3! the d6-pawn is in danger; or 10...a6 11 a4 ♕b6 12 ♕c2 planning a5.

10...♘bd7

Or:

a) 10...a6 11 a4 ♕a5 is met by 12 ♗d2.

b) 10...♗d7 11 ♗g5 ♕e8 12 ♕d2! (12 ♕b3!? also deserves attention)

12...♘h7 13 ♗h6 and White has the initiative – Chernin.

c) 10...h4 11 ♘f1 ♘h5?! 12 g4! ♘f6 13 ♗g5 h3 14 ♕d2 ♘bd7 15 ♘g3 ♖e8 16 0-0 and White is slightly better, Razuvaev-Agrest, St Petersburg 1992.

d) 10...♖e8 should be compared with Line E.

11 ♗e3

Or:

a) For 11 ♗g5 a6 12 a4 see Line A2.

b) 11 0-0 (White does better to postpone castling) 11...a6 (11...♘h7 12 ♘h1 ♘e5 13 ♘f2 f5 14 exf5! ♗xf5 15 ♗e3 a6 {better is 15...♕b6!?} 16 ♕d2 b5 17 ♘ce4 ♘f7 18 ♖ae1 favours White, Korchnoi-Brunner, Switzerland 1991) 12 a4 h4 13 ♘h1 ♘h5 14 ♗e3 ♗d4!? (a risky but dangerous sacrifice with practical chances) 15 ♗xd4 cxd4 16 ♕xd4 ♕g5 17 ♖ad1 f5 with compensation for the pawn, Spassky-J.Polgar, Budapest (7) 1993.

11...h4

11...a6 12 a4, planning ♕d2 and ♗h6, should be compared with Line A2.

12 ♘f1

Now:

a) 12...♘h5?! can be strongly met by 13 g4!.

b) 12...♘e5 13 ♘d2 ♘h7 14 f4 ♘d7 15 0-0 ♖e8 16 h3 f5 17 ♗f2 and now:

b1) 17...fxe4 18 ♘dxe4 ♘b6 19 ♗d3 ♖f8! is a position that occurred by transposition in Razuvaev-Khalifman, Bundesliga 1991/2. After 20 ♕d2 ♗f5 (20...♘f6 21 ♘g5!) 21 ♖ae1 White has the better chances.

b2) 17...♗xc3 18 bxc3 fxe4 19 ♘c4 ♘b6 20 ♘xb6 axb6 21 ♕e1 ±.

E)

9...♖e8 *(D)*

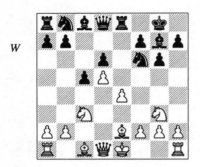

This move follows the rule: put the rook on the open file! Black has ideas of ...b5-b4 together with ...h5-h4. The plan is undoubtedly good, but the question is whether it is fast enough.

10 ♗f4

Or:

a) 10 f3 leads into a reliable line of the Sämisch King's Indian: 1 d4 ♘f6 2 c4 g6 3 ♘c3 ♗g7 4 e4 d6 5 f3 0-0 6 ♘ge2 c5 7 d5 e6 8 ♘g3 exd5 9 cxd5, which is not our topic now.

b) 10 0-0 is a good move, and liable to transpose to Lines A, B or C depending on Black's response.

10...a6

Or:

a) 10...♘bd7 is a surprise. Taking the pawn leads to complications that favour White if he plays well: 11

♗xd6 ♕b6 12 ♗f4 ♕xb2 13 ♗d2! (13 ♖c1 b5! is unclear) and now 13...a6 14 ♖b1 ♕a3 15 ♕c2 or 13...♕b6 14 ♕c2 a6 15 a4 gives White the upper hand since Black's natural play on the queenside is stopped.

b) 10...h5!? (this h-pawn push can often be unpleasant for the g3-knight) 11 f3 h4 12 ♘f1 ♘h5 13 ♗e3 a6 14 a4 ♕a5?! 15 ♕c1! (15 ♕c2 b5!) 15...♗d4 16 ♗g5 ♘d7! 17 ♘d2! (17 ♗xh4 ♘f4!) 17...♘e5 18 ♘b3 ♕b6 (Black should try 18...♕b4 19 ♕c2 f5, taking the risk of 20 ♗d2) 19 ♕d1 h3 20 g4 ♘g7 21 a5 ♗xc3+ 22 bxc3 ♕c7 23 c4 with a clear advantage to White, Jakab-Kerek, Hungarian Cht 1996.

11 a4 ♕c7

11...♕e7 is popular, but is hardly a better place for the queen. Then 12 0-0 ♘bd7 transposes to note 'c2' to White's 12th move in Line A1.

12 ♕c2

This queen move makes the variation distinct. 12 ♕d2 ♘bd7 13 0-0 b6 14 ♗h6 ♗h8 15 h3 ½-½ Szabo-Petrosian, Sarajevo 1972.

12...♘bd7 13 h3

This is not necessary. Better is 13 0-0, when 13...c4 can be met by 14 ♘d1!.

13...c4! 14 0-0 ♖b8 15 a5 b5 16 axb6 ♘xb6

Forintos – Santo-Roman, Lille 1985. Now 17 ♖fc1 is best, planning ♘d1, which leads to just a slight advantage to White.

9 6...c5 7 d5 e6 8 ♗e2 without 8...exd5

1 d4 ♘f6 2 c4 g6 3 ♘c3 ♗g7 4 e4 d6 5 ♘ge2 0-0 6 ♘g3 c5 7 d5 e6 8 ♗e2 ♘a6

There are various other options for Black:

a) 8...h5 9 ♗g5 ♕b6 10 ♕d2 exd5 11 cxd5 (for the alternative 11 exd5 see note 'a' to Black's 9th move in Chapter 7) 11...♘h7 12 ♗f4 ♘d7 (or 12...h4 13 ♘f1 f5 14 ♘e3! planning ♘c4 ±) 13 ♘f1! ♘e5 14 ♘e3 gives White, who is planning h3 and 0-0, the upper hand, Kaposztas-Pinter, Hungarian Cht 1992.

b) 8...♖e8 has no individual significance. It mostly transposes to other lines; e.g. 9 0-0 ♘a6 10 ♗f4 exd5 11 exd5 transposes to note 'd1' to Black's 10th move in Line A2 of Chapter 7.

c) 8...a6 is rather procrastinating, keeping the option of either taking on d5, or playing ...b5:

c1) 9 0-0 exd5 10 exd5 should be compared with lines with ...a6 in Chapter 7, where it is not easy to find a path to equality for Black.

c2) 9 a4 is most significant if White plans cxd5 after ...exd5; see Line A in Chapter 8.

9 0-0

For 9 ♗g5 h6 10 ♗e3 exd5 11 exd5 see note 'b' to White's 10th move in Line D, Chapter 7.

9...♘c7

White has more room and may choose between two bishop moves, amongst other ideas.

10 ♗e3

Not 10 dxe6? ♘xe6!.

10 h3 exd5 11 exd5 transposes to note 'd' to White's 11th move in Line D of Chapter 7.

10 ♗g5 h6 11 ♗e3 exd5 12 cxd5 (12 exd5 should be compared with Line D in Chapter 7) 12...♕e8 (the queen eyes b5 and e4, but 12...a6 is more natural) 13 ♗f4! ♕e7 14 ♕d2 (the chess-player is attracted by winning a tempo, while the philosopher by 14 ♕c2) 14...g5?! (such a weakness may come back to haunt one; 14...♔h7 is necessary) 15 ♗e3 b5 16 f4! b4 (16...g4 17 e5!) 17 fxg5 hxg5?! (17...♘g4!?), Vincze-F.Portisch, Hungarian Cht 1997, and now White should continue his original plan: 18 ♗xg5! bxc3 19 ♕xc3 ±.

10...♖e8

10...exd5 11 exd5 should be compared with Line D, Chapter 7.

11 h3 exd5

Now, instead of 12 cxd5 b5! Soman-Shetty, Indian Ch 1994 with chances for both sides, we suggest 12 exd5, which should be compared with Line D in Chapter 7.

10 6...c5 7 d5: 7...♞a6, 7...a6 and other moves

1 d4 ♞f6 2 c4 g6 3 ♞c3 ♝g7 4 e4 d6 5 ♞ge2 0-0 6 ♞g3 c5 7 d5 *(D)*

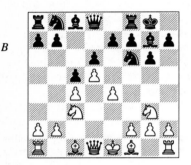

B

Now:

A: 7...♞a6   106
B: 7...a6   108

The other alternatives are mostly bad; the following ones are just about playable:

a) 7...♛a5 (the queen creates a pin on c3 and at the same time it supports the ...b5 pawn sacrifice in Benko Gambit style) 8 ♝e2 b5?! (he might start with 8...a6 as well) 9 cxb5 a6 10 a4 (10 0-0 is also good) 10...axb5 11 ♝xb5 ♝g4 12 f3 ♝d7 13 0-0 ♝xb5 14 ♞xb5 ♞a6 15 ♝d2 ♞b4 16 ♝c3, Farina-Suppa, Nereto 1998. Just like in the Benko Gambit, the fight is against the white pawns on a4 and b2. However, there is not enough compensation

for the pawn here, because White may attack with f4.

b) 7...h5!? is an interesting idea. After 8 ♝e2 h4! 9 ♞f1 h3 10 g4 e6! 11 ♞g3 exd5 12 cxd5 b5!, Black took over the initiative in Efimov-Wojtkiewicz, Warsaw 1988 since 13 ♞xb5 could be answered by 13...♞xg4!. Our recommendation is 8 ♝d3 or 8 h3 h4 9 ♞ge2 not allowing the black pawn as far as h3, when Black has to take care of his h-pawn sooner or later. For example, 9...♛a5 10 ♛c2 ♞a6 11 a3!, when 11...♞b4 12 ♛b1! and ♝g5 wins the pawn.

c) 7...♞bd7 is not best. Although it conforms with the principle of development, it does not support counterplay with either ...b5 or ...e6. Compare with Line B.

d) For 7...e5 see Line A in Chapter 6.

A)
7...♞a6

Nothing else, just "I cannot think of anything good; let's wait to see how White develops". However, White can continue with useful developing moves.

8 ♝e2

8 h4 can be answered by 8...h5, when a black knight will have a good base on g4 or on e5.

8...♘c7 9 0-0

This is best. If 9 ♗e3, 9 ♗g5 or 9 ♗d2, then the ...a6 and ...♖b8 set-up almost equalizes. Black also nearly equalizes after 9 h4 h5! 10 ♗g5 a6 11 a4 ♖b8 12 ♕d2 ♔h7 planning ...♗d7 and ...b5, Alvarado-Also, Mesa 1992.

After 9 0-0 Black may play:

A1: 9...♖b8   107
A2: 9...a6   107

9...e6 transposes to Chapter 9.

A1)

9...♖b8 *(D)*

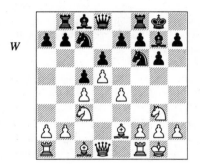

10 ♗e3 ♗d7 11 a4 b6

This plan is really popular. Black prepares ...b5 systematically, while developing his pieces.

12 ♕d2 ♘g4 13 ♗xg4 ♗xg4 14 ♗h6! ♗d7 15 ♗xg7 ♔xg7 16 f4 a6

Black's counterplay on the queenside is too late.

17 e5 ♘e8 18 ♘ce4 b5 19 axb5 axb5 20 ♕c3!? b4 21 ♕e3 ♗c8 22 f5! dxe5 23 fxg6

White opts for an aesthetic solution. 23 ♘xc5 is a practical way to secure a clear advantage.

23...hxg6 24 ♘h5+!!

A beautiful move and plan. Now taking on h5 would lose quickly.

24...♔h7 25 ♕g3 ♖b6 26 ♖a7 f5

The best practical chance in time-trouble, partly because White might have expected 26...f6 (e.g. 27 ♘g5+! ♔g8! 28 ♘f3! ♔h7 29 ♘xe5!)), and partly because White may choose from several winning lines, which is much more difficult in time-trouble than if there is only one good line. The trick worked in Bilek-Yanofsky, Stockholm IZ 1962, as White missed the quick win by 27 ♕xe5! gxh5 28 ♖xe7+ ♔g8 29 d6!, when Black is helpless.

A2)

9...a6 *(D)*

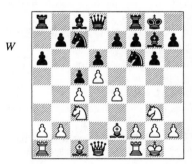

10 a4

The usual scheme.

10 ♗f4 hardly gives any advantage, and it blocks an attack with f4. 10...♗d7 11 a4 ♖b8 12 e5 (12 a5 is the alternative) 12...♘fe8! 13 exd6 ♘xd6 (13...exd6 gives Black a position akin to Chapter 7, which he has been trying to avoid) 14 ♗e3!? b5! 15 cxb5 axb5 16 axb5 ♘cxb5 17 ♗xc5 ♘xc3 18

bxc3 ♗xc3 = Kaposztas-Hohl, Gyongyos 1997.

10...b6

Preventing a5.

11 ♗e3 ♖b8 12 ♖b1! ♗d7 13 b4 h5

The disadvantage of this move is that a later ...f5 may be played only at the cost of weakening the g5-square. The interesting 13...♘h5 can be met by 14 ♗xh5 ♗xc3 15 bxc5! bxc5! 16 ♖xb8 ♕xb8 17 ♗g4, exchanging the good black bishop. Then 17...f5 is no good since ♕c2 wins material after the exchanges on f5.

14 h3 ♗e8

Black plans ...♘d7, but he blocks his back rank just for one second, and White takes advantage of this to secure the b-file. Better is 14...♘fe8 15 ♕d2 e6, risking the ♗g5 continuation after 16 bxc5.

15 bxc5! bxc5 16 ♖xb8 ♕xb8 17 ♕c2 a5

Black opens the way for the c7-knight but it is too late.

18 ♖b1 ♕d8 19 e5!

This makes room for the knight on e4.

19...♘d7 20 exd6 exd6 21 ♘ge4 ♕e7 22 ♖b7 ♘a6 23 ♗g5 ♕e5

23...f6 24 ♗f4.

24 ♕c1! f5 25 ♗f4 ♕d4 26 ♗e3 ♕e5 27 f4 ♕e7 28 ♘g5

White has a decisive advantage, Forintos-I.Polgar, Hungarian Ch 1968.

B)

7...a6 (D)

The other line that sometimes occurs. It often arises by transposition from 6...a6 7 ♗e2 c5 8 d5. This move

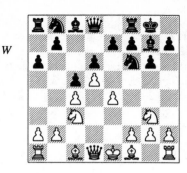

declares that Black is ready to sacrifice with ...b5. This is most frequent after ♗e2, since then ♗xb5 loses a tempo, so the chances of the gambit improve. If 8 a4 is played automatically, then Black may transpose into the 7...e6 system with 8...e6, where a4 is not always awkward.

8 ♗e2

After 8 a4 Black may even omit ...e6 in favour of 8...h5: 9 ♗e2 (better is 9 h4) 9...e6?! (the better 9...h4 is unclear) 10 ♗g5 ♕c7 (after 10...exd5, 11 ♘xd5 is strong) 11 ♕d2 ♘h7 12 ♗h6 e5 13 h4 ♘f6 14 ♖a3 (the rook move prepares the sacrifice on h5, but the immediate 14 ♗xh5 is also good) 14...♕e7 15 ♗g5! (threatening the ♗xh5 sacrifice again) 15...♕e8 16 a5! ♘bd7 17 ♘a4 and with his last two moves White has paralysed Black, Yurtaev-Kempinski, Elista OL 1998.

8...♘bd7

8...b5?! (a pawn sacrifice reminiscent of the Benko Gambit) 9 cxb5 axb5 (9...♘bd7 10 0-0 and 9...♕a5 should be compared with note 'a' to Black's 7th move at the start of this chapter) 10 ♗xb5 h5 11 0-0 ♕a5 (Black threatens ...h4 followed by ...♘xe4)

12 ♗e2 (a2-a4 is not compulsory here, which can mean a kind of weakness) 12...♗a6 13 ♗g5 ♖e8?! (13...♘bd7 is correct) 14 ♕d2 ♗xe2 15 ♘gxe2 ♘bd7 16 h3 (16 f3!) 16...♘b6 17 b3 c4 (better is 17...♘xe4 18 ♘xe4 ♕xd2 19 ♗xd2 ♗xa1 20 ♖xa1 ♘xd5) 18 ♖ab1 cxb3 19 axb3 ♕b4 20 ♗e3 ♘bd7 21 ♘d4 and White has much the better position, Kaposztas-S.Varga, Hungarian Cht 1997.

9 0-0 ♖b8

9...♘e8 is also a natural continuation. 10 ♗e3 e5 (10...♘c7 11 ♕d2 ♖b8 12 a4 and f4-f5 is to White's advantage) 11 ♕d2 f5 12 exf5 gxf5 and now 13 f4 is better than 13 ♗h6 (C.Schneider-H.Ludwig, Swiss Ch 1986), or if we insist on it, then we should choose the move-order 13 ♗g5 ♗f6 14 ♗h6 ±.

10 a4 h5!? 11 f4 (D)

The schematic 11 ♗g5 is also good, but it would not be easy to make a dubious move after that. This is an old joke: the blunder is on the chessboard; it just has to be found.

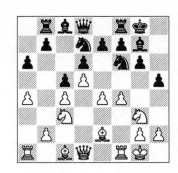

B

11...♘g4?! 12 ♗xg4 hxg4 13 ♗e3!

One should not be greedy: after 13 ♕xg4 ♘e5 14 ♕e2 ♗g4 15 ♕e1 ♘xc4 16 f5 ♗d4+ 17 ♔h1 ♔g7 Black is active.

13...♕b6

After 13...f5 14 ♕d3! Black has many weaknesses.

14 ♖f2 ♕b4 15 a5! b5

15...♗xc3? is met by 16 ♖a4.

16 cxb5 ♗xc3

Black is afraid that 16...axb5 would close out his own queen.

17 bxc3 ♕xc3 18 ♗d2 ♕d3 19 b6

With an advantage to White, A.Garcia-Escobar, Medellin 1994.

11 6...♞c6

1 d4 ♞f6 2 c4 g6 3 ♞c3 ♝g7 4 e4 d6 5 ♞ge2 0-0 6 ♞g3 ♞c6 *(D)*

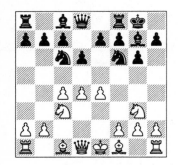

W

If we think it over, Black has only one way to loosen the d5-pawn in the systems after both 6...e5 and 6...c5, which is either ...c6 or ...e6, and that is why it is usually not possible to remove the pawn. The idea behind 6...♞c6 is that the pawn can be lured to d5, and then, following a necessary loss of a tempo (...♞b8 or ...♞e5), both pawns might start to attack against d5 (i.e. by ...c6 and ...e6).

7 d5

Best. Now Black has a choice:

A: 7...♞b8   110
B: 7...♞e5   111

Less advisable is 7...♞b4?! (inviting 8 a3, so that the knight can get to a6 without loss of tempo, but it is not so urgent for White to chase it) 8 ♝e2 c6 9 0-0 e6 (9...e5 10 ♝g5 comes to the same thing) 10 ♝f4!? e5 11 ♝g5 h6 12 ♝e3 c5 13 ♛d2 ♚h7 14 f4 exf4 15 ♝xf4 ♛e7 16 ♞b5 ♞e8 17 a3 ♞a6 18 ♜ae1 with an advantage in Forintos-Ozsvath, Budapest 1961.

A)
7...♞b8

This is clearer but less ambitious than 7...♞e5.

8 ♝e2 c6

This is the best way of attacking the centre. Of course 8...e5?! and 8...c5?! are inadvisable, as they are equivalent to 6...e5 and 6...c5 with the loss of two tempi. 8...e6 is not promising either: 9 ♝g5 (9 0-0 will most likely transpose to the main line) 9...exd5 (Black should force White to clarify what he intends to do with the bishop by playing 9...h6) 10 cxd5 ♜e8 11 0-0 c5 reaches a Benoni set-up with loss of tempo, Ju.Wilson-Sh.Schmid, Elista wom OL 1998. 9...c6 is slightly better, with a likely transposition to lines below.

9 0-0

9 ♝g5 is also good, e.g. 9...cxd5 10 exd5! ♞bd7 11 ♛d2 ♜e8 12 0-0 a6 13 h3 ♞f8 14 ♜ac1 e6 15 dxe6 ♞xe6 16 ♝e3 ♝f8 17 ♜fd1 ♛e7 18 ♝f3 ±, A.Hoffman-Rosselli Mailhe, Cordoba Z 1998.

9...e6

This is one of the basic ideas of 7...♞b8. Other moves:

a) 9...cxd5 10 cxd5 (10 exd5 is more critical; compare the note to White's 9th move) and now:

a1) 10...a6 is feeble: 11 ♗e3 b5 12 b4! ♘bd7 13 a4 with an advantage to White, Kaposztas-L.Lengyel, Gyongyos 1994.

a2) 10...♘a6 11 ♗e3 ♗d7 12 h3 ♕b8! 13 ♖c1 ♖c8 and now 14 ♕d2?! allows Black to equalize with 14...b5!, Szabo-Westerinen, Leningrad 1967. 14 a3 is better, as 14...b5 could be met by 15 b4 with a slight advantage.

b) 9...♘a6 10 ♗e3 ♗d7 11 ♖c1 (11 f4 is also good) 11...♕b8 12 a3 cxd5 13 exd5! (slightly better than 13 cxd5 b5 14 b4 ±) 13...b6 14 b4 ♕b7 15 ♖e1 ♖fe8 16 h3 ♖ad8 (all the rooks are lined up on the files that may become open) 17 ♗f3 ♗c8 18 ♘ge2 ♘b8 19 ♘d4, Ivkov-Nikolić, Vinkovci 1976. White can make plans at his leisure, and also may occupy c6 with a clear advantage.

10 ♗g5

Also good is 10 dxe6 ♗xe6 11 ♗e3 h5 (Black should prefer 11...♕e7 ±) 12 ♗g5!, when Black has development problems, Bertok-Ivanović, Yugoslav Ch (Novi Travnik) 1969. White also threatens e5.

10...h6 11 ♗e3 cxd5 12 cxd5 exd5 13 exd5 ♘bd7 14 h3 ♖e8 15 ♕d2 ♔h7 16 ♕c2!? a6 17 a4 ♖xe3

An enticing offer of the exchange in a difficult position, but it did not prove sufficient in Forintos-Polaczek, Forli 1989.

B)
7...♘e5

Now White has a choice:
B1: 8 f4 111
B2: 8 ♗e2 112

B1)
8 f4 (D)

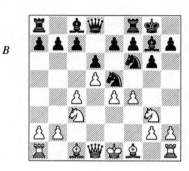

8...♘ed7

8...♘eg4 has gone out of fashion, possibly because of 9 h3! (9 ♗e2 h5) 9...♘h6 10 ♗d3 e6 (10...e5 11 fxe5 dxe5 12 ♗g5 ±) 11 0-0 with a clear advantage.

9 ♗e2

9 ♗d3 is the other way to develop, but 9...♘c5 10 ♗c2 c6 (or 10...e6, Salo-Kanko, Finnish Cht 1990) brings Black close to equality.

9...c6
Or:

a) For 9...e6 see the note to White's 9th move in Line B21.

b) 9...h5 10 ♗e3 c6 and instead of 11 ♗f3 ♘b6 (Nabill-Khait, Moscow 1991), 11 0-0 is necessary, e.g. 11...h4 12 ♘h1 ♘c5 13 ♘f2 ±.

10 ♗e3

10 0-0 makes Black's game easier because ...♕b6+ is not prevented. Then:

a) 10...cxd5 11 exd5 a6 (for the better 11...♕b6+, compare line 'b') 12 a4 a5 13 ♗e3 ♘c5 14 f5 ♗d7 15 h3 ♕b6 16 ♘b5 ± ♖fc8 17 ♗d3 ♕d8 18 ♘d4 ♗e8 19 b3 ♘fd7 20 ♗c2 ♘e5 21 ♕d2 ♘xa4? (this is based on a nice idea, viz. 22 bxa4 ♘xc4 followed by ...♘xe3, ...♗xd4 and ...♖xc2, but White has seen further!) 22 ♗h6!! ♗h8 (22...♘c5 23 ♗xg7 ♔xg7 24 ♘h5+!, and White forces mate) 23 bxa4 ♘xc4 24 ♕f2 ♕b6 25 ♘ge2 left White a piece up in Bozinović-Haselhorst, Biel 1998.

b) 10...♕b6+! 11 ♔h1 h5! 12 ♗f3 and now instead of 12...cxd5 (Vigh-Nemet, Zanka 1977), 12...♕b4 is best, e.g. 13 ♕e2 cxd5! (not 13...h4 14 dxc6 bxc6 15 e5!) 14 e5 dxe5 and in this complicated position the chances are equal.

10...cxd5

Or:

a) 10...h5 can be met by 11 0-0 h4 12 ♘h1 ♘c5 13 ♘f2 ±.

b) 10...a6 11 0-0 cxd5 12 exd5 and now:

b1) 12...b6 13 ♖c1 ♗b7 14 ♕d2 ♖c8 15 ♔h1 ♖c7 16 b3 ± Bertok-Bilek, Budapest 1960.

b2) 12...b5!? is riskier. After 13 cxb5 axb5 14 ♗xb5 ♗b7 15 ♗d4! ♖c8 (Liardet-Finkel, Biel 1995) we suggest 16 ♗xd7 ♕xd7 17 ♕d3, when Black does not have enough compensation.

11 exd5

Or 11 cxd5 a6! (best), and now:

a) 12 a4 ♕a5 13 0-0 and now instead of 13...♕b4? 14 ♘a2! ♕a5 (not 14...♕xb2?? 15 ♗d4 ♕a3 16 ♖f3) 15 b4 ♕d8, Meurrens-Steinbacher, Ostend

1992, we suggest 13...♘c5! with even chances.

b) 12 ♕d2 b5 13 ♖c1 h5! 14 ♗f3 ♘b6 15 b3 ♗g4! and Black equalized in Grooten-Douven, Dutch Cht 1992.

11...h5 12 ♗d4 h4 13 ♘ge4 ♘xe4 14 ♘xe4 ♘f6

The game Zsu.Polgar-W.Watson, Brussels 1987 went 15 ♘xf6+ ♗xf6 16 0-0 ♗f5 17 h3 ♕a5 18 ♔h1 ♗c2 19 ♕xc2 ♗xd4 20 f5 g5! with equality. We consider 15 ♘c3 to give White slightly better chances since keeping more pieces can be advantageous only for White.

B2)

8 ♗e2

Now:

B21: 8...e6   113
B22: 8...h5   114

8...c6 is the other way to attack the centre:

a) 9 f4 can be met by 9...♘ed7 transposing to Line B1. On the other hand, 9...♘eg4 is not good here either, because of 10 h3 ♘h6 11 ♗e3.

b) 9 0-0 and now:

b1) 9...♗g4?! 10 f4! ♗xe2 11 ♕xe2 ♘ed7 12 e5 with a small advantage for White, A.Johannessen-Thoresen, Norwegian Cht 1991.

b2) 9...a5 10 h3 ♘ed7 11 ♗e3 h6 12 ♕d2 ♔h7 (Kaposztas-Kern, Berlin 1984) and now 13 ♖ad1 ± is necessary.

b3) 9...h5 10 ♗g5 cxd5 11 exd5 (11 cxd5) 11...♘h7 12 ♗e3 h4 13 ♘h1 ♗f5 14 f4 (14 ♗d4!?) 14...♘d7 15 ♖c1 ♖c8 ½-½ Novikov-G.Kuzmin,

Finland 1992. White could continue by 16 ♘f2.

b4) 9...a6 10 a4 and now:

b41) 10...♕c7 11 b3 e6 and now, rather than 12 dxe6 fxe6 13 ♗b2 c5 14 f4 ♘c6 15 ♗d3 ♘d4 = Spraggett-Murey, New York 1987, 12 ♗a3 is more promising.

b42) 10...a5 is usual in similar positions. 11 ♗e3 ♕c7 12 ♖c1 ♘ed7 and now instead of the cautious 13 f3 (Verdikhanov-Ovseevich, Nikolaev Z 1993) the more active continuation 13 f4 is better.

B21)

8...e6 *(D)*

This move tries to make use of the fact that White has left out 8 f4.

9 0-0

This is a quieter treatment than 9 f4, but that also has ideas: 9...♘ed7 10 dxe6! fxe6 11 0-0 ♕e7 12 ♗e3 ♘e8 13 ♕d2 c6 14 ♖ad1 a6 15 a4 a5 16 ♗f3 ♗h6 17 ♖f2 (White stands better, so Black now takes a risk) 17...e5?! 18 f5 ♗xe3 19 ♕xe3 ♘c5 20 ♗e2 ♗d7 21 ♖df1 gxf5 22 ♘xf5 ♗xf5 23 exf5 ♔h8 24 g4 with a decisive pawn

march in Forintos-Szabo, Hungarian Ch 1969.

9...exd5 10 cxd5! h5!?

This makes White take a difficult decision. The point is that if White avoids the critical 11 f4, then Black gets good chances. 10...♖e8 is less active:

a) 11 h3 and then:

a1) 11...♕e7 12 ♗g5 a5? (an instructive mistake; it is better to protect b5 with 12...a6, or else to play 12...h6) 13 ♕d2 ♘ed7 14 ♗b5! and the bishop nearly paralyses the black defence, Comas Fabrego-Candela Perez, Spanish Ch 1993.

a2) 11...♘ed7 seems to be better, e.g. 12 ♗e3 a6 13 ♖c1! b5 14 b4!? (14 a3) 14...♘b6 15 ♕b3 h5 16 ♗g5 ♕d7 (Shemeakin-Manik, Hlohovec 1995) 17 ♗d3 ♘h7 18 ♗e3 ±.

b) 11 f4 ♘ed7 (11...♘eg4?! 12 h3 ♘h6 13 f5 gxf5 14 ♗g5!) 12 ♗f3 ♕e7 13 ♖e1 c6 14 ♗e3 with advantage.

11 f4

This gives the most chances; after 11 ♗g5 ♕d7 12 h3 ♘h7 13 ♗e3 h4 14 ♘h1 g5! 15 ♘b5 (15 f4) 15...a6 16 ♘d4 ♕e7 17 ♖c1 ♘g6! 18 ♕c2 ♘f4 Black equalized in Dive-R.Smith, New Zealand Ch 1992.

11...♘eg4 12 h3 ♘h6 13 f5!

This is the most energetic, but it sometimes leads to incalculable complications. We delineate only the more important motifs.

13...c6

Or:

a) 13...h4 14 ♘h1 gxf5 15 ♗g5! shows White's idea: to exploit this pin. Now 15...fxe4 can be met by 16 ♖xf6!

with better chances; or 15...c6 16 ♕c1 ♔h7 17 ♗xh4! ±.

b) 13...♘h7 (Black avoids the pin, but...) 14 f6! ♘xf6 15 ♗g5 (planning ♖xf6) 15...♔h7 16 ♗xh5 gives White the advantage, e.g. 16...gxh5 17 ♘xh5 ♘hg8 18 e5! dxe5 19 ♘e4 +−.

c) If 13...gxf5, then 14 ♘xf5 ± is simplest.

14 dxc6 bxc6!

Or 14...♕b6+ 15 ♔h1:

a) 15...♕xc6 16 ♘d5!.

b) 15...h4 16 fxg6! fxg6 17 ♗xh6 ♗xh6 18 ♖xf6! ♖xf6 19 ♘d5 ♕d8 20 ♘xf6+ ♕xf6 21 ♕b3+ wins.

c) 15...bxc6 16 ♕xd6 ♖d8 (after 16...♘e8 White can play 17 ♕f4) 17 ♕a3 h4 18 fxg6! hxg3 (18...♗f8 19 ♕b3) 19 ♗xh6 +−.

15 ♕d4

15 ♗g5 ♕b6+ 16 ♖f2 is not clear.

15...♕b6

Or:

a) 15...♘fg4 16 f6! c5 17 ♕d5 ♗e6 18 fxg7 wins.

b) 15...c5 16 ♕f2.

16 ♕xb6 axb6 17 ♖d1 ±

The variations in the line starting with 11 f4 are recommended only for those who like tactical complications.

B22)

8...h5 *(D)*

9 0-0

Or:

a) 9 f4 is also playable:

a1) 9...♘eg4 10 h3 ♘h6 11 0-0 ♗d7 12 ♗e3 ♕c8 (Beekes-Dol, corr. 1989) 13 ♕d2 and now the sacrifice 13...♗xh3 is refuted by 14 gxh3 ♕xh3 15 ♖f3 ♘fg4 16 ♘f1 +−.

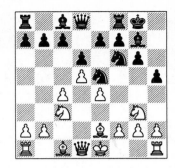

W

a2) 9...♘ed7 10 0-0 c6 11 ♗e3 h4 (11...♘c5 12 b4 ♘a6 13 ♖b1; 11...♘g4 12 ♗d4) 12 ♘h1 ♘c5 13 ♘f2 with a slight advantage for White.

b) 9 h3 h4 10 ♘f1 ♘h7 11 f4? (first 11 ♘h2 and 0-0 is the right plan) 11...♘d7 12 ♗e3 e5! 13 dxe6 fxe6 14 ♘d2 ♗h6 15 0-0 (Dive-De Coverly, British Ch (Norwich) 1994) and now 15...e5! gives Black the advantage.

c) For 9 ♗g5 ♘h7 10 ♗e3 see Line B in Chapter 14.

9...h4 10 ♘h1 c6 11 f4!?

First 11 h3 is more careful.

11...♘eg4 12 ♘f2 ♘xf2 13 ♖xf2 ♕b6! 14 ♕d3!

14 h3 ♘h5 15 ♘a4 ♕d4 16 ♗xh5 gxh5 17 ♕e2 f5 is not clear.

14...♘g4 15 ♗xg4 ♗d4!? 16 ♘d1! ♗xf2+ 17 ♘xf2 ♗xg4 18 c5! ♕xc5 19 ♗e3 ♕b4 20 ♘xg4 cxd5 21 exd5

21 ♕xd5 is better, as it allows less counterplay.

21...♖fc8! 22 ♘h6+ ♔f8 23 f5 ♕c4

In Joyce-Miles, Dublin Z 1993 Black got counterplay after 24 ♕d2?! ♕e4. Instead 24 ♕xc4 ♖xc4 25 fxg6 fxg6 26 ♖f1+ ♔e8 27 ♗g5! gives White the better chances in the endgame.

12 6...♘a6 and Other Rare Knight Moves

1 d4 ♘f6 2 c4 g6 3 ♘c3 ♗g7 4 e4 d6 5 ♘ge2 0-0 6 ♘g3 *(D)*

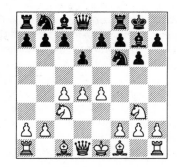

In this chapter we discuss:

A)

6...♘a6

This usually prepares ...c5, which will transpose to lines considered in Part 2. It has independent significance only in connection with ...c6.

7 ♗e2 c6

7...♖b8 is a tricky motif that has not occurred in any game yet.

a) Its idea is 8 ♘b5? c6! 9 ♘xa7 ♗d7 10 ♕b3 ♖a8! (10...♕c7 11 ♘b5 ±) 11 ♕xb7 ♕b8! ∓.

b) 8 ♗e3 c5 9 d5 (or 9 ♕d2 ♘g4 10 ♗xg4 ♗xg4 11 0-0 ±) 9...♘c7 and then:

b1) 10 0-0 a6 11 e5 dxe5 12 ♗xc5 ±.

b2) 10 ♕d2 b5?! (this pawn sacrifice is reminiscent of the Benko Gambit) 11 cxb5 a6 and now the game Westlund-Lind, Ronneby 1998 continued 12 ♗h6 (12 bxa6 is also good) 12...♘xb5 13 ♘xb5 axb5 14 ♗xg7 ♔xg7 15 0-0 e6 16 dxe6 ♗xe6 17 ♖fd1! with an advantage for White.

8 h4

8 ♗e3 and 8 0-0 are also good.

8...h5 9 ♗g5 ♕a5

This was Black's plan with ...♘a6 and ...c6. Instead, 9...e5 10 d5 cxd5 11 cxd5 transposes to note 'a2' to White's 9th move in Line C of Chapter 6.

10 ♕d2 ♘c7

Black's aim is to play ...b5, but on c7 the knight blocks the queen's way back. White can make immediate use of this.

11 ♖b1 b5

The attack on the queenside can be halted, and the weakness on c6 remains.

12 cxb5 cxb5 13 b4

13 ♘xb5 ♕xa2.

13...♕b6 14 0-0 ♘g4!

The g7-bishop also starts working. 14...♗d7 is wrong because of 15 e5.

15 d5! ♖e8 16 ♗xg4 ♗xg4 17 ♗e3 ♕b7 18 ♘ge2?!

The knight aims for the centre, but 18 ♗d4 is more accurate, offering the exchange of the bishops.

18...a5

Black can equalize here by playing 18...♗xe2! and ...e6. With the text-move Black seeks counterplay on the other side, but this is less effective.

19 ♘d4

White keeps some advantage, For-intos-Aalsbersberg, Benidorm 1985.

B)

6...♘fd7 *(D)*

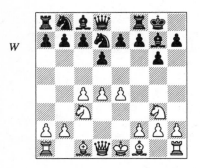

If White does not look after d4, he might get an inferior position.

7 d5

Possibly the best. Others:

a) 7 ♗e3 is a natural reaction:

a1) 7...e5 8 d5 and now:

a11) 8...f5?! 9 exf5 gxf5 10 f4 (a strong move; 10 ♘h5 is the other possibility) 10...exf4 (if 10...♗h6, then 11 ♘xf5!; or 10...♕h4 11 ♕h5) 11 ♗xf4 ♕h4! 12 ♕d2 ♗e5 13 ♗xe5 ♘xe5 14 0-0-0! ♘bd7 (14...♘xc4? 15 ♗xc4 ♕xc4 16 ♕g5+ ♔h8 17 ♖hf1!) 15 ♕d4! gives White a slight advantage, Jenei-Ozsvath, Budapest 1962.

a12) 8...a5 9 ♗e2 ♘a6 10 0-0 (premature; 10 ♕d2 and castling long is better) 10...h5! 11 ♕d2 (11 ♖e1) 11...♘ac5 12 ♖ab1 (Dive-Fadi, Moscow OL 1994) and now Black can take over the initiative by 12...h4 13 ♘h1 ♘f6 14 f3 (14 ♗g5? ♘fxe4) 14...♘h5 planning ...f5.

a2) 7...c5 8 d5 b5!? (as in the Benko Gambit) 9 cxb5 a6 10 ♕d2 (10 bxa6 is the alternative) and now:

a21) 10...axb5 11 ♗xb5 ♗a6 12 ♗xa6 ♘xa6 13 ♗h6!? ♗xh6 14 ♕xh6 ♕a5 15 0-0 ♖fb8 16 f4 (the attack continues) 16...♖xb2 17 ♖f3 (White threatens mate) 17...♕d8! 18 ♘f5 ♕f8 19 ♕g5 ♔h8 20 ♕xe7 gxf5 and Black defended against the attack and nearly equalized in Szabo-Gufeld, Leningrad 1967.

a22) 10...♕a5!? 11 ♗h6 ♗xh6 12 ♕xh6 axb5 13 ♗xb5 ♗a6 14 ♗e2!? ♕b4! and now:

a221) 15 ♕d2?! (this is what Black was playing for, but it is not necessary to retreat the queen) 15...♗xe2 16 ♘gxe2 ♘a6 17 0-0 ♖fb8 18 b3 ♘c7 19 ♖fd1 (to protect the queen and the d4-square) 19...♘b5 20 ♖ac1 ♘xc3 21 ♘xc3 c4! (in the spirit of the Benko Gambit) and Black eventually earned half a point in Bednarski-Wl.Schmidt, Polanica Zdroj 1969.

a222) 15 ♖b1 (more difficult to analyse but better) 15...♗xe2 16 a3 ♖xa3 17 bxa3 ♕xc3+ 18 ♔xe2 ♕c4+ 19 ♔e1 ♘e5 20 ♕d2 ♘d3+ 21 ♔f1 e6 22 ♕e2 exd5 23 ♖d1! with a clear advantage to White.

b) 7 h4!? ♘c6 8 d5! ♘d4 9 ♗e3 (9 h5) 9...c5 (or 9...e5 10 dxe6!? ♘xe6 11

♕d2 with a small advantage, but in a difficult position) 10 dxc6! ♘xc6 (this position is similar to those arising from the Maroczy Bind; the difference is to White's advantage) 11 h5 ♕a5 12 hxg6 hxg6 13 ♕d2 ♘c5 14 ♖c1! ♘e6 (Black does not fall into the trap 14...♗xc3? 15 ♖xc3 ♕xa2?, which is disastrous because of 16 ♗xc5! dxc5 17 ♕h6) 15 b3 ♗d7 and then:

b1) 16 ♗d3!? ♘e5? (it is better to leave e5 free, viz. 16...♖fe8) 17 ♗e2 ♖fe8 (Alber-Degenhardt, Frankfurt 1990) and here 18 ♗h6! ♗h8 19 f4 ♘c6 20 f5 is best, with heavy attack.

b2) Also possible 16 ♗h6 ♕e5! 17 ♘d5 ♗xh6 18 ♕xh6 ♕g7 19 ♕h4 ±.

c) 7 ♗e2 is another good move here:

c1) 7...c6 8 ♗e3 e5 does not equalize, because 9 d5 is not necessary, as there is 9 dxe5! dxe5 10 ♕d6 ±.

c2) 7...♘c6! 8 d5! (better than waiting for ...e5) 8...♘d4 9 ♗e3 ♘xe2 (9...c5?! 10 dxc6 ♘xc6 is a Maroczy set-up where Black has not equalized) 10 ♕xe2 and then:

c21) 10...c5 11 0-0 a6 12 a4 ♘f6 (12...♕a5 can be met by 13 ♗d2!) 13 h3 ♘e8 (in case of 13...e5, 14 dxe6 ♗xe6 15 ♖fd1 ♕b6 16 a5 is advantageous) 14 ♕d2 e5 15 dxe6 ♗xe6 16 ♘d5 ♗xd5 17 exd5 ♕b6 (17...f5 is slightly better) 18 ♖a3! ♘f6 (Pöcksteiner-V.Kostić, Austrian Cht 1989) 19 a5 ♕c7 20 b4 ±.

c22) 10...♗xc3+ 11 bxc3 e5 is also playable, but Black must reckon with 12 ♗h6 ♖e8 13 h4, when the opposite-coloured bishops just strengthen the attack.

We now return to 7 d5 (D):

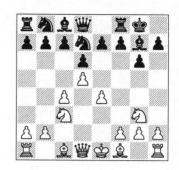

7...c6 8 ♗e2 cxd5 9 cxd5

9 exd5 is also playable. Still, White has to deal with blocked doubled pawns after 9...♗xc3+ 10 bxc3 ♘c5. After 11 ♗h6 ♖e8 12 ♕d4 e5! 13 dxe6 ♘xe6 14 ♕d2 ♕h4 15 ♗e3 f5 16 f4 ♘c5 Black has nearly equalized.

9...a6 10 a4 a5 11 ♗e3 ♘a6 12 0-0 ♘dc5 13 f3

13 f4 seems to be stronger.

13...♗d7 14 ♖f2 ♖c8

14...♘b4 is more accurate.

15 ♗b5 ♘b4 16 ♖d2 ♗xb5

White is better, Remlinger-Young, New York 1995.

C)

6...♘bd7 (D)
7 ♗e2 c6

Or:

a) 7...c5 8 d5 transposes to 6...c5 lines (Part 2) with Black's knight poorly placed. 8...h5 can be answered by 9 h3! (after 9 h4 ♘e5! Black gains use of either e5 or g4) 9...h4 10 ♘f1 ♕a5 11 ♗d2 and White is better.

b) 7...e5 is better, when 8 d5 transposes to Line A in Chapter 1.

W

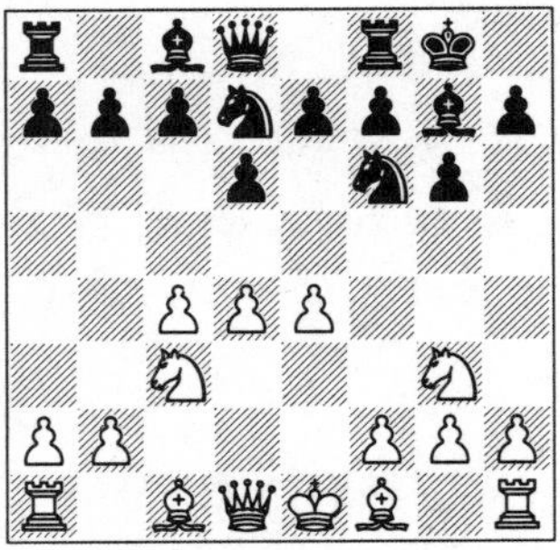

8 ♗g5

White wishes to provoke ...h6. Also good are:

a) 8 ♗e3 a6 and then:

a1) 9 0-0 transposes to line 'b2'.

a2) 9 f4!? ± Veličković.

a3) 9 d5 cxd5 10 cxd5 (here we suggest 10 exd5! with later pressure on the d- and e-files) 10...b5 11 0-0 h6 12 f3 ♘b6 13 ♖c1 e6! with tactical counterplay for Black, Hort-Westerinen, Bochum 1981.

a4) 9 ♕d2 b5 10 ♗h6 bxc4 11 ♗xg7 ♔xg7 12 ♗xc4 d5 13 ♗b3 dxe4 14 ♘gxe4 a5 = Corral Blanco-Illescas, Spanish Cht 1999.

b) 8 0-0 a6 (8...e5 9 d5 cxd5 10 cxd5 transposes to Line A14 of Chapter 5) and now:

b1) 9 ♖b1 b5 10 cxb5 axb5 11 b4?! (better is 11 a3 =) 11...♘b6! (11...♗b7 is feeble because of 12 ♗e3 ♕b6 13 ♕d2 ♖a3 14 ♖fc1) 12 d5? (12 ♕c2! =) 12...cxd5! 13 exd5 ♗b7! (13...♘h5 =) 14 ♗f3 ♕d7 and Black is better, Forintos-Hellers, Malmö 1988.

b2) Better is 9 ♗e3 b5 10 cxb5! (10 a3 bxc4 11 ♗xc4 d5! 12 exd5 ♘b6 =) 10...axb5 11 ♕b3 (planning d5) 11...e6 12 ♖fc1 ±.

8...h6 9 ♗e3 a6 10 ♕d2 h5 11 ♗h6

This is the point of the set-up with ♗g5, ♗e3 and ♕d2. However, this does not mean that the alternative 11 0-0 is worse.

11...h4 12 ♗xg7 ♔xg7 13 ♘f1 b5 14 a3

14 f3 is better – I.Sokolov.

14...bxc4 15 ♘e3

After 15 ♗xc4 d5 16 exd5 ♘b6 the chances are even.

15...♘b6! 16 f4

16 ♘xc4 ♘xc4 17 ♗xc4 d5 18 exd5 cxd5 19 ♗a2 h3 20 g3 ♗f5 and Black nearly equalizes.

16...e5! 17 0-0!

17 dxe5 dxe5 18 ♕xd8 ♖xd8 19 fxe5 should be avoided because of 19...♘fd7! – a common King's Indian motif.

17...exf4 18 ♖xf4 d5! 19 e5

Not 19 ♖xh4? ♘xe4 20 ♘f5+ ♗xf5 21 ♕h6+ ♔f6!.

19...♘h7 20 ♖af1 ♗e6 21 ♗g4 ♘d7!

Black has very good chances, I.Sokolov-Van Wely, Akureyri 1994.

13 Pawn Moves: 6...a6 and 6...c6

1 d4 ♘f6 2 c4 g6 3 ♘c3 ♗g7 4 e4 d6 5 ♘ge2 0-0 6 ♘g3 a6 *(D)*

6...a6 and 6...c6 usually transpose into each other. Since 6...a6 is the subtler of the two, we include all ...a6 and ...c6 lines under 6...a6.

There are just a couple of independent possibilities after 6...c6 7 ♗e2:

a) For 7...e5 8 d5 see Chapter 5.

b) 7...♘bd7 transposes to Line C of Chapter 12.

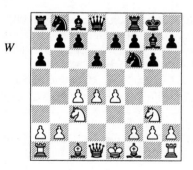

7 ♗e2

Or 7 h4 c5 (7...h5 8 ♗e2 c6 nearly equalizes) 8 d5 e6 9 h5 exd5 10 cxd5 b5 (Black has managed to play ...b5, and White h5; whom does this favour?) 11 ♗e2 ♖e8 12 ♕c2 ♕e7 13 hxg6 fxg6 14 ♗g5 b4 15 ♘d1 ♕e5?! (now the queen becomes too exposed; 15...♘bd7 is more harmonious) 16 f4 ♕d4 17 ♘f2 ♘fd7 18 e5! dxe5 19 ♖d1

b3 20 ♕xb3 c4 21 ♕c2 ♕e3 22 ♘f1 ♕b6 23 ♕xc4 ♘c5 24 fxe5 ♖xe5 25 ♗e3 and White won in Forintos-Hebden, Ramsgate 1984.

7...c6

This is one of the most popular systems. The main lines of 6...a6 and 6...c6 converge here. Otherwise:

a) 7...♘c6?! is not recommended, because after 8 d5 ♘a7 the knight can remain out of play, e.g. 9 0-0 c5 10 a4! e6 11 ♗g5 exd5 12 exd5 ♖e8? (12...h6 is the only chance) 13 ♕d2 ♕e7 14 ♕f4! (there is no defence any more) 14...♕e5 15 ♕xe5 dxe5 16 ♘ge4 ♘d7 17 ♘d6 ♖f8 18 ♗e7 +− Novikov-Kr.Georgiev, Manila OL 1992.

b) 7...h5!? 8 ♗g5 ♘bd7 9 ♕d2 c6 10 0-0 (10 a4 is also playable) 10...b5 (Kosić-Antić, Yugoslav Ch 1999) and now 11 a3, as suggested by Antić, is best.

8 a4

Other moves:

a) 8 d5 b5 9 dxc6 b4 10 ♘d5 ♘xc6 11 0-0 (first 11 ♗e3 and ♕d2 is better) 11...a5 12 ♗e3 ♘d7! 13 ♕d2 ♗b7 14 ♗h6 (14 ♖fd1) 14...♗xh6 15 ♕xh6 e6 16 ♘e3 ♕f6 and Black has at least equal chances, Jenei-Lanc, Budapest 1983.

b) 8 f4!? b5 (8...e5 9 dxe5 dxe5 10 ♕xd8 ♖xd8 11 0-0! ±) 9 e5 ♘fd7 10

♗e3 bxc4 (better is 10...♘b6) 11 ♗xc4 d5 12 ♗d3 e6 13 h4 f5 14 exf6 ♕xf6 15 h5 (this gains a lasting advantage, so Black starts some risky counterplay) 15...e5!? 16 fxe5 ♘xe5 17 dxe5 ♕xe5 18 ♘f1 ♗h6 (18...d4 19 ♗c4+ ♗e6 20 ♕xd4!) 19 ♕e2 ♗xe3 20 ♘xe3 ♕g3+ (20...d4 21 ♘f1) 21 ♔d1 ♖f2 22 ♕e1 ♖a7 23 ♔c1! ♖e7 24 ♘cd1 and White managed to win in Novikov-Kožul, Tbilisi 1988.

c) 8 h4!? e5 (8...h5) 9 d5 b5 10 h5 cxd5 11 cxd5 ♘bd7 12 ♗e3 ♘b6 13 b3 with a small advantage to White, Ermenkov-Topalov, Šumen 1991.

d) 8 0-0 waits to see Black's plan. Then:

d1) 8...♘bd7 9 ♗e3 b5 10 cxb5 axb5 (10...cxb5?! is answered by 11 ♕b3 and ♖ac1 ±) 11 a3 ♘b6 12 b3 ♗e6 13 f4 b4! 14 f5 ♗xb3 15 ♕xb3 bxc3 16 a4 ♖b8 17 ♕xc3 c5! led to unclear play in Arkhipov-A.Schneider, Hungarian Cht 1992.

d2) 8...e5 9 d5 cxd5 10 cxd5 transposes to note 'b' to White's 10th move in Line A2 of Chapter 5.

d3) 8...b5 is the reason why so many people choose the ...a6 and ...c6 treatment. Instead of the feeble 9 a3, there are two interesting lines:

d31) 9 cxb5 axb5 10 b4! and then:
d311) 10...♘bd7 11 a4 e5?! (better is 11...bxa4 and ...♗b7) 12 d5! cxd5 13 ♘xb5 ♘xe4 14 ♘xe4 dxe4 15 ♕xd6 and the advance of the a-pawn decided in Serper-Schroer, Philadelphia 1997.

d312) 10...♘a6 11 ♖b1 ♘c7 12 ♗e3 ♘d7 13 f4 (we suggest 13 ♕d2

with a slight advantage for White) 13...♗b7 14 ♕d2 ♖a3 with a complicated but equal middlegame, A.Hoffman-Tempone, Argentine Ch 1998.

d32) 9 e5 is the other important, active line:
d321) 9...dxe5 10 dxe5 ♘fd7 11 f4 ♘b6 12 c5 ♘d5 13 ♘ce4 a5 14 a3 ♘a6 15 ♗d3 ♘ac7 16 ♘g5 e6 (16...f6? 17 ♘xh7!) 17 ♕e2 b4 18 ♘3e4 ♗a6 19 ♘d6 ♗xd3 20 ♕xd3 f6 21 ♘f3 with an advantage for White in Serper-Levchuk, North Bay 1998.

d322) 9...♘e8 10 f4 ♘d7 and here:
d3221) 11 ♗e3 ♗b7 (or 11...♘c7 12 ♕d2 with an advantage for White in Barczay-Ivkov, Raach 1969) 12 c5! ♘c7 13 exd6 exd6 14 cxd6 ♘d5 15 ♘xd5 cxd5 16 f5! ♕b6 17 ♕d2 ♖fe8 (threatening ...♖xe3) 18 ♔h1 ♕xd6 19 ♗h6 ± Miles-Nunn, Amsterdam 1985.

d3222) The immediate 11 c5 is also good, e.g. 11...dxc5 12 dxc5 ♕a5 13 ♗e3 ♕b4 14 ♕d2! ±.

d323) 9...♘fd7! 10 f4 and then:
d3231) 10...b4 11 ♘ce4 and now 11...d5 12 ♘d2 ± or 11...c5 12 ♗f3 ♖a7 13 ♗e3 ±.

d3232) 10...bxc4 11 ♗xc4 d5 (or 11...c5 12 ♗d5, followed by ♗e3) 12 ♗e2 e6 13 ♗e3 a5 14 ♘a4 ♗a6 15 ♖c1 ♕c7 (Novikov-Wojtkiewicz, New York 1993) and now 16 ♖f2, followed by pressure on the c-file, is best.

8...a5 *(D)*

If ...b5 is not possible, then rather ...a5 and ...♘a6. It may be followed by ...♘b4 or, if permitted, ...♘c5. Black can be happy that the g7-bishop's diagonal is open, unlike in the 6...e5 7 d5 lines.

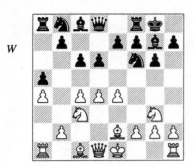

W

9 0-0
Two other ideas:
a) 9 ♗e3 ♘a6 10 ♕d2 e5 11 ♖d1! (the d6-pawn is the target) 11...♕e7 12 d5 and then:
a1) 12...cxd5 13 ♘xd5 ♘xd5 14 ♕xd5 ♘b4 15 ♕d2! (15 ♕xd6? ♘c2+ 16 ♔f1 ♘xe3+ 17 fxe3 ♕g5! and Black is better) 15...f5 16 exf5 gxf5 17 ♗g5 ♗f6 18 ♗h6?! (18 h4!) and now:
a11) 18...♗g7?! (hoping for a draw) 19 ♗g5 ♗f6 20 h4! f4 (20...♖d8 21 ♘h5!) 21 ♘e4 ♗xg5 22 hxg5 ♗f5 23 ♘f6+ and ♕xd6 led to a quick victory in Hort-Nemet, Switzerland 1986.
a12) 18...♖d8 gives White more problems After 19 ♘h5 f4 it is not easy to find the best move, 20 h4!, when after 20...♗xh4 21 g3 ♗g5 22 ♗xg5 ♕xg5 23 gxf4 exf4 White is better in a complicated position.
a2) The 12...♘b4!? pawn sacrifice is our suggestion. Then 13 dxc6 bxc6 14 ♕xd6 ♘c2+ 15 ♔f1 ♘xe3+ 16 fxe3 ♕a7 gives Black a certain amount of compensation on the dark squares.
b) 9 h4 e5! 10 d5 transposes to Line B of Chapter 5.

9...♘a6
Or 9...e5, and now:
a) White should argue that Black has left it too late to play ...e5, and so play 10 ♗e3, avoiding d5. Then:
a1) 10...♕c7?! 11 d5! ♘a6 12 f4! exf4 13 ♗xf4! sets up a nice trap (13...♕b6+?! 14 ♔h1 ♕xb2 15 ♗xd6! ♕xc3 16 ♖a3 ♕b2 17 ♖b3 ♕a2 18 ♗xf8 ♔xf8 19 e5 and ♖bf3). Black already has a bad position, for example 13...cxd5 14 exd5 ♘d7 15 ♘b5 ♕b6+ 16 ♔h1 ♘e5 17 ♘e4 ♘c5 18 ♗e3 ♖d8 19 ♘bxd6 1-0 Efimov-Jakob, Lenk 1991.
a2) The proof of the pudding is 10...exd4! 11 ♗xd4 ♘a6 12 f4, with an unusual position for the King's Indian. White has more room, while Black's counterplay may come on the dark squares.
b) 10 d5 ♘a6 11 ♗e3 ♘c5 12 ♖e1 h5 gave Black reasonable play in the game Verdikhanov-Kruppa, Nikolaev Z 1993.

10 ♗e3 ♘b4 11 h3 ♘e8 12 ♕d2 e6
Black avoids ...e5, preferring a more solid pawn-centre.

13 ♖ad1 d5 14 cxd5 exd5 15 e5 f5 16 ♗g5 ♕d7 17 f4 ♘c7 18 ♗h4 ♘e6
If counterplay accompanied the blockade, we could talk about equality. However, ...c5 cannot be played without material losses.

19 ♘h1 ♗h6 20 ♗f6 ♕c7 21 g3 ♗d7 22 ♗f3 ♖ae8 23 ♘f2
White broke through on the kingside later with ♘e2 and g4 in Forintos-Hansson, Esbjerg 1983.

14 6...h5

1 d4 ♘f6 2 c4 g6 3 ♘c3 ♗g7 4 e4 d6 5 ♘ge2 0-0 6 ♘g3 h5 *(D)*

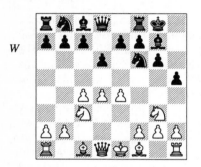

Black thinks that ...h5 fits in with every method of development. White must immediately decide whether to allow ...h4.

A:	7 h4	122
B:	7 ♗g5	122
C:	7 ♗e2	123

A)

7 h4

The mechanical blockade is typical. Still, it should not be played lightly, since the h4-pawn may become weak.

7...♘c6

After 7...e5, 8 d5 ♘h7 transposes to Line B21 in Chapter 6, while 8 dxe5 dxe5 9 ♕xd8 ♖xd8 10 ♗g5 c6 is harmless to Black.

8 d5

It is not advisable to let the knight in to d4: 8 ♗e2? e5 9 d5 ♘d4 10 ♗g5

c6 gave Black the initiative in Merlini-Lamorelle, Cannes 1995.

8...♘e5 9 ♗e2 c6 10 ♘f1

Or:

a) 10 ♗g5 ♕b6! 11 ♕d2 ♕b4 12 b3 cxd5 13 exd5 ♘h7! 14 ♖c1! ♘xg5 15 hxg5 (Oei-Berend, Bad Mondorf 1991) and now 15...a6 nearly equalizes.

b) 10 ♗f4 ♕b6 11 ♕d2 and then:

b1) 11...♘fg4 12 ♘d1 f5? (better is 12...cxd5) 13 exf5 ♗xf5 14 f3 ♗d3? (Black falls into his own pit) 15 fxg4 (15 ♗xd3? ♖xf4) 15...♘xc4 16 ♗e3 ♗e5 17 ♗xb6 ♗xg3+ 18 ♗f2 ♘xd2 19 ♗xd3 ♗xf2+ 20 ♘xf2 cxd5 21 ♗xg6 ♖f4 22 ♘h3 1-0 Kaposztas-Levačić, Eger 1989.

b2) 11...♕b4! 12 a3 ♕b3 13 c5 cxd5 14 exd5 ♗g4 15 f3 ♗d7 and Black at least equalizes.

10...e6

10...cxd5 also possible.

11 ♗g5 ♕e8 12 ♘e3 exd5 13 exd5 ♘h7 14 ♗f4 ♕e7 15 ♕d2 c5 16 0-0-0 a6 17 f3 f5 18 ♖df1 b5 19 g4

Both sides have chances in a complicated position, Teng Wei Ping-Manninen, Kuala Lumpur 1996.

B)

7 ♗g5 ♘h7 8 ♗e3 *(D)*

This set-up is directed against ...e5, as we shall see.

8...♘c6

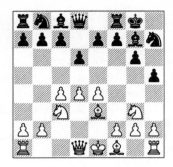

It is advisable to support ...e5, as we see from the following lines:

a) The immediate 8...e5 can be strongly answered by 9 dxe5 – compare line 'b'.

b) 8...h4 9 ♘ge2 e5?! is premature since it can be met by 10 dxe5!?. Then:

b1) 10...dxe5?! 11 ♗c5! ♕xd1+ (11...♖e8? 12 ♕xd8 ♖xd8 13 ♘d5 ♘a6 14 ♗e7 wins a pawn) 12 ♖xd1 ♖e8 13 ♘b5 ♘a6 14 ♗e3 with a small advantage.

b2) 10...♗xe5 is better, but it does not fully equalize: 11 ♕d2 ♖e8 12 f3 ♘c6 13 ♖d1 ♗g7 14 ♘f4 with a slight advantage for White.

9 d5 ♘e5 10 ♗e2

This is a position that can also be reached from Line B22 in Chapter 11.

10...c6

Another possibility is 10...c5 11 h3 (we suggest 11 f4 ♘g4 12 ♗xg4 ♗xg4 13 ♕d2 h4 14 h3 ♗d7 15 ♘ge2) 11...e6 12 ♕d2 (12 f4? ♕h4) 12...h4 (12...exd5 13 ♘xd5! ±) 13 ♘f1 f5 (Remlinger-Manninen, Gausdal 1991) and now 14 f4 ♘f7 15 exf5 is best, e.g. 15...exf5 16 0-0-0 or 15...gxf5 16 g4! with activity on the kingside.

11 0-0

11 f4 is also possible, as above after 10...c5.

11...h4 12 ♘h1 cxd5 13 cxd5 h3 14 g3 ♘f6 15 f3

Black's position is clearly worse as the h3-pawn can be captured sooner or later.

15...♕c7!? 16 ♖c1 ♕a5

Black has diverted the rook from defending the a2-pawn with an interesting idea which gives him some counterplay.

17 ♘f2

White is in a hurry and that is why the rest is instructive. 17 ♖b1! is simpler.

17...b5! 18 ♗xb5 ♖b8 19 a4?!

After 19 ♕e2! a6 20 ♗a4 ♕b4 21 b3! Black does not have enough compensation.

19...a6

Liardet-Wielicki, Biel 1998 soon finished as a draw.

C)

7 ♗e2

It is practical to start by developing the bishop, and to decide how to continue after Black's answer.

7...e5

Or:

a) 7...h4 (the advance of the h-pawn is also popular) 8 ♘f1 and now:

a1) 8...h3?! 9 g4 ♘c6 10 d5 ♘e5 11 g5 (11 ♖g1! c6 12 f4 ±) 11...♘h7 12 f4 ♘d7 13 ♗e3 ♘c5 14 ♘g3 e5! 15 f5 ♘xg5 16 ♕d2 and White has compensation on the g-file for the pawn, A.Martin-J.Littlewood, Birmingham 1985.

a2) 8...e5 9 d5 ♘h7 10 ♗e3 ♘a6 11 ♘d2 ♗d7 (11...f5 can be met by 12 exf5 gxf5 13 f4) 12 ♘b3 b6 13 ♕d2 ♘c5 14 ♘xc5 (this is not so urgent; 14 0-0 is better) 14...bxc5 15 0-0 ♗f6 16 ♖ab1! a5 17 ♘b5 and now 17...♖e8 18 b3 ♗xb5 19 cxb5 ♗g5 20 a3! ♗xe3 21 fxe3! ± Shemeakin-Prokhorov, Yalta 1995, as Black's position can be attacked from two directions (after b3-b4 on the c-file, or on the f-file). The immediate 17...♗xb5 is better, and the rook should stay on f8.

b) 7...♘h7!? must be met by 8 ♗e3 as after 8 0-0?! h4 9 ♘h1 (Mäki-Manninen, Jyväskylä 1994) Black can play 9...♘c6! 10 ♗e3 e5, when the black knight can come into the centre.

8 d5 *(D)*

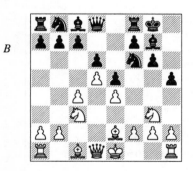

B

8...♘a6

The disadvantage of this move is that the knight can get to c5 only with White's help. Other moves:

a) For 8...h4 9 ♘f1 see note 'a2' to Black's 7th move.

b) 8...♘h7 prevents the pin.

b1) 9 0-0 and then:

b11) 9...h4 10 ♘h1 ♘d7 11 f3 f5 12 ♘f2 (allowing ...f4, which could be prevented with 12 exf5 gxf5 13 ♘f2) 12...♘df6 13 exf5 ♗xf5 14 g4! hxg3 15 hxg3 ♘h5! and now:

b111) 16 g4? ♘f4 17 ♗xf4 exf4 18 gxf5 ♕g5+ 19 ♘g4 (the only move) 19...gxf5 and Black is better.

b112) 16 ♔g2! ♗d7 17 ♘ce4 ♖f7 18 ♗e3 ♗f8 19 ♕d2 ♗e7 20 ♖h1! favours White, Fokin-Gleizerov, Kursk 1987.

b12) For 9...♘d7 10 ♗e3 see line 'b3'.

b13) 9...a5 10 ♗e3 ♗f6 (10...♘a6 is more logical) 11 c5! ♗g5 12 cxd6 cxd6 13 ♕d2 ♘a6 14 ♗xa6 (luring the rook to a6) 14...♖xa6 15 ♘ge2 (better is 15 f4) 15...♗xe3 16 ♕xe3 ♗d7 17 ♔h1 (preventing ...♕b6 after f4) 17...b5 18 f4 b4 19 ♘d1 ♗b5 = Naumkin-A.Kuzmin, Moscow 1988.

b2) 9 h4 transposes to Line B21 of Chapter 6.

b3) 9 ♗e3 ♘d7 10 0-0 h4 11 ♘h1 f5 12 exf5 gxf5 13 f4 exf4 14 ♗xf4 ♘e5 15 ♘f2!? ♗g5 (15...♘g6 16 ♘h3) 16 ♘b5! ♗f6 17 ♘d4 and White has the advantage due to his centralized knight, Novikov-Gleizerov, Pavlodar 1987.

9 ♗g5 ♕e8

Now:

a) 10 ♘f1 (this helps the black knight get to c5) 10...♘c5 11 ♘d2 a5 12 0-0 ♗d7 13 b3 ♘h7 14 ♗e3 ♗f6 15 ♗h6 ♗g7 with a repetition of moves, Novikov-Ibragimov, Bled 1996.

b) 10 h4 (this is our suggestion) 10...♘h7 11 ♗e3 ♕e7 12 ♕d2 ♗f6 13 0-0-0 ♗xh4 14 ♘xh5 gxh5 15 g3 ♗f6 16 ♖xh5 gives White a dangerous attack for the sacrificed piece.

15 Can Black Delay Castling?

Black castles in more than 90% of the games in this opening (after **1 d4 ♘f6 2 c4 g6 3 ♘c3 ♗g7 4 e4 d6 5 ♘ge2**), although original ideas might be tried to avoid 5...0-0. Most of them are either aimed against the knight on g3, by playing ...h5-h4, or intend play on the queenside with a quick ...b5. We consider:

A: 5...e5   125
B: 5...c6   126

These are the most substantial lines, as 5...♘c6?! and 5...♘bd7 do not cause White any problems.

After 5...a6, 6 ♘g3 c6 transposes to Line B, but this move-order is only worth playing if we suspect that White would not play 6 g3!, as suggested by Korchnoi, which transposes to advantageous Fianchetto systems. White may also switch to a form of Sämisch by playing 6 f3, when he maintains possibilities of either ♗e3 or ♗g5.

A)

5...e5 6 d5 *(D)*
Instead, 6 f3 is akin to the Sämisch (though Black might try 6...♘fd7 7 ♗e3 ♗h6), while 6 ♗g5 can be met by 6...h6 7 ♗h4 g5 8 ♗g3 ♘h5 9 dxe5 ♘xg3 followed by 10...♗xe5.
Now:

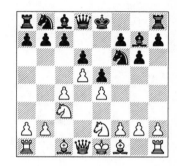

B

a) 6...♘h5 (this move tries to obstruct the 7 ♘g3 plan) 7 ♗e3 and now:
a1) 7...0-0 8 ♕d2 a6 9 ♘g3 ♘f4!? (I did not accept this pawn sacrifice because I considered that it would have been too risky against one of the greatest King's Indian experts of the time) 10 ♘ge2 ♘h5 11 ♘g3 ♘f4 12 ♘ge2 ½-½ Forintos-Geller, Budapest 1973. Repeating moves also meant a kind of respect of the opponent. Accepting the sacrifice by 10 ♗xf4 is playable, e.g. 10...exf4 11 ♕xf4 f5 12 exf5 ♗xc3+ 13 bxc3 ♗xf5 14 ♕d2 ±.
a2) 7...f5?! 8 exf5 gxf5 9 ♘g3 and now 9...♘f4? (Eising-Oechslein, German Cht 1970) allows 10 ♗xf4 and ♕h5+. The slightly better 9...♘f6 can be met by 10 ♘h5 ±.
b) 6...♘a6 7 ♘g3 h5 and then:
b1) 8 h4 c6 9 ♗e2 ♗d7 10 ♗g5 ♗h6 11 ♗xh6 (11 c5! looks strong)

11...♖xh6 12 ♕d2 ♖h8 (Bianchi-Bettalli, Siena 1997) 13 dxc6 ♗xc6 14 ♖d1 ±.

b2) 8 ♗e2 h4 9 ♘f1 ♘c5 10 f3 (10 ♕c2 a5 {10...h3 11 g3} 11 h3 is better) 10...a5 11 ♗g5 ♖h5 and rather than 12 f4? ♖xg5! 13 fxg5 ♘fxe4 ∓ Jakab-Szük, Budapest 1999, 12 ♗e3 is right.

B)
    5...c6 6 ♘g3 *(D)*

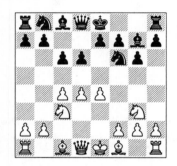

This is not the only possibility in this position, but it is consistent with the main theme of this book.

6...a6
Other possibilities:
a) 6...h5 7 ♗e2 (7 h4 a6 8 a4 is likely to transpose to the main line) and now:
a1) 7...a6 should also be compared with the main line.
a2) 7...h4 8 ♘f1 and the h4-pawn will need protection after White plays h3.
a3) 7...♘bd7 8 0-0 a6 (Black avoids both ...e5 and ...0-0) 9 ♖e1 (9 a4) and here:
a31) 9...e5 10 ♗g5 ♕c7 (if 10...♕b6 11 dxe5 dxe5 then 12 ♖b1 planning

♘a4 and c5; however, 10...h4 deserves attention) 11 d5! c5 12 ♖b1 ± Piket.
a32) 9...b5 10 a3 0-0 (Black has managed to achieve ...b5 by delaying castling) 11 ♗g5 ♘h7 12 ♗e3 ♖b8 13 ♕d2 e5 14 d5 ♘c5 15 dxc6!? ♘b3 16 ♕c2 ♘xa1 17 ♖xa1 bxc4 18 ♘d5 ± M.Gurevich-Van Wely, Tåstrup 1992.
b) In the case of 6...♘bd7 7 ♗e2 a6, 8 a4 is advisable (as in the main line).
7 a4
To stop Black playing ...b5, but White thereby weakens b4, and allows the ...a5, ...♘a6 manoeuvre. Alternatively, the ...b5 plan may also be permitted, viz. 7 ♗e2 b5 8 0-0, when 8...0-0 transposes to note 'd3' to White's 8th move in Chapter 13.
7...a5 8 ♗e2 e5
8...0-0 is a bit better, and transposes to Chapter 13.
9 d5 h5 10 h4 ♘a6 11 ♗g5 ♘c5
Black recognizes that castling does not work any more: 11...0-0 12 ♗xh5 ± Gaborit-Reinderman, Cappelle la Grande 1993.
12 ♖b1
12 ♕c2 is more natural.
12...♗h6! 13 ♗xh6 ♖xh6 14 ♕d2 ♖h8 15 b3 ♗d7
Now 16 f3 led to chances for both sides in Forintos-Gofshtein, French Cht 1998. Instead, 16 dxc6 ♗xc6 17 ♗d3 would have given White slightly more comfortable play.

Conclusion:
Castling can be delayed but it is not really beneficial. Black must also be alert to possible transpositions to Sämisch and Fianchetto lines.

Index of Variations

A1: 9...♘bd7 *59*
A11: 10 h4 *59*
A111: 10...a6 *60*
A112: 10...h5 *62* 11 ♗g5 a6 *62*: 12 a4 *63*; 12 ♗xh5!? *64*
A12: 10 ♗e3 *65*
A13: 10 ♗g5 *67*
A14: 10 0-0 *68*
A2: 9...a6 *69*
B: 8...a6 *70* 9 a4 a5 10 h4 *70*:
10...♘a6 *70*; 10...h5 *71*
C: 8...h5 *72*

6   6...e5 7 d5: Other Moves
6...e5 7 d5 *73*
A: 7...c5 *73*
A1: 8 h4 *73*
A2: 8 ♗d3 *73*
A3: 8 ♗e2 *74*: 8...a6 *75*; 8...♘a6 *75*; 8...♘e8 *76*; 8...♘bd7 *77*
B: 7...h5 *77*
B1: 8 ♗g5 *78*
B2: 8 h4 *79*: 8...♘h7 *79*; 8...♗g4 *80*
B3: 8 ♗e2 *80*
C: 7...♘a6 *81*

7   6...c5 7 d5 e6 8 ♗e2 exd5 9 exd5
6...c5 7 d5 e6 8 ♗e2 exd5 9 exd5 *83*
A: 9...♖e8 *83*: 10 ♗f4! *84*; 10 0-0 *85*
B: 9...♘bd7 *86*
B1: 10 0-0 *87*: 10...♖e8 *87*; 10...♘e8 *88*
B2: 10 ♗f4 *89*
C: 9...♘e8 *90*: 10 ♗e3 *90*; 10 h4 *90*
D: 9...♘a6 *91* 10 0-0 ♘c7 *91*: 11 a4 *92*; 11 ♖e1 *93*

8   6...c5 7 d5 e6 8 ♗e2 exd5 9 cxd5 (Benoni line)
6...c5 7 d5 e6 8 ♗e2 exd5 9 cxd5 *94*
A: 9...a6 *94* 10 a4 ♘bd7 *94*: 11 0-0 *95*; 11 f3 *96*

B: 9...♘a6 *97* 10 0-0 *98*
B1: 10...♖e8 *98*: 11 ♗g5 *98*; 11 ♗f4 *98*
B2: 10...♘c7 *99*: 11 ♖b1 *99*; 11 a4 *100*; 11 f3 *101*
C: 9...b6 *101*
D: 9...h5 *103*
E: 9...♖e8 *104*

9   6...c5 7 d5 e6 8 ♗e2 without 8...exd5
6...c5 7 d5 e6 8 ♗e2 *105* 8...♘a6 *105*

10   6...c5 7 d5: 7...♘a6, 7...a6 and other moves
6...c5 7 d5 *106*
A: 7...♘a6 *106* 8 ♗e2 ♘c7 9 0-0 *107*: 9...♖b8 *107*; 9...a6 *107*
B: 7...a6 *108*

11   6...♘c6
6...♘c6 *110* 7 d5 *110*
A: 7...♘b8 *110*
B: 7...♘e5 *111*
B1: 8 f4 *111*
B2: 8 ♗e2 *112*: 8...e6 *113*; 8...h5 *114*

12   6...♘a6 and Other Rare Knight Moves
6...♘a6 *115*; 6...♘fd7 *116*; 6...♘bd7 *117*

13   Pawn Moves: 6...a6 and 6...c6
6...a6 *119* (6...c6 *119*) 7 ♗e2 c6 *119* 8 a4 a5 *120* 9 0-0 *121*

14   6...h5
6...h5 *122*: 7 h4 *122*; 7 ♗g5 *122*; 7 ♗e2 *123*

15   Can Black Delay Castling?
1 d4 ♘f6 2 c4 g6 3 ♘c3 ♗g7 4 e4 d6 5 ♘ge2 *125*: 5...e5 *125*; 5...c6 *126*